TREASURES
OF SCOTLAND

above The 'moon gate' of the walled garden at Leith Hall.
endpaper 'Prospect of Falkland from the East' by Slezer, *c.*1680.
frontispiece The high hall of Crathes Castle.

TREASURES OF SCOTLAND

Magnus Magnusson

NATIONAL TRUST FOR SCOTLAND
WEIDENFELD AND NICOLSON · LONDON

ISBN 0 297 77898 6

Designed by Martin Richards and Heather Sherratt
Typeset in Great Britain by Keyspools, Golborne,
Lancashire
Printed in Italy by LEGO, Vicenza

CONTENTS

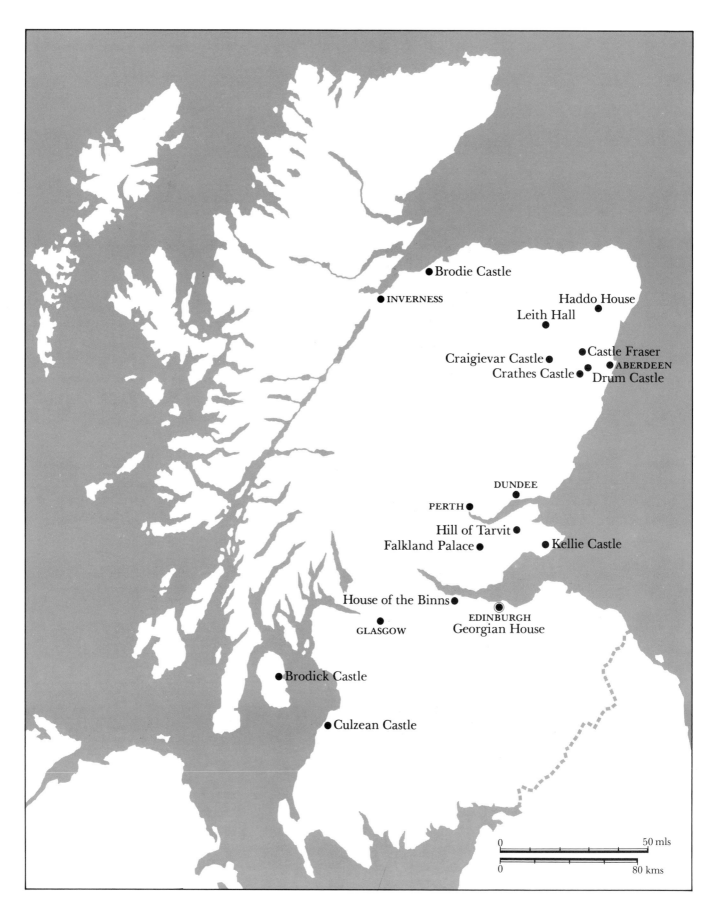

Locations of properties covered by this book.

INTRODUCTION

Every house, however great, however humble, is essentially a drama of life and love, of ambition and achievement, of failure and despair, of happiness and tragedy. Every house in the world is the backdrop to humanity, and every house has a story to tell. In this book I have tried to tell the human story of fourteen castles, palaces, mansions and country houses in the care of the National Trust for Scotland.

Sir Richard Bulstrode, the early eighteenth-century essayist, observed in his *Miscellaneous Essays* (1715) that 'there are four different Actors on the Theatres of Great Families: the Beginner, the Advancer, the Continuer and the Ruiner . . .'. When I first came across that dictum, it helped immeasurably to put the stories of the houses I visited into new order and perspective. A house never stands still. A house, paradoxically, is always on the move, always having its ups and downs. However solid and immovable its stones may appear, a house has insubstantiality built into its very fabric.

This book is called *Treasures of Scotland* not simply because many of the houses featured in it are treasure-stores of priceless works of art and fine furnishings, like Brodick Castle on the Isle of Arran with its Beckford Collection, but because they are all treasures in themselves. Each one is a microcosm of the social and political and economic history of Scotland, as well as reflecting the history of architecture in Scotland down the long centuries.

All the major landmarks of history are represented by these great houses. At Drum Castle in the Grampian Region we feel ourselves in the intimate presence of Scotland's liberator, King Robert the Bruce, after his victory at Bannockburn in 1314, for it was Bruce who gave the charter for the Royal Forest of Drum to the Irvine family which had faithfully supported him in his struggle for Scotland's independence, and Bruce may well have stayed there himself.

The unhappy accession of Mary Queen of Scots and the long-drawn-out troubles of her reign are recalled by the forty years it took to build Crathes Castle on Deeside in the second half of the sixteenth century. The whole unhappy history of the romantic, doom-ridden Stuart dynasty from James I to James VI of Scotland and I of England sighs in the wind that breathes on the partly-restored ruins of the Palace of Falkland in Fife. The short-lived prosperity that invaded Scotland after the Union of the Crowns in 1603 is celebrated by a clutch of splendid Jacobean houses like Kellie Castle in Fife, Craigievar Castle in Grampian Region and the House of The Binns in Lothian, as well as several Renaissance extensions to older buildings like Castle Fraser. The bloody strife of the Civil Wars of the Covenanting period of the mid-seventeenth century is reflected in the destruction or financial ruin of many great houses and an almost complete halt to new building, with the notable exception of Leith Hall in Aberdeenshire which became the home of generations of distinguished soldier lairds.

The eighteenth century, with the traumatic 1745 Rebellion led by Bonnie Prince Charlie, is writ large in the story of these houses, with great Jacobite estates forfeited and new families arising from the ashes of defeat. It gave us Haddo House in Grampian, designed by William Adam, and the present shape of Culzean Castle, designed by his even more celebrated architect son, Robert Adam. The nineteenth century, with its new money from agriculture and industry, and the social pretensions of the Victorian age, is faithfully mirrored in the major and often drastic extensions to the older houses. It was the same in the cities, and the Georgian House at 7 Charlotte Square, Edinburgh, built in 1796 by a Highland clan chieftain who bankrupted his clan lands in the process, is a living example of how a house, through its owners and tenants, can chart with intimate accuracy changing fashions and aspirations.

The youngest of this collection of treasure-houses is the Edwardian country house in Fife known as Hill of Tarvit: a monument to the huge wealth engendered by the jute industry in Dundee in the second half of the nineteenth century. It is only seventy-five years old, but already it is a fascinating period piece, memento of an age that was swept away for ever by the First World War.

I can no longer think of these houses simply as architectural specimens, as handsome façades to adorn a coloured calendar. The more closely I came to know them, the more I came to associate them with the human beings who had built them or added to them or pulled them about or destroyed them – all the Beginners, Advancers, Continuers and Ruiners, all the Actors on the Theatres of Great Families.

At Craigievar Castle, that quintessence of how a castle should look, I find everywhere the presence of a man called Danzig Willie – William Forbes, younger son of landed gentry who made good in his own right as a merchant and celebrated his fortune by building himself a dream castle.

At The House of The Binns I meet the shade of General Tam Dalyell, scourge of the Covenanters, who was reputed to roast his prisoners alive in the huge baking-oven in the barrel-vaulted kitchen.

At Castle Fraser, a shapely wooden leg on display in the dining-room belonged to a great nineteenth-century laird, Colonel Charles Mackenzie, who lost a leg in the Peninsular War and 'improved' the castle with boundless but disastrous enthusiasm.

Kellie Castle is haunted by a pair of red slippers said to have been worn by a lovelorn daughter of the house who jumped to her death when trying to elope; but it is also the story of the remarkable Lorimer family of Edinburgh who rescued it from total ruin in the nick of time late last century.

At Leith Hall, home of the martial Leith-Hays, the spirit that pervades the house is that of a gentle Jacobite giant, John Hay, exiled for years after the 1745 Rebellion, who saved the estate and house from bankruptcy by sacrificing his own home.

Brodie Castle, home of the Brodies for more than four centuries, is a living gallery of memorable characters, but none more so than Alexander Brodie, Lord Lyon King of Arms in the first half of the eighteenth century, who lived so extravagantly and improved the castle so exuberantly that he left his ancestral estate bankrupt.

Haddo House and the Prime Minister Earl of Aberdeen who presided over the Crimean War and died a sad and heartbroken old man after a youth of golden promise; Falkland Palace, and the royal bedchamber in which the dying James v breathed his bitter epitaph on the Stuart dynasty – 'It cam' wi' a lass, and will gang wi' a lass'; Hill of Tarvit and the wealthy jute financier, Frederick Sharp, who built it to house his collection of *objets d'art* but whose line was cruelly snuffed out when his only son was killed in a rail disaster in the 1930s; Brodick Castle and the nineteenth-century sporting Dukes of Hamilton who brought society to Arran but nearly ruined their birthright with their wild gambling. . . .

For all these great houses, the twentieth century has created a new future for their past, through the National Trust for Scotland. With one or two exceptions such as Haddo House and Brodie Castle, where the twenty-fifth Brodie still resides in kilted splendour and is almost as great a tourist attraction as the castle itself, the ancestral families no longer live in their ancestral homes. Their place has been taken by a new generation of Trust representatives, who are as varied and interesting as the former owners. At Brodick Castle, John Forgie, who is joint representative with his wife Wilma, was formerly picture editor on *The Scotsman* newspaper. At Craigievar, the representative is Miss Raeburn Murray, an Edinburgh-born nurse who served in the Queen Elizabeth's Overseas Nursing Service, in Uganda. The administrator at Culzean Castle, Captain John Mott, is a retired naval officer. At Leith Hall the representative, Sandy le Gassick, is a former military man – most appropriately, in a house that enshrines so many military memories. Haddo House has a representative, Mrs Iona Maclean; but one wing is still occupied, busily, by Lady Aberdeen, who with her late husband turned Haddo into the musical mecca of the north – which it still is. The representative at Kellie Castle is the distinguished sculptor Hew Lorimer, grandson of that first Lorimer who saved the place from utter ruin. And so on.

There seem to be no formal qualifications needed to win the job of being a representative – only an intense love of the place, a deep interest in history, and a positive enjoyment of meeting people. Very few of them had any pretensions to being historians before they were appointed; they did their homework afterwards – and they are still doing it. After a short time in office they become formidably knowledgeable, for a great house is an endless quarry for historical research. They learn from books and family papers, they learn from chance visitors who recognize a piece of furniture, or have a story to pass on. They all look on 'their' houses as homes, and treat them as such; and this makes every visitor feel like a guest, not a tourist. Without exception, they gave me unstintingly of their time and knowledge, and I am deeply grateful to them all.

I am also greatly indebted to the authors of the National Trust for Scotland guidebooks on the specific properties which are the subjects of this book; these guidebooks are available at all N.T.S. centres. In them, the avid pilgrim will find detailed information about the contents of the houses – the art treasures, the furnishings, the keepsakes – which I have tended to omit in my pursuit of the houses themselves. They are written with enormous erudition, and I have plundered them shamelessly.

This book has been written to celebrate the Golden Jubilee of the National Trust for Scotland and its achievements. The Treasures of Scotland singled out in these pages are only a section of what the Trust holds in care for the Scottish nation, and thereby for the world at large. Membership of the Trust has just broken through the magic 100,000 mark. Over a million visitors now come to savour and enjoy Trust properties the length and breadth of Scotland – castles, palaces, gardens, coastlines, battlefields, mountain areas, historic houses and cottages. The story of the formation of the National Trust for Scotland fifty years ago by a dedicated group of eleven Scots is an inspiring tale in itself; it is thanks to their foresight and patriotism that in the 1980s millions of people will be able to share the Treasures of Scotland that the Trust has saved from the ultimate. Ruiners, time and neglect.

The imposing southern facade of Brodick Castle on the island of Arran.

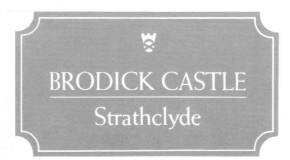

BRODICK CASTLE
Strathclyde

THE GENERATIONS of children who have built sandcastles on Brodick beach and knocked them down again with triumphant cries of 'I'm the king of the castle!' were merely re-enacting, if they only knew it, what kept happening to Brodick Castle over a period of nearly a thousand years. Brodick Castle is the story of Scotland carved in sandstone, a story of trying to impose order upon chaos, century by century, layer upon layer. Today it is one of the oldest habitable houses owned by the National Trust for Scotland, in part going back to the fourteenth century, to the time of King Robert the Bruce himself. It's the sandstone castle that wouldn't lie down.

As it stands now it is a magnificently imposing mansion, solid and unshakeable, commanding the wide sweep of Brodick Bay. Around it lie sixty-five acres of spectacular gardens that help to attract 50,000 visitors a year; behind it lie 7300 acres of mountain, hill and moor that form a microcosm of Scotland's geology. Inside it resides a spectacular collection of pictures and *objets d'art*, remnants of the hoard of treasures garnered by one of England's richest and most eccentric connoisseurs, William Beckford. Altogether, Brodick Castle today presents an alluring face of effortless serenity, of wealth and privilege buttressed by good taste and hard work. But behind that smiling façade is a very different story.

The building wasn't always a castle, but there must have been some sort of fastness there on the north side of Brodick Bay on the island of Arran as far back as the fifth century AD, when Celts from Ireland came over to found the kingdom of Dalriada in south-western Scotland. Arran had considerable strategic importance on the western sea-routes, lying fifteen miles off the Ayrshire coast in the estuary of the Clyde. And so, throughout all the turbulent years of Scotland's history, the stronghold at Brodick was harried and plundered, besieged and assailed, stormed and captured by a succession of Celts, Vikings, Lords of the Isles, Macdonalds and Campbells, Stuarts and Douglases, king's men, Covenanters and Cromwellians. Its ownership by a series of Scottish kings and then by the most powerful family in Scotland – the Hamiltons, themselves of royal descent – made it a natural target in every conflict. Time and again it was pronounced 'utterly destroyed', but every time it was knocked down someone else raised it up again, ready for the next onslaught. The last person to rebuild it as a fortress was none other than Oliver Cromwell who, having beheaded the first Duke of Hamilton in 1649 (shortly after King Charles I himself was beheaded) ordered his Ironsides to add a battery and a garrison wing to the castle. It was never knocked down, and it was still standing as Cromwell's men had left it when, two hundred years later, the tenth Duke of Hamilton decided to upgrade the castle from a luxury hunting-lodge to the splendid mansion house it is today.

It was only then, in 1844, when the accommodation in the old keep was more than doubled, that Brodick Castle really came into its own. With a couple of judicious marriages into English wealth and European royalty, the Hamiltons gave Brodick a heady heyday in the Victorian age, when the rich, the titled and the talented flocked to

Arran. But it was not to last. The Hamiltons had always had a historic compulsion to gamble for the very highest stakes. In the old days they had gambled for crowns, and sometimes lost their heads; now their gambling energies turned to horses, and soon they were faced with financial disaster. Yet when their other castles and palaces were empty or in ruins, the red sandstone castle on the island of Arran that had withstood the slings and battering-rams of ancient battles now survived the modern onslaught of death duties and inflation. In 1958 the castle and its contents were accepted in lieu of estate duty by the Commissioners of Inland Revenue, and the Treasury conveyed them to the National Trust for Scotland to become the focal point of a thriving island tourist industry. Refurbished and painted, cleaned and cossetted by a tiny but devoted staff, Brodick Castle is now making up for the centuries of violence, ill-treatment and neglect that almost laid it low for ever.

But where does one start the story of Brodick? There was the ebb and flow of Celts, followed by the Norsemen in the ninth century who made Arran part of a loosely supervised island empire (the Hebrides and the Isle of Man) until any direct Norwegian influence was ended as a result of the Battle of Largs in 1263. Whatever fort or keep guarded Brodick Bay at that time passed into the possession of the Scottish Crown, and seems to have been rebuilt or strengthened not long afterwards. The oldest masonry in the present castle, in the round tower in the south-eastern corner, dates back to the thirteenth century.

After the tragic and untimely death of King Alexander III of Scotland (he fell with his horse from a cliff at Kinghorn in Fife in 1286), Scotland was racked with violent struggles for the succession. In 1307, according to the near-contemporary account of John Barbour in *The Bruce*, Robert the Bruce paused on Arran while on his way from Rathlin Island (off Ireland) to start his seven-year campaign on the mainland to consolidate, at Bannockburn, the crown he had been awarded at Scone in March 1306. In advance of his arrival in Arran, Bruce had authorized a raid on the English garrison at Brodick Castle; but the castle held fast, and Bruce had to be content with roughing it in a nearby glen until he felt the time was ripe for his comeback. There is no record of Bruce ever having entered the castle, although traditional wishful thinking would have it so. In Brodick Castle, in the old tower up a winding turnpike stair, there is even a vaulted chamber rather fancifully known as Bruce's room. The Trust makes no such claim for it now; the room has been done up as a prison cell, complete with a rotting skeleton (a 'rickle o' banes') in the corner to represent a certain gentleman called Yellow John who was starved and then stabbed to death there in 1715, and may have scratched on the wall the legend 'May 1715 had barley'.

For nearly two centuries after Bruce's victory at Bannockburn, Arran and Brodick Castle was royal property again. But that didn't make it invulnerable (or inalienable, as it is under the Trust today). It was destroyed by an English fleet in 1406. It was 'stormed and levelled to the ground' again in 1455 by the Lord of the Isles.

In 1503 the castle and much of the island of Arran passed to the Hamilton family, and Brodick as it now stands is almost completely the creation of that family. It came about in a manner as bizarre and wayward as anything else in Scottish politics at that time.

In 1467 Sir Thomas Boyd of Kilmarnock married Princess Mary, sister of King James III who was still a minor and under the control of the ambitious Boyd family. Sir Thomas was created Earl of Arran to match his new status as the young king's brother-in-law. Two years later, as soon as the king reached his majority at the age of eighteen and married Princess Margaret of Denmark, he turned against his 'guardians'. The Earl of Arran was stripped of his lands and titles while he was a refugee in Denmark, his wife was ordered home for a divorce, and she was then given in marriage to the elderly James, first Baron Hamilton, by whom she had a son called James, who succeeded as second Baron Hamilton. In August 1503 King James IV married Princess Margaret, daughter of

above The entrance hall of
Brodick Castle lined with
eighty-seven stags' heads, all
but one of them red deer shot
on the island. Above the
fireplace is the carved device
of the dukes of Hamilton.

right The bedroom on the
south-west front, as used by
Mary Louise, Duchess of
Montrose. The four-poster
bed is by Hepplewhite; the
adjustable rosewood bed table
is early Victorian.

13

The dining-room, hung with sporting pictures acquired by the gambling dukes of Hamilton.

Henry VII of England. Prominent among the guests was his cousin, James Hamilton, who attended with a splendid retinue. In the tournament that was held to mark the occasion, the young Hamilton tilted so nobly that the king, carried away by enthusiasm, conferred upon him on the spot the earldom of Arran of which his aunt's first husband had been stripped.

That was how the Hamiltons, who had been climbing the ladder of political power for a long time, came into the royal succession and landed estate. Throughout the sixteenth century they were to play a major part in the power struggles around the Scottish throne as one infant royal Stuart after another succeeded to the throne. It was to be a century of vicious violence and sordid intrigues for power. As a descendant of James II through his daughter, Princess Mary, any Hamilton Earl of Arran was an heir presumptive to the throne if a Stuart died without issue; and for much of the century the Hamiltons were only, as the saying goes, a heartbeat from the throne.

The new Earl of Arran, so fortuitously elevated by his prowess at the lists, set about rebuilding the keep at Brodick, and displayed an over-optimistic faith in future peace by adding a great hall on the west side (the forerunner of the present dining-room). But in 1529, a year before his death, the castle was 'destroyed' yet again in a feud between Stuarts and Hamiltons over the possession of the young King James V. It happened again in 1554, in the course of another feud over the possession of the infant Mary Queen of Scots.

What a dreadful time it was! Poor James V of Scotland had died in December 1542, leaving a week-old infant, Mary, heiress to the throne. At once the intrigues began. The second Earl of Arran, who was next in line to the throne if Mary should die, was appointed Regent. It would have surprised nobody if an 'accident' had befallen the baby to enable Arran himself to assume the crown. Instead he agreed to overtures from King Henry VIII of England to betroth the child to his five-year-old son, the future King Edward VI. The Scots, however, repudiated the treaty, whereupon Henry VIII sent armies to devastate Scotland in retaliation – the so-called 'rough wooing'. In the course of these incursions Arran's rival, the Earl of Lennox, was entrusted with an invasion of the Clyde aimed at capturing Dumbarton Castle; this he failed to achieve but 'he did great execution in the Regent's lands in Arran, utterly destroying Brodick'.

Not surprisingly, Arran's enthusiasm for the English connection cooled rapidly as a result, and he started fostering the French connection, the 'Auld Alliance', as represented by the infant queen's mother, Mary of Guise. In 1548, at the age of five, little Mary Queen of Scots was dispatched to France to be affianced for eventual marriage to the dauphin of France; and in that same year the Earl of Arran was rewarded for his services by the dauphin's father, King Henry II, with the dukedom of Chatelherault. In 1554 Arran surrendered his Regency to the Queen Mother, Mary of Guise. When the sixteen-year-old Mary Queen of Scots eventually married the dauphin in 1558, England's wrath boiled over again; and once again Brodick Castle was burned down during a punitive expedition by the Earl of Sussex.

Nothing daunted, the Earl of Arran immediately started rebuilding Brodick Castle, and it was this remodelling and enlarging that forms the kernel of the castle today, with the main round tower at the east end. But Arran himself still had royal dynastic ambitions; when Mary Queen of Scots returned to Scotland a widow in 1561 (her husband, by then King Francis II of France, had died after the briefest of reigns in 1560), Arran had high hopes of marrying her to his eldest son, James, the future third Earl of Arran. Alas for his hopes: Queen Mary chose instead to marry her cousin, the appalling Lord Darnley, son of Arran's bitterest foe, the Earl of Lennox.

Baulked of the greatest prize of all, the Hamiltons were to take bloody revenge and suffer revenge in turn. The birth of the future King James VI of Scotland and I of England in August 1566 put paid to Arran's dreams of a Hamilton dynasty that might one day have ruled not just Scotland but the United Kingdom too; but the family was still prepared to gamble everything in a reckless quest for power. When Mary Queen of Scots was forced to abdicate in 1567 in favour of her baby son, another Regent was required. Once again the Earl of Arran (and now Duke of Chatelherault), who was still heir presumptive after the infant King James VI, thought his turn had come. Instead, the Regent chosen was Mary's illegitimate half-brother, James Stewart, Earl of Moray. Early in 1570, Moray was assassinated in Linlithgow by a Hamilton – James Hamilton of Bothwellhaugh – who was subsequently given refuge in Brodick Castle.

Even now the Regency did not come to Arran, as the Hamiltons had hoped; it went to the Earl of Lennox, father of Darnley and grandfather of the child king. Within a year he too had been murdered. It still did the Hamiltons no good. Other Regents were appointed in rapid succession; and one of them, the implacable Earl of Morton, broke the Hamiltons and their dreams of glory soon after the death of the second Earl of Arran in 1575. His sons were arraigned for complicity in the murders of Moray and Lennox and stripped of their lands and titles.

The eldest son, James, erstwhile suitor of Mary Queen of Scots, and by this time an imbecile, was imprisoned. His brothers fled into exile. It was not until 1599 that the Hamiltons got back into royal favour with King James VI. In that year John, the middle son, on the occasion of the baptism of the king's daughter Margaret, was created the first Marquess of Hamilton.

For nearly four decades, after the Union of the Crowns in 1603, Scotland (and Brodick) enjoyed a period of rare peace and prosperity. But by the time of the third Marquess of Hamilton, Scotland had plunged headlong into strife again over the National Covenant. Hamilton, a staunch Royalist, got himself appointed King's Commissioner in Scotland. He strengthened Brodick's defences, but to no avail; in 1639 the Marquess of Argyll, the Covenant's Warden of the West, captured the castle and installed a Campbell garrison. The Campbells were later driven out, and in 1643 King Charles I, by now embroiled in the Civil War against the Parliamentarians, rewarded Hamilton for his loyalty by making him the first Duke of Hamilton.

That loyalty was to cost him dear: in 1649, just a few weeks after the execution of Charles I, the Duke of Hamilton was beheaded as well. He was succeeded by his brother, William, the second duke, whose portrait hangs in the drawing-room; but he did not have long to enjoy his inheritance. He attended the coronation of King Charles II at Scone on 1 January 1651, and was with the king at the crushing defeat of the Scots army at Worcester in September 1651. He was severely wounded during the battle, and died a few days later. There were no male heirs to the dukedom.

Cromwell had no difficulty in subduing Scotland after the Battle of Worcester – and now something unusual happened to Brodick Castle. Instead of being knocked about again, it acquired a new occupier in the unlikely person of Oliver Cromwell himself. He put in a garrison of Ironsides and English levies with orders to turn the castle into a mini-fortress. First they built a new battery with loopholes for artillery at the east end, commanding the Firth of Clyde. Then they conscripted Scottish stonemasons to add an extension on the west side, presumably as extra accommodation for the garrison. The upper floor of this Cromwellian extension is now the old library, while the ground floor with its heavy barrel-vaulted ceiling has been converted into a tea room for visitors. Architecturally, the extension is almost indistinguishable from the older tower that had been built a century earlier by the second Earl of Arran, slightly set back but matching it in height and in three courses of corbelling under the battlements. The castle was to remain as Cromwell's men left it for some two hundred years before the Hamiltons made it the spendid house it is today.

Meanwhile the Hamilton fortunes were at a very low ebb. There was no male heir. The estates were heavily in debt, the family had been fined by the Commonwealth government and some of their lands forfeited. It was now that a very remarkable lady came on the scene – Anne, daughter of the first Duke of Hamilton who had died on the scaffold in 1649. Under the terms of the original creation of the dukedom in 1643 she inherited the title as Duchess of Hamilton in her own right after her uncle's death in 1651. In Arran she is always remembered, fondly and respectfully, as 'Good Duchess Anne'.

Her portrait, by David Scougal, hangs above the fireplace in the boudoir: a striking woman in a satin dress and blue and grey wrap. Not beautiful (the nose is too long), she had an arresting appearance, strong featured and brimming with character. She married William Douglas, second son of the Marquess of Douglas, who took the name of Hamilton, and on the Restoration of Charles II in 1660 he was (at Duchess Anne's request) invested with the title of third Duke of Hamilton.

Good Duchess Anne added nothing to the castle itself, but she restored the fortunes of the Hamilton family and of the island of Arran. She paid off the fines that had been imposed. She persuaded the restored king to repay a loan her father had made to his father. Through Parliament she forced the Campbells to pay reparations of 3000 Scots merks for the damage they had done to the island during their occupation in the 1640s. She built roads on the island, and a small pier and basin at Lamlash known as Duchess Anne's Quay. She was the first Hamilton laird to treat Brodick as a home rather than just as a fastness to retreat to in times of trouble or as a hunting-lodge. Shrewd and tough-minded, she passed on to her family more of the island than it had ever owned before. A remarkable lady, she also had fourteen children.

The fourth duke, James Douglas, came to an unhappy end – and it was his second wife, Elizabeth Gerrard (whose portrait hangs in the gallery), who was the indirect cause of it. She and her cousin were co-heiresses of the extremely wealthy Earl of Macclesfield; the cousin was married to a notorious rake, Lord Mohun (pronounced Moon), a brawler and dueller who was twice tried and acquitted by the House of Lords for murder. Hamilton and Mohun disputed the Macclesfield inheritance in a court case that dragged on for years. Eventually a chance remark in court in the year 1712 led to a duel, which was fought by the pond in Kensington Gardens; both protagonists were killed. This episode was featured by Thackeray in his novel *Henry Esmond*.

One way or another, marriages were to continue to play a highly significant part in the fortunes of the Hamiltons and of Brodick Castle itself. The fifth duke, for instance, had three wives; after his death, his third wife, Anne Spencer, married into the family of Orange Nassau (Richard Savage Nassau, younger son of the third Earl of Rochford), establishing the first of the exotic family connections that were to provide Brodick with the marvellous art treasures that distinguish it today. The widow of the sixth duke, Elizabeth Gunning, having given birth to two future dukes of Hamilton, later married the fifth Duke of Argyll and thereafter gave birth to two future dukes of Argyll, which must be some kind of a record.

The nineteenth century brought spectacular changes to Brodick and to the Isle of Arran. It was the century of the 'Clearances', of Victorian aggrandisement, of conspicuous wealth and conspicuous poverty. The story of Arran tells it all.

The second half of the eighteenth century had seen the introduction of large-scale agricultural changes on the ducal estates, abolishing the old run-rig system of small farms and enclosing them into larger units at higher rents. In 1829, when the tenth duke was laird, all the people from the farms in the north end of the island – seventeen families in all – were evicted to make way for a single sheep-farm and packed off to Canada, the duke paying half their fares. This was a Clearance writ large in island memories. In 1978 a memorial was unveiled at Lamlash to commemorate those who had been forced to emigrate to 'Scotch Settlement' in Megantic County. Descendants of those clearance victims came back for the ceremony; according to John Forgie, the Trust representative at Brodick Castle, 'Those who survived certainly appeared to have prospered'.

The dukes of Hamilton prospered too. They had a new source of wealth apart from

above Porcelain sweetmeat boxes from the display cabinet in the flower room.

above left Part of the superb collection of china and porcelain on display in the flower room, also called the china room.

far left The 'Brodick Owls': part of a set of thirty drinking horns of walrus tusks with silver mountings.

left From the Beckford Collection: one of a set of six Venetian stools in the form of crouching Nubian boys supporting upholstered cushions.

agriculture – the Lanarkshire coalfields around their main ducal seat of Hamilton Palace. And this was sensationally augmented when the tenth duke married Susan Euphemia Beckford in 1810; for Susan Euphemia Beckford happened to be the younger daughter and co-heiress of the fabulously rich and eccentric art collector, William Beckford of Fonthill.

Beckford, whose macabre deathbed portrait by Willes Maddox hangs in the boudoir landing, was one of the more extravagant products of the sybaritic Augustan Age. He was the son of an immensely wealthy alderman and Lord Mayor of London who had inherited a 'plantation fortune' in Jamaica, a luxurious and licentious man whose country house in Wiltshire was known as Fonthill Splendens. In 1770, at the age of only ten, the boy Beckford inherited the whole of his father's huge fortune. He was intensely precocious and sensitive as a young man (at the age of five he was given lessons in musical composition by Mozart, who was himself only nine at the time), and soon became obsessed with hedonism and the occult; in a scandalous age, his voluptuous bisexual orgies at Fonthill scandalized society sufficiently for him to be ostracized. Yet he was also a man of considerable literary ability, and an art collector of genius. Today he is remembered as the author of some lively travel journals and an 'Arabian' novel, a Gothic fantasy written in French while he was in his twenties, entitled *The History of the Caliph Vathek*. He is remembered also for the building of the ultimate in follies, the palace of Fonthill Abbey with its huge octagonal tower (over 260 feet high), which collapsed into ruin soon after it was completed. There is a magnificent watercolour of it, by Turner, in the boudoir landing. He was a strange and complex man, intelligent and deeply read, but soured by experience and contemptuous of the world. His enormous collection (despite the sale of Fonthill Abbey and most of its contents in 1822) embraced paintings, books and *objets d'art* of every conceivable kind; and this was what Susan Euphemia, Duchess of Hamilton, inherited when her father died in 1844 at the ripe old age of eighty-four.

It was a fortunate time in which to come into a massive inheritance. In the previous year the duke and duchess (their portraits, also by Willes Maddox, hang at the head of the staircase) had celebrated the most glittering Hamilton wedding yet, when their eldest son William, Marquess of Douglas and Clydesdale and the future eleventh duke, married Princess Marie of Baden, daughter of the Grand Duke of Baden. Her mother was Stephanie de Beauharnais, niece of the Empress Josephine and adopted daughter of Napoleon Bonaparte. The Hamiltons decided that Brodick Castle should be transformed into a fitting home for the young couple, and so after five hundred years of ups and downs the old house was to be extended and renovated.

The man commissioned to carry out the renovation was the Edinburgh architect James Gillespie Graham, who had a large practice throughout Scotland in the middle of the nineteenth century. Starting where Cromwell had left off, he extended Brodick westwards, contriving not to stick a Victorian monstrosity on to the simple older buildings but to blend old and new in a style that harked harmoniously back to the indigenous Scots baronial style. Using the same local red sandstone as was used in the older building, he put up two towers which were linked to Cromwell's old library and dining-room by a magnificent drawing-room, flanked by a gallery thirty yards long that ran the length of the building to the old tower and Cromwell's battery. The end result was what Schomberg Scott described (in *The National Trust for Scotland Guide*) as 'a building such as only Scotland can show, making its effect, like its seventeenth-century prototypes, by height and the almost stark simplicity which at first belies and then enhances the richness within'.

'The richness within' now includes the remnants of the great Beckford Collection, on display in practically every room. At the time the future eleventh Duke of Hamilton ushered his German bride across the threshold of the 'new' Brodick, 'the treasures within' meant superb and elaborate decoration. The new entrance hall in the west tower boasts a large carved fireplace bearing the device of the dukes of Hamilton – an oak tree practically cut through by an old-fashioned woodman's saw. It commemorates a legendary incident in 1323 when Sir Gilbert Hamilton, one of the early founders of the family, was being pursued by a posse of king's men through a wood. Sir Gilbert and his companion changed clothes with some woodcutters who were working in a clearing, and as their pursuers arrived they shouted 'Through!' (the equivalent of today's 'Timber!'), meaning that the saw was almost through; the soldiers thought it meant the fugitives had gone on through the wood, and rushed on after them.

The lofty drawing-room, the social hub of the house, has a magnificent white and gold plaster ceiling on which Italian craftsmen worked the Hamilton family history in heraldic terms from the time of James II and the first Baron Hamilton. New plaster ceilings, less ornate but no less elegant, adorn the old library and the dining-room. The panelling in the dining-room comes from Letheringham Abbey, near Easton Park in Suffolk, an estate that came to the Hamiltons through the Nassau family.

The portraits of the eleventh duke and his German princess hang in that splendid drawing-room today. Princess Marie was painted with Goatfell, the highest peak on Arran, in the background. It is a little sad to relate that she never really enjoyed her magnificent new home; she was lonely and unhappy, for there was no one with whom she could speak German.

The fortunes of the Hamilton family were now at a conspicuous peak; but in reality they were being seriously undermined by generations of 'sporting' dukes, from the eighth onwards, who plunged heavily into the sporting life with manic enthusiasm – horse-racing, prize-fighting, bear-baiting, cock-fighting, anything on which they could gamble. Between them they accumulated a hoard of sporting trophies, now at Brodick, and a vast sporting library; they commissioned and bought paintings and cartoons which are a historical record of the most colourful events and characters of a vanished era. Most of this fine collection of sporting memorabilia is now in the dining-room. A painting of the fight between Gentleman Jack Jackson and Daniel Mendoza at Hornchurch in 1795 shows the eighth duke standing in the front row of spectators. The eighth and ninth dukes won the St Leger no fewer than seven times in twenty-eight years (1786–1814).

But it was an expensive business, and in 1862 the tenth duke held a huge sale at Hamilton Palace including much of the Beckford Collection that his wife Susan Euphemia had inherited. But even this was hardly enough to satisfy the gambling mania of the Hamiltons. In 1863 the eleventh duke died, to be succeeded by the most spectacular sporting duke of them all, William Alexander, the twelfth duke, then a young man of eighteen. A bust of him, with his hair severely parted in the middle, stands on the staircase in the entrance hall. He had made himself a reputation as a compulsive gambler at Oxford, and now he started cutting a great dash on the racecourses of England and France with a string of horses of his own. He won the Grand National with Cortolvin in 1867, but his losses were so sensational that even he had to cut back on his racing activities. Back he came, however; his great horse Friday (painted by John Duval) won him the Chesterfield Cup at Goodwood in 1878 – a splendid silver trophy of an American Indian in hot pursuit of a bison, now at Brodick. Four years later he won it again, with Vibration; this time the trophy represented Lady Godiva on horseback. They didn't skimp on trophies in those days.

It all had to be paid for, however. In the year he won the Chesterfield Cup for the second time, he held another huge sale of the Beckford Collection in London that lasted three days. The list of 'pictures, works of art and decorative objects' covered 234 pages of a leather-bound catalogue, and it realized £700,000. In effect, he was exchanging a major part of the Beckford Collection for the outstanding collection of nineteenth-century sporting mementoes that make Brodick today such a fascinating historical document.

What was left of the Beckford Collection came to Brodick Castle, which had blossomed anew with the advent of steam, steamships (most of them named after the Hamilton family) that connected with mainland railway trains to bring the famous and the fashionable to shoot and stalk on Arran. Robert Browning holidayed on the island, and so did Lewis Carroll. Asquith called Corrie one of the prettiest villages in Europe.

There were also new continental relations. The twelfth duke's sister, Lady Mary, married Prince Albert of Monaco; her great-grandson, Prince Rainier, was to spend happy summer holidays at Brodick as a little boy, running around the battlements and shouting down the old chimneys to give the cook a fright. Lady Mary later married Count Tassilo Festetics de Tolna, a Hungarian prince, and a huge stag's head he shot in Hungary is one of the overpowering collection of eighty-seven heads that cover the walls of the entrance hall.

But now the direct Hamilton line was coming to an end. When the twelfth duke died in 1895 he had no male heir. He had an eleven-year-old daughter, Lady Mary Louise, but unlike her ancestor the Good Duchess Anne she was not allowed to assume the title in her own right, so a new Hamilton line had to be traced back to James, the fourth duke, to produce a thirteenth Duke of Hamilton. His son, Douglas, who became fourteenth duke in 1940, was the first man to fly over Mount Everest, and was the man whom Rudolf Hess was trying to contact when he made his bizarre flight to Scotland in 1941. The fifteenth duke inherited in 1973, and now lives at Lennoxlove, near Edinburgh.

But at least the twelfth duke had bequeathed Brodick Castle to his daughter, Mary Louise. In 1906 she married the sixth Duke of Montrose, and from then until her death in 1957 at the age of seventy-two, Brodick Castle enjoyed a last flourish as a private family home – and gained a new and inestimable treasure, the 'wild' woodland garden down the hill between the castle and the bay.

The part of the house most closely associated with Mary Louise, Duchess of Montrose, is the suite of three rooms that leads off the landing at the head of the staircase: the dressing-room and bedroom on the west front, the boudoir overlooking the garden, and its associated boudoir landing. These rooms reflect an interesting blend of personal memories and choice items from the Beckford Collection – paintings, porcelain and furniture. This was typical of the family life of the Montroses: their four children (two sons and two daughters) grew up surrounded by priceless treasures, yet as Lady Jean Fforde, the youngest of the family, says: 'They were just things we used every day, silver cutlery, candlesticks, china, porcelain serving-dishes. They were always in use.' The present Duke of Montrose (the seventh), who lives in Zimbabwe, recalls how as children they used to have races along the gallery on the backs of a pair of Chinese goose-shaped soup-tureens of the eighteenth-century Chien Lung period!

The Duke and Duchess of Montrose were essentially homely people, in the best sense of that term. The duke was an enthusiastic inventor, and has been credited with the invention of the aircraft carrier. The duchess was an artist and musician; a splendid portrait of her, looking very beautiful at the age of twenty-eight and painted by Philip de Laszlo, hangs in the drawing-room above her Bechstein piano. She was also an enthusiastic dog breeder, and at one time there were seventy dogs in the Brodick kennels. But above all she was a skilled and knowledgeable gardener, and it was she who was responsible for creating at Brodick one of the finest rhododendron gardens in Europe.

There had been a walled garden immediately below the castle at its eastern end since early in the eighteenth century; this the duchess restored, with rose-beds, shrubs and herbaceous borders (the Trust simplified it twenty years ago but is now redesigning it to the way it was in Victorian times). But her great joy, and greatest achievement and lasting memorial, is the woodland garden. It was planned and planted early in the 1920s by the duchess and her much-loved son-in-law, Major John Boscawen; together they brought in palm trees and exotic shrubs that would thrive in the temperate climate of the North

The view over Brodick Bay from the castle gardens.

Atlantic Drift that caresses Scotland's west coast, and an enormous selection of rhododendrons. Brodick, you might say, *is* rhododendrons. Ironically it was the twelfth duke who introduced the first rhododendrons to Arran and planted them with great ceremony; today, true to his track record, wild rhododendrons now run riot all over the estate and up the hillsides, ruining large tracts of land for forestry.

With the death of her husband in 1954, the duchess realized that the castle and estate could have no future as a family home – death duties would cripple it irredeemably. So this remarkable heritage came to the National Trust for Scotland in 1958, via the Treasury; a public appeal for £10,000 made it possible for the Trust to accept the property, and Lady Jean Fforde, who moved into Strabane House on the estate, added her own generous gift of 7300 acres of mountainous land that includes Goatfell, Cir Mhor ('The Great Comb'), one of Scotland's finest rock-climbs, and lovely Glen Rosa. It has given Brodick a fairy-tale setting of mountain and sea, exotic flowers and treasures, that enhances it immeasurably – the old pile that refused to lie down, and now never will.

Brodie Castle, Grampian.

BRODIE CASTLE
Grampian

It was Alexander, nineteenth Brodie of Brodie, who introduced the Bulstrode Scale for assessing the role played by successive owners of great houses in the ebb and flow of their fortunes. Alexander's elder brother James had succeeded to the family castle and estates, midway between Forres and Nairn in Morayshire (now part of Grampian), as eighteenth Brodie of Brodie in 1714. Alexander himself was not yet the laird of Brodie, nor had he any realistic expectation of becoming so, when he wrote to James in December 1717:

I hope you will bear with me a little and allow yourself to read what I have read and collected from books and the little I have seen of the world in relation of Great Families.

Sir Richard Bulstrode in his *Miscellaneous Essays* [1715] observed that there are four different Actors on the Theatres of Great Families: The Beginner, the Advancer, the Continuer and the Ruiner...

Little did he know that within three years his brother would be dead without issue, and he himself laird of Brodie; and that in his extravagant attempts to become the Advancer, he would end up as Brodie's Ruiner. But at least he was a Ruiner in glorious style and scale. As Lord Lyon King of Arms, Member of Parliament for Elgin, he lived exuberantly and far beyond his means, leaving debts of £18,268 15s 4½d when he died in 1754.

Fortunately for the Brodies of Brodie, however, there was another 'Actor on the Theatres of Great Families' that Bulstrode never mentioned – the Rescuer. Time and again the estates were to be almost miraculously rescued at the eleventh hour, to allow the family to survive in the house they have inhabited for more than four hundred years.

Four centuries is a long time for one family to have lived in the same house, making it a kind of domestic time machine. But the Brodies, or Brothies, have been living in the Laigh of Moray for at least twice as long as that, certainly from the twelfth century and quite possibly long before that, making them one of the oldest untitled landed families in the country. Some historians, notably Dr Ian Grimble, are convinced that the Brodies are descended from King Brude, the king of the northern Picts who was converted to Christianity by St Columba late in the sixth century. Less speculatively, monastic records of the eleventh century make a mention of a long-established family of 'Brothies' in that part of Morayshire, suggesting that the name may have derived from a Gaelic word meaning 'ditch' or 'mire' – an apt description of the lands first bestowed by King Malcolm IV in 1160 on a family from the ancient Moraviensis line. There was a thane of Brodie in the reign of Alexander III in the thirteenth century, and another in the fourteenth century who received a charter from Robert the Bruce in 1311.

From the time of the Beginner, Alexander, twelfth Brodie of Brodie, who built the original house in the 1560s, to Ninian, twenty-fifth Brodie of Brodie, who lives there today, there is a well-documented and almost unbroken male line of Brodie lairds. The only hiatus came with James, the sixteenth laird, who left only daughters – nine in all; but one of them promptly married a cousin, thus keeping the line more or less intact. And whether the family took their name from King Brude or from the miriness of their land, the laird of Brodie became the Brodie of Brodie, and in the good Scots way he was addressed correctly – as Ninian the twenty-fifth laird is to this day – simply as 'Brodie'.

Brodie Castle, or Brodie House as it was first called, dates back to 1567, as a carved stone in the south-west tower indicates. The Beginner, Alexander Brodie, had been a supporter of Lord Huntly against Mary Queen of Scots and had fought with him at the Battle of Corrichie, near Aberdeen, in 1562, where Huntly fell; and though Brodie himself escaped with his life, the Brodie lands were confiscated. He was pardoned in 1566, however, and got his estates back, and it was in the following year – the dramatic year in which Mary's husband, Lord Darnley, was murdered in Edinburgh and the queen herself forced to abdicate – that Alexander Brodie, the twelfth laird, began to build his castle.

He built it to the standard sixteenth-century design familiar throughout the north-east of Scotland, a tall tower house on the so-called 'Z'-plan, rising straight and solid over the flat Morayshire landscape: a central hall-building reinforced by two towers set diagonally at opposite corners. The house was entered by a door directly into the high hall (now the red drawing-room) on the first floor; food was brought up from the kitchens below (now the entrance hall), and Brodie could step straight from his seat at the high table through a door into his private sitting-room and to a stairway leading to the laird's apartments above.

Brodie House was not to stay unchanged for long. Early in the seventeenth century a new wing was added to provide more living accommodation. This had the effect of shifting the focal point of the house from the high hall to a more sophisticated suite of rooms associated with the laird's drawing-room (now the dining-room) in the new block. But it was the original laird's chamber (now known as the blue sitting-room) in the old keep or main tower that provided Brodie House with the first of the many treasures for which it is renowned today – an exuberant if somewhat crude strapwork plaster ceiling.

This was the work of the fifteenth laird, another Alexander Brodie. He had succeeded his father in 1632 at the age of fifteen. No sooner had he come of age in 1635 than he married Elizabeth Innes, and it was to celebrate this double event that he had the ornamental plasterwork of the ceiling installed; their lovingly entwined monogram appears in the embrasure of the south window. It was probably of Scottish workmanship. From the boss in the centre of the ceiling a hand protrudes grasping a bunch of arrows, but since the craftsmanship is different it is probable that it was added later.

That ceiling must have been completed in the late 1630s, for in 1640 Elizabeth Innes died, leaving Alexander a twenty-three-year-old widower with a son and a daughter to raise. It seems to have been a shattering blow, for he never married again. This private sorrow, combined with the disturbances of the Covenanter period, appears to have affected him deeply, and the rest of his long life (he died in 1680 at the age of sixty-three) was much preoccupied with religion and religious politics.

Alexander Brodie was a Covenanter, to such effect that the Marquess of Montrose sent Lord Lewis Gordon to teach him a lesson: in 1645 Brodie House was burned and plundered by Gordon, but apparently it escaped severe structural damage. Repairing the house must have absorbed much of Brodie's energies. Undeterred, he became Member of Parliament for Moray and in 1649, after the execution of Charles I, Brodie was appointed one of the five Scottish commissioners sent to treat with Charles II in exile. Charles at first refused to sign the Solemn League and Covenant, but in the following year he agreed. Just before his brief foray to be crowned at Scone and routed at Worcester, the man who had helped to change his mind, Alexander Brodie, was created a Lord of Session in June 1650.

It was now that Lord Brodie began to keep a diary which he continued until his death.

opposite The dining-room at Brodie Castle with its exuberant plaster ceiling of the early eighteenth century, painted and grained to look like wood in the 1820s. Above the sideboard, oval-framed, hangs the portrait of the man who is thought to have commissioned the ceiling, Alexander Brodie, the Lord Lyon.

It was a devotional diary, the story of the spiritual struggle of a lonely and tormented man, in which he recorded the nightmares and temptations and agonizings suffered by those of zealous conscience who strove to live by the severe Calvinist doctrines of the time. It was a private diary and never meant for publication, but two centuries later it was discovered and in 1863 was published by the Spalding Club of Aberdeen, along with the diary of his son James, the sixteenth Brodie of Brodie. It was this posthumous publication that ensured him a wider fame than he had acquired for his role in Scotland's political history.

Until quite recently it was generally believed that Alexander had been responsible for a second and even more spectacular plaster ceiling – the one in the new laird's drawing-room, now the dining-room. It is an astonishing piece of workmanship, a riot of ornamentation, with unusually deep ribs decorated with a profusion of vines and grapes in full relief. Four great cornerpieces seem to represent the four elements (earth, air, fire and water). It was originally white, but in the 1820s it was carefully painted over and grained to make it look like wood. Despite this, it is still a magnificent masterpiece of its kind, making the dining-room much the most powerful room in the whole house.

But was it the work of tormented Alexander Brodie, the fifteenth laird? Do these rich and voluptuous female figures square with his austere Calvinism? It is now thought much more likely that this crowning glory of Brodie Castle should instead be credited to his great-grandson Alexander, nineteenth Brodie of Brodie, the Lord Lyon King of Arms, the Advancer who turned Ruiner.

After Alexander's death in 1680, his son James, sixteenth Brodie of Brodie, as spiritually tormented as his father had been, made no significant changes to the castle. Nor did his successor, his cousin George, seventeenth Brodie of Brodie, who married the fifth of James's nine daughters and died in 1715. It was George's eldest son James, eighteenth Brodie of Brodie, who received the celebrated 'Bulstrode letter' from his younger brother Alexander in 1717 and was succeeded by him in 1720.

Alexander, nineteenth Brodie of Brodie, inherited just after he had completed his education at Aberdeen (and possibly Leyden), and immediately plunged into politics. He was MP for Elginshire from 1720 to 1741, for Caithness from 1741 to 1747, and for Inverness from 1747 until his death in 1754. His steady support for Walpole and the Whigs earned him the appointment to the office of Lord Lyon in 1727.

Today his portrait, oval-framed, hangs above a sideboard in the dining-room with the massive ceiling he is now thought to have commissioned – the earliest family portrait to have survived at Brodie. It shows a fleshy-faced man with a florid complexion, blue eyes and full lips, a man clearly addicted to the good things of life. It was this addiction that eventually beggared the Brodie estate.

Not that he himself was solely to blame. In 1724 he had married Mary Sleigh, whose grandiose plans for landscaping the grounds and extravagant hospitality matched her husband's aspirations but not his means. During the Jacobite Rising of 1745, while Alexander was away on duty with the Duke of Cumberland's army, Mary was left to run the estate and help provide for the occupying troops. We are told that 'The Gentlemen were all extremely welcome to the best this House could afford'.

She was an exceptionally energetic and capable lady, was Mary Sleigh Brodie. According to the *Statistical Account of Scotland* she was a pioneer in training women for cottage industries, she raised flax and built a flax-mill and worked hard at improving the agricultural standards of the estate. She ordered a huge landscape garden with broad avenues radiating out from the house. The western avenue stretched as far as the horizon, and there was a formal canal which ran into a circular basin. Only vestiges of this great vanished garden now remain, but recently discovered surveys and estate plans drawn up in 1770 should make restoration of the grounds a feasible prospect – if anyone could afford it.

opposite The strapwork plaster ceiling of the blue sitting-room dates from the 1630s. The central boss, with a hand clutching arrows protruding from it, is of different workmanship and probably of later date. Originally the laird's room, this chamber with its 160-year-old blue flock wallpaper was used as a sitting-room by the mother of the present Brodie of Brodie.

The Lord Lyon was just as busy inside the house as his wife was outside it. Apart from the extravagant ceiling of the dining-room, he had made extensive structural changes in 1732 – a straight staircase to replace a spiral one, and the removal of the battlements and corner turrets of the tower. And always the personal bills kept pouring in, bills for clothes, bills for doctors, bills for materials . . . The great estate sagged and groaned under a mountainous pile of debts; what remained of it on his death in 1754 was to be beggared for the next hundred years. Not that he had ever meant to be the Ruiner; it was simply that in his rash enthusiasm to be the Advancer he had never known when to stop.

He was succeeded by his only son, a sickly child of thirteen who died soon after being sent to school in England, and the bankrupt estate passed to a fifteen-year-old cousin, James Brodie of Asleisk, twenty-first laird of Brodie. James had barely reached his majority when he eloped, in 1767, with Lady Margaret Duff, daughter of the first Earl of Fife. As it turned out, the elopement was quite unnecessary, for the earl proved himself a man of remarkable benevolence and generosity. His reaction to the elopement was a model of dignified restraint. In a letter preserved in the muniment room in Brodie Castle he wrote:

I am informed Mr Brodie and Lady Margaret have stolen a marriage. I wonder neither one nor the other chose to drop me a little civil note. However, their want of discretion gives me no pain. I wish they may pass a happy life together.

The omens for a happy life together did not look promising, however, in view of Brodie's parlous financial position. The contents of the house had had to be sold off to pay the creditors, but the estate was still deeply in debt and eventually, in 1774, it had to be put up for sale. It was now that the second Earl of Fife, son of the unaggrieved father-in-law, became the Rescuer: before the auction he agreed to bid up to £31,000 for the whole property. He then handed the ancient barony of Brodie back to his sister and brother-in-law, keeping the rest for himself. Brodie had been saved for the Brodie family – but only just.

There is a painting in the dining-room of Lady Margaret, posing with her finger held up as if testing the wind. There is also a portrait there of her husband looking shrewd and clever, as befitted a Fellow of the Royal Society of Edinburgh, but not particularly attractive.

Twelve years after the rescue by the Earl of Fife, a dreadful tragedy struck the house of Brodie. The story is told in a vivid letter in a pink-ribboned bundle in Tin Box 18 in the muniment room. On a February evening in 1776 Mr Brodie and two friends returned to Brodie House, where they found Lady Margaret in 'uncommon good spirits':

That evening they all retired to their bedrooms, about 11 o'clock; when Mr Brodie accompanied her to her room he saw she had a good fire . . . The instant he lay down he fell asleep, from which he was soon awakened by the most dismal shrieks . . . He rushed naked downstairs and . . . was met by the flames. At the risk of his life . . . he pushed forward and sought the dear unfortunate in vain. Suffocation and flame drove him (back) . . . then, frantic, he again pushed in, for the whole room to the very cornice and furniture was in a blaze, and in his second attempt, found the lovely sufferer distended on the floor. He thinks then he found her heart once leap. She was all on fire. He carried her into the dressing-room and rolled her in a carpet but ere then her soul had fled forever. Oh! Madam, what a sight was here, the lovely, the once admired Lady Margaret in a few minutes a disfigured corpse, for death and the element had done their work.

Family tradition has it, without proof, that the room in which this calamity took place is the chamber now known as the best bedchamber. Today it is a lovely room, furnished with choice Chinese lacquer cabinets dating from about the same period as the fire, the late eighteenth century; and even though it may not have been the room in question, it is impossible to enter it without a pang of pity for that night of horror.

Ill-fortune was still to dog the house of Brodie. Their only son and heir, James, was forced to emigrate to seek a profitable career with the Honourable East India Company at Madras; but just when he had started to prosper, he was drowned in a sailing accident in 1802. He left seven children – two sons and five daughters – who are depicted in a magnificent canvas, by the Cornish painter John Opie, of 1804 or thereabouts. It now hangs on a side wall in the elegant nineteenth-century drawing-room that was to be built by the boy in a red suit being held aloft by one of his sisters. This was William Brodie, now his grandfather's heir, who twenty years later would inherit Brodie Castle and turn it into a Victorian mansion, the Brodie Castle that we see today.

Grandfather James died in 1824, and William became the twenty-second Brodie of Brodie. He was only twenty-five years old, but he was determined from the start to develop the estate, apparently totally undeterred by the huge debt – amounting to £12,706 12s 2d – that still crippled it. He at once set about repairing and enlarging the dilapidated house, as well as buying a few Dutch paintings to cheer up the walls: a pair of portraits by N. Elias, another pair by J. G. Cuyp dated 1647, and a large portrait by Ferdinand Bol, all now in the drawing-room; a charming study of *The Young Artist* by Vaillant, dated 1656, now hanging on the staircase; and a striking painting of *A Philosopher and his Pupils*, now attributed to Volmarijn, which hangs in the red drawing-room.

Encouraged, somewhat irresponsibly, by his estate factor, Neil Maclean of Inverness, William Brodie called in the much sought-after Edinburgh architect William Burn to design large-scale extensions for the house. There was to be an eastern extension housing a magnificent and spacious dining-room, and a western extension incorporating a new drawing-room. After three years of work on the eastern extension, however, the soaring costs forced a stop. The estate factor who had been so keen on the idea now had distinctly cold feet; he wrote to William:

It has become a matter of . . . necessity and even *duty* for you to make a *prudent* marriage and that as soon as possible . . . I dread the awful consequences of your creditors being driven to desperation, of which I had observed some symptoms . . .

However desperate the creditors, Brodie avoided marriage for the time being and managed to stave off the inevitable auction of his chattels until he had privately disposed of his pictures, books and silver among members of his family. But although most of his remaining possessions had to go to help pay the debts, the house itself was beginning to look the way he wanted it; before William Burn had gone back to Edinburgh he had completed quite a lot of refurbishing of the older rooms. It was under his guidance that the magnificent plaster ceiling in what is now the dining-room was grained to look like wood. The original high hall had been completely redecorated, with a new heavily compartmented ceiling, and its walls covered with a fine red flock wallpaper that gave it its present name of the red drawing-room. The blue sitting-room, with its fine plaster ceiling installed by the fifteenth laird in the 1630s, now got its name, from the blue flock wallpaper hung during that first rapturous fit of decoration by the twenty-second Brodie in the 1820s – and still only a little faded after more than 150 years.

Somehow or other, Brodie managed to survive the bankrupt years, made so much worse by his early profligacy, without losing the house itself. In 1838 he finally made the 'prudent' marriage his estate factor had been praying for – to a wealthy heiress, Elizabeth Baillie, of Redcastle on the Beauly Firth, who would prove to be another Rescuer for Brodie. His bride brought a dowry large enough to pay off the outstanding debts and allow a resumption of building work. In 1843 a new architect, James Wylson, was called in to adapt, modify and complete William Burn's original scheme.

Wylson remodelled the entrance hall with Romanesque columns and formed a new library out of two storerooms beyond it, a handsome chamber that seems to be permanently filled with dusk. That had been Wylson's express intention:

above left A portrait by John Opie of William, twenty-second Brodie of Brodie, and his brother and five sisters. William is the boy in the suit, held aloft by one of his sisters. This splendid canvas hangs in the drawing-room which William Brodie added in the nineteenth century.

above A copy of a Romney portrait of the beautiful Duchess of Gordon (the one who raised the Gordon Highlanders regiment with kisses and shillings) and her son, who became the fifth and last Duke of Gordon. His childless marriage to a Miss Elizabeth Brodie brought a treasure-trove of *objets d'art* to Brodie Castle. The painting hangs in the drawing-room.

left Alexander Brodie of Brodie, Lord Lyon King of Arms 1727–54.

I should fear the appropriateness of white painting in a library, which appears rather to want a subdued light (if not the dim-religious, which is so often quoted) and there should be no want of light in the new library: I should also doubt its harmonizing with the tone of the buildings.

If the light became too dim to tell the time, one corner houses a special clock which, when you pull the repeater device, chimes in such a way as to tell you the hour. This is only the first of an astonishing collection of ornate clocks to be found in practically every room which audibly reinforces the impression that Brodie Castle gives of being a time machine.

In the red drawing-room Wylson installed a monstrous Gothic chimneypiece to take pieces of seventeenth-century Flemish carvings that Brodie had acquired abroad, thus giving the room a curious chapel-like air.

Burn's planned western extension, with its new drawing-room, was abandoned, and the original laird's chamber, with its massive plaster ceiling installed by the Ruiner in the 1730s, was converted into a dining-room instead. This left Burn's planned dining-room in the eastern extension free to become the new drawing-room – and what a superb room it is, lovely and airy with tall windows, a very large room that somehow contrives to feel cosy, even intimate. The ceiling was ornately decorated in stencil work in blue, pink and gold (unfortunately, it was painted over in the 1930s by mistake, but it is hoped that the original scheme will be restored in the near future). The carpet was bought at the Crystal Palace Exhibition of 1851, its leaf-and-trellis pattern in white on rose elegantly reflecting the painted decoration on the doorcases. The drawing-room is the present Brodie's favourite room – and no wonder.

So, once again, Brodie Castle was back on the crest, after having been so nearly destroyed by the Ruiner a century previously. A family portrait from about 1845, called *Mr and Mrs William Brodie in the Dining Room*, with his drowned father's portrait by Opie on the far wall and a glimpse of that heavy, wood-grained plaster ceiling, depicts a carefully posed Victorian family, once again used to the best things in life.

As William and Elizabeth settled themselves comfortably into their splendid 'new' mansion with their four children and (later) their many grandchildren, all that was missing was the obligatory collection of treasures that make a fine house into a great house – the pictures, the ornaments, the family heirlooms, the antique furniture to replace the things that had perforce been sold off to keep the estate intact. And once again Providence provided, in the person of a Miss Elizabeth Brodie who had married the last Duke of Gordon.

Her husband had predeceased her, and now, just as the rebuilding of Brodie was completed, the last duchess died, leaving all her chattels to William, twenty-second Brodie of Brodie. To his refurbished castle came a treasure-trove of French antique furniture, priceless paintings, vases, candelabra and an amazing collection of historical bric-a-brac: Bonnie Prince Charlie's broadsword, Bonnie Dundee's sword from the field of Killiecrankie, a tomahawk and pipe of peace, a lantern rather dubiously alleged to have belonged to Guy Fawkes, and one truly exceptional item – the coronation robe of Queen Adelaide, William IV's consort, which she wore at his coronation in 1831. The last Duchess of Gordon had been Mistress of the Robes to Queen Adelaide, and this was the only coronation robe in private hands in Britain.

William's heir, the twenty-third Brodie of Brodie, was the grandfather of the present laird. Neither he nor his son, Ian Ashley Morton Brodie, the twenty-fourth Brodie of Brodie, made any further changes to the castle building; but Ian Brodie and his wife, Violet Hope, made a special and distinctive contribution to the ever-evolving Brodie heritage. During the 1920s and 1930s they formed a notable collection of paintings, particularly of early eighteenth-century English watercolours (now on display in the blue bedroom and dressing-room) and twentieth-century French, Scottish and English paintings (now in the long room). These additions have given Brodie Castle one of the most catholic collections in any Scottish country house – some two hundred paintings in all, ranging from a Van Dyck of Charles I to moderns like MacTaggart and Dufy and L'Oiseau.

Ian Brodie also became an expert on the cultivation of daffodils, producing over four hundred varieties in his lifetime. He changed the outside face of Brodie by covering the grounds with golden drifts of blooms, many of which he had developed himself. Many varieties have now died out and cannot be found in any nurseries, but the twenty-fourth laird (as the Brodies have always done) kept meticulous records, and gardeners are now working on the lost varieties in order to restock the estate with Brodie daffodils.

And so we come to the present laird, Ninian Alexander, twenty-fifth Brodie of Brodie, a real 'Actor on the Theatres of Great Families'. He was born in 1912, and succeeded his father in 1943. He was educated at Eton, served in the Royal Artillery during the war, and was a stage actor who also appeared in films and television before he and his late wife returned to Brodie Castle to run the estate in 1950. What role was he to play in the drama of Brodie? It looked as if he might be landed with the unenviable part of the Finisher, faced as he was with rising costs and a castle that once again badly needed refurbishing. The strong oak timbers of the old tower were still sound enough; but his great-grandfather, William, the twenty-second laird, despite his lavish expenditure on the house, had been constrained to exercise a little economy by using softwood instead of oak. As a result there was now woodworm and decay throughout all the later parts of the house. Leadwork had worn thin and needed replacing, and the roof needed repairing. Externally, the soft sandstone had weathered badly and needed reharling. The prospect looked bleak. There was a real possibility that when Brodie's son, Alastair Ian Ninian, Younger of Brodie, came to inherit, he would be forced to sell all the contents of the castle to meet the inevitable death duties, leaving Brodie Castle an empty, uninhabitable shell.

But once again there was a Rescuer to hand, this time in the shape of the National Land Fund which had been established in 1945 by the then Chancellor of the Exchequer, Hugh Dalton, to acquire land or buildings of outstanding historic or architectural interest. Later legislation enabled the Secretary of State for Scotland to be reimbursed by the Land Fund for any such acquisitions he might make. This was the avenue Brodie decided to explore. He had set up a trust with his son as beneficiary to own and manage the castle and estate; and now in 1973 the trustees approached the then Secretary of State for Scotland and offered to sell him the castle and its essential contents for eventual transfer to the National Trust for Scotland.

It took more than five years of negotiation, but in December 1978 the then Scottish Secretary, Mr Bruce Millan, announced that he had purchased Brodie Castle and its grounds for £130,000, together with the contents of the castle from Brodie himself for £275,000, out of which Brodie would provide an endowment fund to enable the National Trust for Scotland to accept the castle and open it to the public. The total sum of £405,000 was then paid back to the Scottish Secretary by the National Land Fund. It was the last transaction of any importance to be made by the National Land Fund, which was replaced on 1 April 1980 by the National Heritage Memorial Fund.

It all sounds very complex, but the end result was simple and straightforward: Brodie Castle now belonged to the nation in perpetuity and its future was assured. The occasion was celebrated on 28th June 1980, when Brodie Castle, repaired and refurbished by the National Trust for Scotland, was opened to the public for the first time. On the first Sunday no fewer than 973 visitors trooped through the house; in the first summer period the number of visitors totalled 32,000.

Brodie himself, now a widower, elected to live in a wing of the castle and help show visitors around his old home. His fellow guides are the resident Trust representative, Mr Bill Cockburn, and the youngest, bonniest flock of guides in the country – nearly all of them are sixth formers at Forres Academy. The twenty-fifth Brodie of Brodie, now in his late sixties, wears the green Hunting Brodie kilt and yellow stockings, entrancing all and sundry with his deep, softly modulated actor's voice. He insists that he loves to 'share the lovely things of Brodie with all the people who come – I'd rather share the treasures with the general public than see them dispersed'.

He knows every nook and cranny in the castle, which to him is not a castle but simply a home. The blue sitting-room, with its 1630s plastered ceiling, is simply his mother's writing-room. The nineteenth-century bed in the best bedchamber, where Lady Elizabeth had burned to death, was his late wife's bed. The old schoolroom upstairs was where he and his brother had lessons from their governess before going to prep school. He can show you the curious faults in the magnificent armorial china service in the dining-room, on which the family motto 'Unite' has been mis-painted 'Untie' by Chinese craftsmen on one of the plates and on the soup tureen. He demonstrates the curious chair in the library that unfolds into a set of library steps. He knows and loves every one of the strange and beautiful clocks in his time machine of a house – especially the grandfather clock made by Clidsdale of Edinburgh which is simply 'the one that's been going all my life'.

It all seems an immensity of time since the days of King Brude in the sixth century, or even of the twelfth Brodie of Brodie, who built himself a tower house in 1567. Yet a Brodie still lives at Brodie. What would the Lord Lyon Brodie, who almost ruined it, think of that? Would he have wanted to add yet another category to the Bulstrode Scale to accommodate his descendant? What about the Survivor?

Castle Fraser, grandest of all the great houses of the north-east.

CASTLE FRASER
Grampian

FOR A DECADE or more before the National Trust for Scotland was founded in 1931, Aberdeenshire had a sort of one-man National Trust of its own – Weetman Dickinson Pearson, first Viscount Cowdray. He was a remarkable man, considerably larger than life, who carved out a prodigious fortune at the turn of the century as a contractor on a global scale. He built the Sennar Dam across the Blue Nile above Khartoum to give Sudan hydroelectricity. He built the great Mexican drainage schemes. He completed the Blackwall Tunnel under the River Thames. He built the harbour at Vera Cruz and extended Dover Harbour. He built the Tehuantepec railway in Mexico, a country in which he acquired huge tracts of oil-rich land. He was the greatest entrepreneur-contractor of his era.

Nearly all dynamic multi-millionaires of his type develop a besetting weakness of some sort – for luxury yachts, or young girls, or both. Lord Cowdray's besetting weakness was for old castles and historic ruins. Whole or decayed, grand or merely great, he had a true collector's passion for castles. He loved restoring them. He loved buying them and distributing them among members of his family. Above all he loved buying up castles in north-eastern Scotland. Local legend has it that it was his avowed ambition to own every castle between the Dee and the Don. He bought the ruins of Dunnottar Castle, and his equally remarkable wife Annie restored part of them. He bought and restored the Castle of Birse. He bought Raemoir House, outside Banchory, and his wife transformed it into what is now an elegant and inviting hotel. He tried hard to buy Craigievar Castle, but was brusquely baulked by Lord Sempill. He expressed a hungry interest in the Glentanar estates. He bought Dunecht House, still the family's Scottish retreat, and in 1921 bought Castle Fraser, some fifteen miles to the west of Aberdeen, grandest of all the great houses of the north-east.

As a building it is a splendid piece of sculpture: solid and bulky, yet seeming to soar lightly upwards, a massive bole that flowers into a gay exuberance of decoration like some aureole. It has been hailed as a supreme example of native genius using local materials, a masterpiece of art fashioned by men who could make even the most intractable granite look as pliable as putty. And this artistic homogeneity is all the more remarkable because it is not the work of a single architect but the outcome of several separate building-periods. Castle Fraser is a historical jigsaw puzzle carved in stone.

There is a great deal of learned argument about who founded Castle Fraser, and when; but there is no doubt about which of the castle's owners put his finishing touches to the building as it stands today. That was in 1636, the last year of real peace and prosperity before Scotland was plunged into the turmoil of the Covenanting quarrels and the Civil War, the end of a great flowering of Scottish architecture.

But when did it all start? The Frasers of Castle Fraser were originally descended from a French family called Frisel (from the French 'fraise', meaning 'strawberry' – hence the strawberry motifs discernible on the castle walls), who came to England in the wake of

King Henry II late in the twelfth century, or perhaps even with William the Conqueror a hundred years earlier. They moved steadily northwards until by the late thirteenth century they were extensively settled in central Scotland, with their principal seat at Cornton in Stirlingshire. Then, in 1454, a certain Thomas Fraser resigned the lands of Cornton to King James II and received in exchange the united barony of Stoneywood and Muchall-in-Mar in Aberdeenshire. This Thomas Fraser thus became the first Fraser Laird of Muchall, the estate on which Castle Fraser stands.

Was it at this time, in the middle of the fifteenth century, that Castle Fraser was started? Was there an even earlier house on the site, perhaps? Or was there no laird's house at all on the Muchall estate for another hundred years? The dating of Castle Fraser has long been a vexed question among antiquarians and architectural historians, with some favouring a fifteenth-century start and others plumping for a sixteenth-century date. The latest expert to enter the fray is Mr Harry Gordon Slade, with a cogently argued paper, 'Castle Fraser: a seat of the antient family of Fraser' (from *Proceedings of the Society of Antiquaries of Scotland,* Volume 109). In it he comes down firmly and convincingly on the side of an earlier date. He thinks that the core of the present building was a substantial stone tower with a vaulted basement and a vaulted hall, evidence of which is still to be seen (the north wall of the hall and the inner west wall of the vault beneath the hall). According to Mr Gordon Slade, this tower was probably built by Thomas Fraser, first laird of Muchall, if it were not in existence already.

I'm not qualified to pass judgement on this question of dating the earliest structure in Castle Fraser, and I have no way of knowing whether Mr Gordon Slade's dictum will be the last word on it. But in view of the confusion and uncertainty, I think it prudent to award the accolade of founder to both Thomas Fraser, the first laird, *and* to the man whom we know succeeded to the estates of Stoneywood and Muchall in 1565, Michael Fraser, the fifth laird. What is certain is that this Michael Fraser embarked on an ambitious building programme in the mid-1570s, either starting from scratch or remodelling an existing structure. We know that the fabric of the square tower (now called the Michael Tower) was under construction in the year 1576, for that is the date carried on the Royal Coat of Arms that was formerly located above its entrance (it is now on the south, or 'back', wall of the house).

Michael Fraser died in 1588-9 before his tower and any other building-plans he had envisaged were completed, and now followed a hiatus of some years. His son, Andrew Fraser, the sixth laird, was under age when he inherited, but he would later prove himself to be the Advancer in the fullest sense of Bulstrode's meaning.

In 1592 Andrew Fraser married Lady Elizabeth Douglas, daughter of the Earl of Buchan, and was soon at work reviving and, it seems, considerably extending his father's half-finished project. The house he built was designed to a traditional plan looking rather like a fattened Z – a central rectangular block with the great hall (remnants of the fifteenth-century original?) occupying the whole of the first-floor area, with projecting towers at the opposite corners of each end, square to the north-west (the Michael Tower) and round to the south-east. This is the so-called 'Z-plan' or 'three-stepped' castle. By the time the castle proper was finished, around 1618, it was apparently much larger and taller than his father had originally planned. By 1622 the internal finishes were still being installed, and a few years later the building as we see it was completed with the addition of two low service wings to form an entrance courtyard – the traditional 'laigh biggins' (low buildings) for servants' quarters, here forming an integral part of the architectural design.

The work seems to have been done by two exceptionally gifted families of Aberdeenshire master masons – the Bells and the Leipers. Thomas Leiper, the father, is associated with the early stages of construction commissioned by Michael Fraser in the mid-1570s; his son, James Leiper, was employed to pave the hall in 1622. John Bell

(I.Bel), who in all probability was involved with the building of Crathes, Craigievar and the extension to Drum Castle, was certainly responsible for the magnificent upper works of Castle Fraser, with the great belt of profuse corbelling that crowns the whole building. It was John Bell who was also responsible for the great armorial frontispiece or table of the Royal Arms in deep red freestone high up in the centre of the north façade of the main block, trumpeting its presence to all who approached the entrance. Underneath it is the modest tablet, dated 1617, of John Bell himself. It reads I BEL MMF, with Bell's own heart-shaped manual, and can be interpreted as standing for 'John Bell – *murifex me fecit*' ('the mason who made me', meaning either the building or his own mark).

The sixth laird, Andrew Fraser, was not just the Advancer, however; he was also the Advanced, for in 1633 he was created the first Lord Fraser by King Charles I. There are two sets of portraits of him and his wife in the great hall (as he was married twice his second wife may be represented in one of them, although the two portraits look similar). He was a fine-looking man with a handsome red beard and moustache, a high forehead and thinning hair. In the second portrait he wears a hat – perhaps to conceal eventual baldness? He died in 1636, three years after his ennoblement and forty years after inheriting from his father. He had obviously been an immensely wealthy man. Despite the huge cost of building Castle Fraser he had also been able to afford to buy Cairnbulg Castle, near Fraserburgh, from Fraser of Durris (a branch of the family now headed by Lord Saltoun), and later to buy Durris as well.

With the death of the first Lord Fraser the high tide of fortune began to ebb for the Frasers of Muchall. His son Andrew, the second Lord Fraser, was soon in the thick of the bloody conflicts of the Covenanting wars. He was 'a pryme Covenanter', according to John Spalding's *Memorialls of the Trubles* (although it should be remembered that Spalding, Aberdeen diarist and commissary clerk, was a staunch Royalist himself). He came out against the king as early as 1638, and in May 1639 he was involved in the very first action of the Civil War in which blood was shed in the north-east, when he helped to repulse a Royalist raid on Towie-Barclay Castle. A month later, according to Spalding, the Royalists took their revenge when Lord Aboyne attacked Castle Fraser itself:

Upon the 12th Junij they ride to the Lord Fraser's house of Muchallis, bot he wes fled fra hame. The soldiouris mellis with and plunders his horse, oxen and ky and all other goodis that they culd get. They threw down haill stakis corne amongis their horss feit to eit and destroy. Those who war within the place schot out some muskites but did no skaith.

Bot he wes fled fra hame. Lord Fraser clearly knew when discretion was the better part of valour! But of his genuine valour there need be little doubt: at the Battle of Aberdeen in September 1644 Lord Fraser led two cavalry charges against the right wing of Montrose's royal forces, and even Spalding allowed that he 'showed himselfe lyke a brave and valiant gentleman'. After sacking Aberdeen, Montrose took a lazy swipe at Castle Fraser in retaliation; on 18 October he burned all the corn-yards and 'spolzeit his ground', but apparently made no assault on the castle itself. After the Royalists had eventually laid down their arms, Lord Fraser's unswerving devotion to the Covenant was recognized when he became a member of the Committee of Estates in 1645. In 1649 he was one of those responsible for 'putting the Kingdom in a Posture of Defence' against Cromwell after Scotland had offered the crown to the future Charles II.

The second Lord Fraser died some time between 1656 and 1658 while in his early sixties, and was succeeded by his son, yet another Andrew. Not much is known about the third Lord Fraser, but he must have been spectacularly profligate. He married well; his first wife was the daughter of Lord Lovat and widow of the Viscount of Arbuthnott, his second wife the daughter of Lord Seaforth and widow of the Earl of Mar. Even so, in fifteen years or so he ran through the family fortune that his grandfather had amassed; it

above The great armorial table of Royal Arms high up in the centre of the north façade of the main block of the castle. Below it is the modest tablet, dated 1617, of the master mason John Bell: I BEL M M F (John Bell, the mason who made me).

right Castle Fraser, showing the entrance courtyard in its restored form.

was only by the narrowest of squeaks – and the shrewd help of his second wife – that Castle Fraser itself wasn't sold off to pay his debts. When he died in 1674 his twelve-year-old son inherited an estate that was seriously impoverished.

This was Charles Fraser, ninth laird of Muchall and fourth and last Lord Fraser. As soon as he came of age in 1683 he married a widow, Lady Marjorie Erskine, who was considerably older than he was; she had been married to Simon Fraser of Inverallochy, a cadet of the Lovat line, by whom she had had a son, William Fraser of Inverallochy. And with that the dynastic plot of Castle Fraser thickens and ravels into a dynastic jigsaw puzzle to match its architectural puzzle.

The fourth Lord Fraser was as prime a Jacobite as his grandfather had been a 'pryme Covenanter'. As a result he was not only struggling with debt all his life, but he was also on the 'wrong' political side as well. Castle Fraser was 'disponed' (mortgaged or made over) to his own stepson, William Fraser of Inverallochy, from whom he leased it (his only child, a son, died in 1690) and meanwhile the hapless laird of Muchall was constantly getting into trouble for his overt support of the Jacobite cause. In 1692 he was fined £200 for drunkenly proclaiming as true king the exiled King James VII of Scotland and II of England at the Mercat Cross at Fraserburgh; and although he took the oath of allegiance to William and Mary in 1695 and supported the Act of Union in 1707, as soon as he sniffed Jacobitism in the air again in 1715 when the standard was raised for the Old Pretender, James II's son, he was pawing the ground again like an old warhorse. The Great Cause failed, ingloriously; Lord Fraser, on the run from government troops, was 'lurking' near the fishing village of Pennan on the coast in 1716 when he fell over the cliffs to his death.

With the death of the fourth Lord Fraser, childless, the direct male line of the Frasers of Muchall died too, and Castle Fraser passed into the full possession of his stepson, William Fraser of Inverallochy. Not long afterwards, and certainly by 1721, it passed to *his* son, Charles Fraser of Inverallochy, who came to be known as 'Auld Inverallochy' because of the ripe old age he attained – he was in his eighties when he died in 1787. He married Anne Udny, daughter of the laird of Udny, and one of the treasures on display in a recess in the great hall is a massive sixteenth-century iron strongbox, of German origin, which is thought to have contained her family possessions and trousseau. It is known as 'Jamie Fleeman's Kist'; Jamie Fleeman (James Fleming) had been fool to the laird of Udny when Knockhall Castle caught fire one time, and tradition has it that Jamie threw this strongbox single-handed out of the window to safety. Today it takes four strong men to lift it.

'Auld Inverallochy' and his wife Anne had five children – three sons and two daughters. This would seem to be quite enough to ensure a long and orderly succession. But no. The eldest son, Charles, who was then only twenty-one, commanded the Fraser Regiment at Culloden, where he fell wounded in the field. He was spotted the next day by one of the government commanders (probably Hawley), who ordered the future General James Wolfe to shoot Fraser. Wolfe refused, and so did every other officer, until eventually a common soldier was found to dispatch the wounded man. It was with that same General Wolfe that 'Auld Inverallochy's' second son, Simon Fraser, fell during the assault on Quebec in 1759. By the time 'Auld Inverallochy' himself died there was only one son alive, William, who died childless in 1792, five years after inheriting Castle Fraser. So now the line of succession took another swerve. Of the two daughters, only the elder one, Martha, had married; her husband was Colin Mackenzie of Kilcoy. And now, on her brother's death, the properties were divided, Inverallochy going to Martha Mackenzie and Castle Fraser to her younger unmarried sister, Elyza Fraser, who was then aged fifty-six.

She was a remarkable character, Miss Elyza. Mr Gordon Slade records a delightful legend about her giddy youth, to the effect that she had been in love with her uncle, the

Trophies of the hunt in the master's room.

laird of Udny, and had been sent abroad by her disapproving father. Mr Gordon Slade takes up the tale:

When she returned she brought with her a maid who was not known by any of her family or by any on the estate. For many years they lived together in the rooms over the Great Hall until this maid died. Gossip having been at work suspicion was aroused, and on the coffin being opened it was found to contain the body of a man.

Her 'shrine' at Castle Fraser is the 'worked' room above the great hall, so called because of the needlework bed-hangings, curtains and seat furniture, much of which is believed to have been done by Miss Elyza herself. Her portrait, 'after Raeburn' (made around 1900) hangs over the fireplace.

Two other portraits in the worked room commemorate deep and abiding friendships. One is of the antiquary James Byres of Tonley (with whom she is said to have been also in love), whom she had met during her extensive travels in Italy. It was Byres who designed her magnificent classical mausoleum in Cluny churchyard, and in her will she left him her carriage and best pair of horses. Her other great friend was Miss Mary Bristow, who lived with her at Castle Fraser until her death in 1805. Miss Bristow (there is no suggestion in the folklore that she too was a man in disguise!) seems to have been an extremely able and energetic lady who took a particular interest in the parkland around the castle. According to her extant journals she spent a lot of her own money buying and planting the sycamore trees that now lend such charm to the castle environs. Her portrait, with a red pinched nose (the castle was probably chilly), hangs to the left of the door of the worked room; it is by George Chinnery and is considered one of the best paintings in the castle. Miss Bristow is commemorated further on a pyramidical granite monument in 'Miss Bristow's Wood', a copse south of the castle:

Sacred to the memory of a Friendship which subsisted forty years. Elyza Fraser erects this monument in the groves planted by her late lamented friend.

After her 'late lamented friend' died in 1805, Miss Elyza took to her bed and stayed bedridden in the worked room for the last nine years of her life until her death in 1814. She had done a lot for her property, although not perhaps as much as she liked to claim ('... the whole Restored and Beautified by Elyza Fraser 1795'). Most of her work (with Miss Bristow's help) was connected with the policies and the building of a new stable court to the west of the castle (now the home of the last of the lairds). She seems to have intended more than she actually did, for a surveyor's map of the policies shows a new entrance hall at the castle, a new round tower, and considerable remodelling of the courtyard buildings, but none of these projects was carried out in her lifetime. She is also supposed to have enlarged the west window of the great hall, the better to enjoy the sunset.

The main question that was exercising Miss Elyza's mind was who should inherit Castle Fraser? Whatever romantic associations she may or may not have had in her youth, she was still a childless spinster. The closest kin she had were the sons of her sister, Mrs Martha Mackenzie of Kilcoy. Of the two, her favourite nephew was the elder son, Charles Frederick Mackenzie of Kilcoy and Inverallochy, and he was her first choice as heir to the castle; but he incurred her wrathful displeasure on one occasion by sending her a bulldog when she had asked him for a lap-dog, so he was promptly disinherited. That left the second son, Major-General Alexander Mackenzie, whose military portrait dominates the great hall above the fireplace, wearing the inscribed sabre which is on display directly below the painting. The sole condition she made was that he should assume the additional name of Fraser, which he obligingly did. But alas, the bold major-general predeceased her in 1809. So when Miss Elyza herself died in 1814 Castle Fraser was inherited by the major-general's elder son, her great-nephew Charles Mackenzie

above Major-General
Alexander Mackenzie Fraser:
this portrait, after Raeburn,
hangs in the high hall at
Castle Fraser.

above left The worked room,
with furnishings that are
thought to have been
embroidered by the
remarkable Elyza Fraser. A
copy of a Raeburn portrait of
her hangs over the fireplace.

below left The dining-room.
On either side of the
Georgian mahogany
bookcase, with its Chinese
export service of the Chien
Lung period, hang portraits
of Colonel Charles
Mackenzie Fraser and his
bride, Jane Hay.

Fraser, then aged twenty-two. Over the next fifty-seven years of strenuous activity at Castle Fraser, he was to be the Continuer who also turned out to be the Ruiner on a quite disastrous scale.

During Miss Elyza's last bedridden years, the downstairs chambers had been systematically plundered of their pictures and furnishings by her friends, kinsmen, or servants – or all three. We get the impression of a great castle gradually sliding into dilapidation below and around the helpless Miss Elyza. This was the inheritance received by the gallant Captain Charles Mackenzie Fraser (late of the Coldstream Guards), a Continuer to the core, with a boiling well of energy, a beautiful and utterly devoted seventeen-year-old bride, and a wooden leg that is now on display in the dining-room. And thereby hangs a tale.

The story of Charles Mackenzie Fraser and his young bride, Jane Hay, can be read at length in an enchanting booklet written by Mrs Lavinia Smiley (granddaughter of the first Viscount Cowdray) called *Life at Castle Fraser 150 years Ago*. Their portraits can be seen in the dining-room – Charles (by B. R. Faulkner) looking very strong and virile, Jane a picture of doe-eyed gentle beauty (her portrait is a copy of an original by Sir Thomas Lawrence that is now in the Pennsylvania Museum of Art, Philadelphia). There is also a portrait of an unknown girl, possibly one of the fourteen children that were born to Charles and Jane Fraser in the first sixteen years of their marriage.

The dining-room, which was handsomely redecorated by Mrs Smiley in 1977 as a gift to the Trust, is full of fascinating pieces of furniture from different periods. But my own favourite display is an ebonized show-table that vividly tells the story of how Captain (as he then was) Charles Mackenzie Fraser of the Coldstream Guards lost his right leg at the age of twenty in the Peninsular War, during the assault on the castle of Burgos in northern Spain in September 1812. In a box under the table is one of the articulated wooden legs he wore for the rest of his life, the foot surprisingly small and neat for a man of his height. Also on display are a bullet-holed cockaded hat and two musket-balls – and Fraser's handwritten diary, which reveals all too tellingly what a botched operation the Burgos campaign actually was.

The cockaded hat saved his life – because it was too large for him. To make it fit, he had stuffed his folded handkerchief into the lining. As he approached the walls of Burgos, a musket-ball caught him on the side of the head, but the accidental padding inside the hat stopped its force and it broke only skin, not bone. Captain Mackenzie Fraser was knocked over, but in a trice he was up and leading his men up the scaling-ladders. This time he got a bullet on the inside of his right knee, whereupon he tumbled down into the ditch below and was eventually carried to safety. With the ball still lodged in his knee the leg became so infected that it was amputated on 4 November 1812. The two bullets on display are the ones that struck him on head and knee; in the entrance hall under the great hall we can see the wheelchair that he would use on occasion.

Not that the loss of his leg was allowed to affect or incapacitate him in any way. After retiring from the army he entered Parliament and sat for Ross and Cromarty from 1815 to 1819. He was also appointed colonel of the Ross-shire Militia, a post he held for fifty-six years. He married his adoring Jane Hay, daughter of Sir John Hay, fifth Baronet of Hayston and Smithfield, in 1817, and no sooner were they installed in Castle Fraser than Colonel Mackenzie Fraser 'plunged into altering and improving his property with boundless – at time regrettable – enthusiasm' (Mrs Smiley). Or as Mr Gordon Slade puts it:

His effect on the Castle was immediate, incessant, and disastrous, although he must have made it in many ways a more convenient place to live in.

The alterations that Colonel Mackenzie Fraser made were little short of drastic. He began with the great hall. In the west window which Miss Elyza is said to have enlarged he now

The smoking-room in the round tower.

installed an organ (it was removed in 1938 and given to St Anne's Church in nearby Kemnay). This major 'improvement' not only obliterated the view of the setting sun; it also destroyed the bottom end of a shaft leading from one of the most interesting – and disputed – architectural features of Castle Fraser: the so-called 'laird's lug', or listening-room.

Upstairs in the worked room (traditionally the laird's bedroom) there is a wall closet with a trapdoor in the floor leading down by ladder to a constricted cell measuring six feet by three feet and hidden in the deep-arched recess of the west window of the great hall. It had a ventilation hole leading to the hall itself. There has been great argument about the purpose of this curious chamber. Some authorities believe that it had been used as a safe deposit, or muniments room, for the laird's papers. Mr Gordon Slade thinks that it may have been used as a prison cell. But others, notably the early nineteenth-century antiquarian James Skene of Rubislaw, believed that it was a secret listening-post from which the laird could eavesdrop on conversations and conspiracies in the great hall itself. This may have been the story heard, and believed, by Sir Walter Scott, who seems to have used it as the model for the 'Dionysius Ear' in the Tower of London in his novel *The Fortunes of Nigel*; in it, King James VI had this sort of device constructed and tried it out for himself, but found it so uncomfortable that he had it dismantled.

It was the shaft leading from this intramural chamber to just above the one-time windowseat in the great hall that the Continuer destroyed with his alterations to accommodate the new organ (a pencilled outline on the wall to the left of the window recess indicates the position of the chamber). We shall now never know what the true nature or purpose of the cell was; but despite the admitted lack of evidence, the Trust representative at Castle Fraser, Mrs Catriona Webster, thinks that it may be nothing more romantic than the relics of a very early stone staircase which became 'lost' in subsequent alterations.

The Continuer now embarked on an extensive scheme of improvements which destroyed all the existing seventeenth- and eighteenth-century interiors in the interests of 'modernization'. He also demolished the main external staircase and replaced it with a domed internal stair hall in the courtyard, to give access to the whole first floor; the courtyard itself was transformed by building arcades with a corridor over them to serve both storeys of the 'laigh biggins', and the north end was closed off with an arched entry.

In their private life the Frasers suffered tragedy after tragedy; one by one their huge brood of children died, either in infancy or through tuberculosis in their teens or twenties. It was as if the great castle had been struck by some morbid blight that took away young lives at will. When Jane Mackenzie Fraser died in 1861, only three of her fourteen children were still alive. Colonel Mackenzie Fraser himself, who became something of a martinet in his old age, died ten years later in his eightieth year. He had made no further alterations to the castle for some years; but what he had done with his boundless enthusiasm and love for the castle was to ruin it architecturally.

Of the three surviving children, only one was a son: the seventh, Colonel Frederick Mackenzie Fraser, who succeeded to Castle Fraser and Inverallochy in 1871. He lived at the castle for twenty-six years, but all the sunshine and laughter had now fled. Socially he was a virtual recluse, and the castle was closed to any but private visitors. He seems to have been abnormally sensitive to the presence of servants; it's said that any housemaid who was tactless enough to be found dusting was dismissed on the spot. It was around now that stories began to circulate about a murdered princess who had allegedly been done to death in the green room in the round tower; her body had been hidden in the cupboard behind the door, and then dragged unceremoniously down the stone staircase for disposal. On the way down, however, the body left a tell-tale trail of bloodstains which, no matter how hard the housemaids scrubbed, would not go away. For that reason, so the story goes, the stone stairs were covered with wood. There is no indication of who this mysterious princess may have been, or in which century the dastardly deed is alleged to have taken place.

The story first appeared in print in the *Ladies' Field* of 22 September 1900, in an article on Castle Fraser by one of the Continuer's granddaughters, May Tomlinson. But since the stone stairs of the Michael Tower were *also* at one time covered with wood, it is much more likely to have been an attempt by Colonel Frederick or a predecessor to deaden the sound of servants' feet on the staircases. From such mundane material is the stuff of legend woven.

Colonel Frederick Mackenzie Fraser married twice, but died still childless in 1897. A granite memorial stone in the woods bears this gloomy epitaph:

> The last of this race to live and die
> In this his Ancient Stronghold.

On the west gable of the castle, under Miss Elyza's window, his widowed second wife, Theodora Fraser (Theodora Lovett Derby, of Leap Castle, County Dublin), put up a plaque with a single word that said it all: FINIS.

And finis it was, to all intents and purposes, for Castle Fraser as a lived-in family home. Colonel Frederick had been a keen sportsman, and it is probable that the collection of stuffed birds and animal heads – including two stuffed pet dogs – now in the so-called master's room was made by him. It is symbolically appropriate in a way, because after the colonel's death in 1871 it is as if the taxidermist had taken over Castle Fraser itself.

With Colonel Frederick's death in 1897 the succession once again reverted to the female line. His eldest surviving sister, Eleanor Mackenzie Fraser, had married the first Bishop of Gibraltar, the Reverend George Tomlinson, in 1855; the castle was now inherited by her grandson, Thomas Fraser Croft Fraser, who was then still a child – but the estate had been left in the hands of trustees with the life rent going to Colonel Frederick's second wife, Theodora. Thomas Fraser Croft Fraser seldom visited Castle Fraser, and showed little interest in it; he himself became Privy Chamberlain to the Pope and Master of Ceremonies at St Peter's, Rome (he died in 1956).

So when the first Viscount Cowdray started on his castle-buying spree in Aberdeenshire, Castle Fraser and its estates were ready to fall into his lap. After protracted negotiations he eventually bought it in 1922 at a public auction, and handed it over to his second son, the Honourable Clive Pearson. And this turned out to be the saving of Castle Fraser, for Mr Pearson was just as hooked on old castles as his father was. With the help of the Aberdeen architect and antiquarian Dr William Kelly, he embarked on a long and careful course of architectural detective work in an attempt to restore it to its former state.

It was not before time. Mrs Lavinia Smiley (Mr Pearson's daughter) remembers it from her early youth as a sad and sadly dilapidated place:

Peeling paint and crumbling plaster, leaky roofs and a terrific smell of paraffin lamps ... very dark, very creepy, everything painted dark brown. My father had to tread carefully because old Mrs Young, the housekeeper (who wore all the keys of the Castle round her waist on what was known as a *chatelaine*) was still there, remembering the Old Days, and he did not want to hurt her feelings ...

Throughout the thirties, Mr Pearson and Dr Kelly carefully unpicked the Victorian embellishments bestowed by Colonel Mackenzie Fraser, in particular in the Michael Tower and the great hall, in order to discover how the castle had developed. In 1947 Mr Pearson made the castle over to his second daughter, Lavinia, and her husband, Major Michael Smiley, and they continued the restoration work. In 1950 there came a hidden stroke of luck: one night thieves stripped all the lead from the roofs of the nineteenth-century additions filling the courtyard, as a result of which all the additions were removed, thus restoring the courtyard to its original form.

opposite Brodick Castle from the north-west: on the left is the arched entrance under the north-western tower.

left The drawing-room of Brodick Castle. One of the finest rooms in Scotland, it was the key to the nineteenth-century extension of the castle. The magnificent plaster ceiling, of Italian workmanship, tells the heraldic history of the family from James II, whose daughter married Sir James Hamilton of Cadzow, to the eleventh Duke of Hamilton. The chandelier was brought from the Duke of Montrose's home at Buchanan Castle before its demolition some years ago. The room is superbly furnished with Italian and French pieces. On the left, between the windows, is a pair of neo-classical marquetry commodes, probably Piedmontese, from about 1780. On them stands a pair of spectacular Chinese porcelain soup tureens of the Chien Lung period (1736–95), modelled as ducks or geese, one with an eel in its beak, the other with a fish. They are mounted on silver bases made in Rotterdam. Above them hang Venetian looking-glasses. The giltwood seat furniture is Louise-Philippe, dating from the 1830s.

p 51
below The lofty drawing-room of Brodie Castle, designed by William Burn for William Brodie. The carpet with its leaf-and-trellis pattern in white on rose was bought at the Crystal Palace Exhibition of 1851. The French furniture was brought to Brodie after the death of the last Duchess of Gordon.

In 1976, exactly four hundred years after Michael Fraser put up the Royal Arms on the tower he had started to build, Major and Mrs Smiley inaugurated a new chapter in Castle Fraser's history when they made a gift of it, along with twenty-six acres of surrounding parkland, to the National Trust for Scotland. By then they had completed a thorough and painstaking restoration of the whole castle, and wanted to have it safeguarded for posterity.

The restoration work has had one curious side-effect, however. By opening up old doorways and old walls – doors that were never in use all at the same time – Castle Fraser now gives the impression of being even more of a labyrinth than it ever was in real life. One can see now, more clearly than ever before, the fascinating jigsaw puzzle that is the story of the grandest of the great houses of the north-east.

The great hall at Castle Fraser.

The north side of Robert Adam's Charlotte Square, Edinburgh.

7 CHARLOTTE SQ
Edinburgh

THE STORY OF 7 Charlotte Square in the west end of Edinburgh is a story of birth and rebirth. It encapsulates in a single house the birth of the New Town in Edinburgh – one of the finest achievements of civic planning in Europe – and the kind of modern rebirth at which the National Trust for Scotland has so often acted as devoted midwife.

The Georgian New Town, striding with measured tread down the slopes from the tenement-crowded Royal Mile of the medieval Old Town, was built in the hundred years between 1760 and 1860. It gave Edinburgh the gracious and ordered aspect of a romantic classical city that has excited the admiration of the world ever since. The culmination, the crowning architectural flourish, of the first New Town plan was Charlotte Square, described by the late Sir Basil Spence as 'civic architecture at its best, created by a master'. That master was Robert Adam, the foremost classical architect of his generation, then in his sixties and nearing the end of his distinguished career. In 1791 he was commissioned by the town council to design a unified scheme for the frontages of the proposed square, for which he was paid the princely fee of two hundred guineas; in 1975 the cost of recreating the Georgian interior of just one of his houses, 7 Charlotte Square, was £80,000!

Little more than two centuries ago, Edinburgh consisted entirely of the Old Town, a huddled burgh of teeming tenements, urban towers of up to ten or eleven storeys, that fledged the ridge that sloped from the rock of Edinburgh Castle down to the Palace of Holyroodhouse: the historic Royal Mile. It was crowded, insanitary, extremely smelly, but also rather cosy, where people of all social ranks, from lords to the lower orders, lived cheek-by-jowl in a fetid *mélange* of humanity. By the middle of the eighteenth century, however, with Edinburgh's population and prosperity increasing rapidly, the constrictions of the Old Town were becoming intolerable. Edinburgh was bursting at its seams, and simply had to expand; the fact that it expanded into the controlled, polished elegance of the New Town was entirely due to the shrewdness and initiative of one outstanding Edinburgh burgher – George Drummond, Lord Provost for no fewer than six terms of office between 1725 and 1764.

The ideal area for a major expansion programme lay to the north, on the undulating fields (then known locally as the 'Barefoots' Parks') that stretched towards the Firth of Forth. In 1752 a pamphlet entitled *Proposals for carrying on certain Public Works in the City of Edinburgh* expressed the vision of a new town there, to be distinguished by 'the neatness and accommodation of its private houses; the beauty and conveniency (sic) of its numerous streets and open squares, of its buildings and bridges, its large parks and extensive walks'. This was Provost Drummond's dream, which he had been nursing for years. There was a formidable topographical obstacle in the way, however: a large and noxious lake called the Nor' Loch, used for boating in summertime and skating in winter, that lay at the roots of the Castle Rock.

Provost Drummond's scheme involved the draining of the Nor' Loch in 1759 (it is now better known as Princes Street Gardens), and building the North Bridge over the ravine from the old High Street (the Royal Mile) to what is now the east end of Princes Street. This was begun in 1763, but not completed until 1772 after an unfortunate collapse while under construction. Meanwhile, in 1766, the town council announced an architectural competition for the layout of its proposed new 'housing scheme for the affluent', as it has been called. It was won by a young and unknown Edinburgh architect, James Craig, whose modified plans were adopted by the town council in 1767; Craig received 'as a reward of merit a gold medal, with an impression of the Arms of the City of Edinburgh, and the Freedom of the City in a silver box'.

James Craig's plan was orthodox simplicity itself: a rectilinear area laid out on a grid system between Princes Street and Queen Street. Between them, on the crest of the field of 'Barefoots' Parks', there was to be a spacious thoroughfare (George Street) with an elegant square at each end. A significant feature of his design was that the two outer terraces (Princes Street and Queen Street) should have houses on one side only: Princes Street looking southwards and upwards at the Castle Rock, Queen Street looking northwards and downwards over the Firth of Forth.

Building started at once at the eastern end of the scheme, closest to the North Bridge, and St Andrew Square was completed by 1781; it included the fine mansion designed by Sir William Chambers for Sir Lawrence Dundas (now the headquarters of the Royal Bank of Scotland). Progress was slow elsewhere, however; many people were reluctant to 'emigrate' from the Old Town to the New across the windswept North Bridge, and speculative builders who took feus from the town council knew it was a gamble. The town council was gradually tightening up its regulations about the size and style of the buildings that could be erected (a little later, a feuar who built a house which departed from the overall plan was compelled to pull it down).

In order to get the western part of the New Town moving, the Lord Provost of the day, Sir William Stirling, decided on a bold gesture: after much discussion and many proposals by other architects, he called in Robert Adam to design an exemplary square at the empty western end of George Street. Adam was then the most famous architect in Britain, having designed great mansions in England and Scotland (such as Culzean Castle) and streets and squares in London (such as Fitzroy Square); in Edinburgh he had recently designed two monumental public buildings, Register House at the east end of Princes Street and the 'Old Quad' of Edinburgh University. Robert Adam had also proved himself a master of designing unified house frontages with simple but vigorous and varied ornamentation.

So Adam set to work to earn his two-hundred-guinea fee. He had to design a square as a single architectural unit, each side five hundred feet long. The most conspicuous aspects were to be the north and south sides, each with a matching 'palace front' tying the houses together on either side of an imposing central unit with grouped columns jutting forward slightly. Basil Skinner, now the Director of Extra-Mural Studies at Edinburgh University, explained the concept admirably for laymen in *The National Trust for Scotland Guide* (1976):

The avoidance of monotony was to depend upon composition, the idea that a block of tidy, ironed-out houses in an urban terrace could be given rhythm by composing the façade as one would the balanced image of a stately home. This is the contribution, the object-lesson, of Robert Adam's north side of Charlotte Square. It is a block of eleven separate houses; its occupants could be assumed to have no common interests beyond the superficial, but many separate tastes; yet the autonomy of design is complete and the eleven owners are for ever knit together in a unified, composite whole...

The mechanics of the thing are obvious. The central house has the benefit of strong emphasis in its colonnaded pediment; the wings protrude and have the dignity of garlands and roof-top sphinxes, and the intervening houses just run along in exquisite good taste, pulled together by

opposite The Georgian House façade. To the right is the imposing colonnaded front of number 6, now the official residence of the Secretary of State for Scotland.

these dominating features. Yet the whole composition is extremely subtle in its reconciliation between vertical demands and horizontal necessity. Eleven houses built together must imply a strong horizontal ... Yet each house itself is a vertical unit, basement and four upper levels of domestic accommodation, and each level is varied in the nature of its stonework and the dignity of its openings according to aesthetic and room-use considerations.

One of these eleven houses on the north side, right beside the dominant central house, was to be 7 Charlotte Square.

Robert Adam died in 1792, to be buried in Westminster Abbey, and never saw his magnificent square take shape. The sale of feus started in 1792, however, and the first house had its roof on by September of that year, thereby winning for its builder a premium of £10. But other buildings were slow to follow. The outbreak of the Napoleonic Wars in February 1793 made money dear and people cautious. In the event, Charlotte Square as a whole was not to be completed until 1820. The truly astonishing thing is that so much of it conformed to Adam's original designs, especially the north side. The houses were built singly by individual feuars, and one can still see the joins in the stonework where the houses were knitted together.

These feuars were a curiously assorted bunch of speculators, and included two architects, a mason, a painter, a wright, two upholsterers, and a 'writing master' called Edward Butterworth. It was Butterworth who bought the feu of 7 Charlotte Square, having already bought and built on nine other feus elsewhere in the New Town (he was later to buy another five feus in Charlotte Square). It is not known whether or not he started building there 'on spec', but in 1796 the feu charter of 7 Charlotte Square was granted by the town council (with the consent of Edward Butterworth) to John Lamont of Lamont (1741-1816), eighteenth chief of Clan Lamont, of Ardlamont in Argyll. And with that the story of the Trust's Georgian House in Edinburgh begins. The feu of the central building-plot – the present number 6, now known as Bute House, the official Edinburgh residence of the Secretary of State for Scotland – had already been sold, and the building had been erected to Adam's original specifications, both inside and out. Lamont's architect had to fit number 7 to number 6. It was a much more modest building, but even so it cost the eighteenth chief of Clan Lamont some £1800.

'John xviii', as he is called in the *History of the Lamont Clan* by H. McKechnie (1938), seems to have been a typical chief of his time, when Highland society was changing fast after the *débâcle* of the 1745 uprising. McKechnie described him, more in sorrow than in anger, as 'the last of the patriarchs and the first of the moderns'. It was a time when Highland clan chiefs were eagerly discovering the joys of city life as opposed to the rough and tumble of a country lairdship, and John Lamont was an almost totally absentee laird: 'From his youth he was known in the coffee-houses of Pall Mall,' wrote McKechnie – and what could be more damning than that? He inherited from his father in his twenties in 1767, and in no time was falling into the contemporary pattern that Dr Samuel Johnson was to comment on so percipiently during his entertaining tour of Scotland in 1773:

Chiefs being now deprived of their jurisdiction have already lost much of their influence; and as they gradually degenerate from patriarchal rulers to rapacious landlords, they will divest themselves of the little that remains.

McKechnie put it bluntly:

The old order was changed and gave place to the new at the ruthless bidding of John xviii ... If appearances mattered all and sentiments nothing he was a brave chief, for he kept the state of a wealthy landlord, though it meant rack-renting his estates ... Alas! he introduced sheep-farming to the grief of his people ... Many a hearth-stone has been cold since the time of John xviii.

He was seldom seen at Ardlamont. While his clansmen's hearth-stones were cooling, he was warming his feet at more luxurious fireplaces. In 1773 he married Helen, only daughter of the late Duncan Campbell of South Hall in the Kyles of Bute, and there he stayed for several years. He also liked to cut a dash in Edinburgh. He had been elected to the King's Bodyguard (Royal Company of Archers) in 1770, and was an early member of the new Highland Society of Edinburgh: 'John XVIII moved abroad, escorted by his piper and standard-bearer . . .'

In 1788 John the eighteenth moved to Edinburgh with his wife and five children, staying first at 4 St Andrew Square and then at 19 Princes Street in the New Town – presumably in rented property. He had taken possession of his new house, 7 Charlotte Square, by 1797, because in the summer of that year his twenty-one-year-old daughter Amelia was married from there.

Compared with number 6, with its magnificently preserved Adam interiors, number 7 was positively skimpy. Lamont had to conform to the exterior specifications laid down by Robert Adam and the town council, but what he did inside was a matter of his own inclination and his pocket. And it is quite clear that his means were already stretched to the limit. His net income from his estates was £2800 a year, but this was not nearly enough to support his lifestyle. In 1799 he sold off half of the clan lands, including Castle Toward, for £40,000, but most of that went towards paying off his debts.

He flew to the winds the economy by which his three forebears had redeemed their patrimony . . . and at his death the estate was bankrupt [wrote McKechnie]. Certain it is that he ruined the fortunes of the family, reducing it (for the time at least) from wealth to poverty . . . But he had lived well and with enjoyment, and it is an old maxim alike in Highlands and Lowlands that 'what's in your wame [belly] is no' in your testament'.

His portrait by Henry Raeburn around 1800 shows a bluff oldster in black enlivened by a yellow cravat. In 1811 there is news of him making alterations to 7 Charlotte Square. But five years later, in April 1816, he sold it for 'above £3000 sterling' to Mrs Catherine Farquharson of Invercauld. He died later that year, 'having ridden rough-shod over the remnants of his clan for half a century . . . The luxury of a city dwelling was never again the lot of any chief . . . From his time on, the tide has been ever on the ebb for the *clan Laomainn*'.

By this time, Charlotte Square was definitely becoming a prestigious address. The next-door neighbour in number 6 had been Sir John Sinclair, the Caithness laird and agriculturalist who compiled the first *Statistical Account of Scotland* in the 1790s (he sold number 6 in 1816 for £3700). Number 5 had been bought by the Grants of Rothiemurchus as soon as it was built and in 1797 had been the birthplace of Elizabeth Grant, author of the enchanting *The Memoirs of a Highland Lady*. On the west side of the square, number 13 was the home of Sir William Fettes, tea and wine merchant and general entrepreneur, twice Lord Provost of Edinburgh, and later to be the founder of Fettes College with an endowment of £166,000. Next door to him, at number 14, lived Henry Cockburn, later to be Lord Cockburn and Senator of the College of Justice, a wit, sage and Whig reformer whose *Memorials of his Time* (1856) were to become a classic observation of Edinburgh life in the first half of the nineteenth centry. Charlotte Square was already a microcosm of the changing social life of Scotland.

The new owner of number 7, Mrs Catherine Farquharson of Invercauld in Aberdeenshire, 'Eleventh of Invercauld', had inherited from her father in 1805. She was born in 1774, the youngest of a family of eleven children, ten of whom predeceased their parents. The New Spalding Club's *Records of Invercauld* (1901) traces her ancestry back to a Finlay Mhor who died bearing the Royal Standard at the Battle of Pinkie in 1547, and whose male line came to an end with Catherine Farquharson some two and a half centuries later.

At length a gloom overcast the once happy household at Invercauld. First a little baby died, and soon after her, another; and so on, one by one as they grew up . . . The mother, worn out with

The dining-room of the
Georgian House, facing on to
Charlotte Square.

watching, anxiety and sorrow, followed her children (1779), leaving only, of all their eleven offspring, the youngest, a little girl of five years of age, to be the care and comfort of the bereaved father for the rest of his life.

Catherine Farquharson married a Captain James Ross RN, who obligingly took the name Farquharson as his new surname; but since the Invercauld family was now represented through the female line, the titular chiefship of the clan went to another branch, even though Mrs Farquharson, who seems to have been a lady of forceful personality continued to be regarded as the 'real' chief until her death in 1845. So, ironically, yet another Highland clan heritage dissipated itself behind the elegant urban symmetry of Edinburgh's new Charlotte Square.

After Mrs Farquharson's death, number 7 was bought by a brilliant up-and-coming Edinburgh advocate, Charles Neaves, later to be appointed a judge of the Court of Session in 1854 following the death of Lord Cockburn. Neaves was one of the greatest case lawyers of his day, a man with a ferociously tenacious memory who could cite apposite precedents with unfailing accuracy, and he was one of the foremost authorities on criminal law in Scotland. Out of court he enjoyed a large reputation as a literary man, both as a serious classical scholar and a satirist; for more than forty years he was a contributor to *Blackwood's Magazine* (now, alas, defunct). He was a prominent figure at all the major literary functions that so enlivened the Edinburgh scene. He was present at the Theatrical Fund banquet in 1827 when Sir Walter Scott first publicly acknowledged his authorship of the *Waverley Novels,* and at a similar function given in honour of Charles Dickens in 1841. It was from number 7 that he sallied forth in full fig to attend the banquet held in recognition of Thackeray in 1857.

We catch an enchanting glimpse of Lord Neaves, host and entertainer, in the diary of the Reverend David Aitken DD, who lived at 4 Charlotte Square from 1864 to 1875 (*The Book of the Old Edinburgh Club*, vol. 23, 1971). On 17 March 1866 he dined at number 7 with a small but select company. In the drawing-room on the first floor after dinner, Lord Tennyson's sister, Mrs Lushington, 'repeated in a sort of recitative her brother Tennyson's "Charge of the Light Brigade" & another of his poems – given with great feeling standing apart in the doorway. An amusing contrast was Lord Neaves singing a song of his own, "Philology", very droll.'

Lord Neaves' occupation of number 7 presents a picture of nineteenth-century Edinburgh society at its most brilliant – lively, witty, intellectual, intensely literary. The next prominent occupant of number 7 was to reflect another and deeply significant aspect of Scottish life in the second half of the nineteenth century – the great religious debates and ructions over the independence of the established Church of Scotland and the Disruption of 1843 that split the Kirk in two.

Lord Neaves died in 1876, but number 7 remained in his family's possession until it was bought in 1889 by the Reverend Dr Alexander Whyte. Dr Whyte, one of the most distinguished clergymen of his day, was a son of the catastrophic Disruption when 451 of the Kirk's 1203 ministers walked out to form the Free Church of Scotland in protest against Government interference in what they considered their proper spheres of control – in particular over the question of the right of congregations and presbyteries to choose their own ministers.

Dr Whyte was an influential and pacific voice in the Free Church in the move towards reunion with the Church of Scotland at the end of the nineteenth century. He had been 'called' to Free St George's Church (now St George's West) in Shandwick Place, just around the corner from the original St George's in Charlotte Square, in 1870. It had been built when his great predecessor, Robert Candlish, had 'come out' in the Disruption, and its congregation now included some of the ablest professional men in Edinburgh. Dr Whyte was elected Moderator of the General Assembly of the Free Church for 1898; in 1909 he was appointed Principal of the Free Church's New College at the crest of the

Mound in Edinburgh. He retired in 1918 and went south, where he died in 1921. In number 7 he used the former drawing-room as his study, with high bookcases lining the walls, as can be seen in two photographs in his biography (*The Life of Alexander Whyte* by G. F. Barbour, 1923). These photographs are very telling. They show Dr Whyte surrounded by busts of Homer, Plato and Dante, a statuette of Thackeray, and portraits of Thomas Carlyle and Cardinal Newman – a revealing reflection of the studious, broad-minded interests of a top Free Churchman of his time, before the eventual reunion in 1929.

In 1922 number 7 was bought by a company called Mountjoy Ltd; and with that, the Georgian house entered a new and significant phase in its chequered life, and one that was to lead indirectly to its rebirth in 1975.

Mountjoy Ltd was then a company of trustees acting under settlement by the fourth Marquess of Bute, whose family seat was Mount Stewart at Rothesay in the Isle of Bute, off the west coast of Scotland. He inherited the title and the vast Bute estates (more than 100,000 acres) in Scotland and Wales in 1900; but he also inherited his father's reverence and pioneering concern for Scotland's historic heritage. The third marquess, who is supposed to have been the model for the subject of Disraeli's novel *Lothair*, had salvaged many ancient historic monuments, including Falkland Palace; his son was to continue this passionate and positive interest. In 1903, at the age of twenty-two, he bought 5 Charlotte Square (now the headquarters of the National Trust for Scotland) as his Edinburgh town house; twenty years later this would gestate into a scheme for restoring the frontage of the whole north side of Charlotte Square back to Adam's original design. But he was not concerned just with the conspicuous monuments of the past, the castles and great houses, as his father had been. He was just as concerned, perhaps even more so, about the neglect and destruction of much more humble domestic architecture, the 'little houses' of Scotland's heritage. There was nothing élitist about his attitude. In a clarion speech in Edinburgh in 1936 he declared: 'In my opinion it is the working man who, of all people, takes the greatest interest in our ancient buildings, and well he may, for he is best able to understand the solidity and care with which they were built and the excellence of their workmanship.'

He personally initiated and financed the listing, by acknowledged experts, of houses of architectural and historic merit all over Scotland, the original 'Bute List', which became the basis for official government listing of buildings that deserve to be preserved. In that same speech in Edinburgh he expressed the credo that had inspired the formation of the National Trust for Scotland five years earlier:

The destruction that is taking place now is just as great and just as real as the destruction that took place years ago in the case of our old castles and churches, the remains of which we are now, when too late, doing our best to preserve. The destruction that is now taking place will be no less a loss to our children and to our country than the loss we now deplore caused by that former vandalism.

Like his father, the fourth marquess was more than prepared to 'put his money where his mouth was'. In the 1920s his trustee company, Mountjoy Ltd, purchased 6, 7 and 8 Charlotte Square. These properties were bought for leasing, but the primary purpose was to apply a scheme of unified restoration. In the 1920s the roofs were restored to Adam's original elevation by removing the dormer dindows that had been added haphazardly by earlier owners, and in the 1930s the Marquess of Bute persuaded all the other proprietors on the north side of Charlotte Square to unite in restoring the whole frontage to the Adam design. This involved lifting the lower sills of many of the drawing-room windows, which had been lowered in accordance with Victorian practice, and reinstating the Georgian front doorways. And with that the north side of Charlotte Square began to look more like its old self again.

Inside it was a different story, however. Number 7 was leased to various tenants, until

above The parlour, or back drawing-room, of the Georgian House; furnished as it would have been at the end of the eighteenth century, with chairs drawn up round a central table. On the left, the barrel organ in its Sheraton-style mahogany case dates from about 1880 and plays a selection of Scottish airs.

left The drawing-room on the first floor of the Georgian House.

right The dresser in the kitchen carries a comprehensive collection of copper pots and pans – probably larger than it ever was in reality.

right The kitchen is a masterpiece of inspired restoration. None of the original fixtures or fittings had survived: the open fire range was rescued from a demolition skip in the street. The elaborate spit mechanism in front of it is operated by a fan in the chimney that rotates in the rising heat. To the right is a separately fired oven for baking.

in 1934 it was taken over, at a nominal rent, by Messrs Whytock & Reid, a distinguished Royal Warrant firm of antique-dealers and furnisher/decorators. Some of the other proprietors were distinctly sniffy about 'trade' being allowed into the square; but in fact several houses in the square had been converted into small private boarding-schools, number 6 had been a hotel for a time (Oman's Hotel, with an annexe in number 4, in the middle of the nineteenth century), number 28 had been a lodging-house for seventeen paying guests, and numbers 38 and 39 had been 'twinned' to found the Roxburghe Hotel – not to mention the number of houses that had been taken over as offices by insurance or financial firms.

Whytock & Reid, who have done and still do an enormous amount of specialized restoration work in furnishings for the National Trust for Scotland, occupied number 7 from top to bottom. In the basement, where the Trust has now recreated the kitchen, there were rooms for upholstery, sewing and cutting. In the upper floors, now converted by the Baird Trust into the official Edinburgh residence of the Moderator of the General Assembly of the Church of Scotland, there was a drawing-office. On the ground floor, the old bedchamber at the back was the general office, partitioned to accommodate a receptionist, while the managing director had his office in the old dining-room at the front. Upstairs, the splendid drawing-room looking out over the square, which Dr Whyte had converted into a study, was used as the saleroom for soft furnishings, fabrics and wallpapers. The old place buzzed with activity, employing at its height some twenty-five people.

Although it was 'trade' it was very genteel, catering for upper-middle-class Edinburgh or country clients looking for top quality plenishings. But it was also extraordinarily dowdy. As tenants, Whytock & Reid had no incentive to 'do up' the place. Their clientele would come in, on their way home from Binns at the west end of Princes Street, perhaps, to discuss curtains or cushion-covers or to commission a piece of hand-made furniture. It was a dying world, in a dying square.

The regeneration began after the Second World War. The fourth Marquess of Bute died in 1947, to be succeeded by his son John, a very shy, sensitive man, intensely interested in ornithology; but John had also been imbued with the (by now) traditional Bute passion for preservation. In 1931 he had bought the celebrated archipelago of islands far out west in the heaving Atlantic known as St Kilda, which had been evacuated by its inhabitants in 1930, and he bequeathed it to the National Trust for Scotland when he died in 1956 as an area of nature conservation.

His eldest son John, the sixth marquess, became formally involved with the Trust's work as a member of Council in 1964 and has been an extremely active chairman of the National Trust for Scotland since 1969. The Trust had had its headquarters (on lease) in his grandfather's former town house at 5 Charlotte Square since 1949; so it was a matter of great mutual satisfaction when the three houses in the centre of the north block – numbers 5, 6 and 7 – along with certain chattels, were accepted in 1966 by the Commissioners of the Inland Revenue in part satisfaction of the estate duties arising from the death of the fifth marquess ten years earlier. They passed to the National Trust for Scotland through the Land Fund procedures operating at the time. One provision of the agreement was that number 6 should be restored and furnished as the first official residence of the Secretary of State for Scotland, and this was completed in 1970.

Number 6 is a magnificent Adam house, but it is not, of course, open to the public. Number 5 was in use as the Trust's headquarters. That left number 7 as an opportunity and a challenge to recreate something unique: a Georgian show house displayed and arranged as it might have been when the house was first occupied by John Lamont of Lamont in 1796.

An appeal for £100,000 was launched for the purpose, which to everyone's surprise and delight raised £117,000 in a remarkably short time. There was clearly a keen desire to be able to see behind the Adam façade and visualize what life was like in Edinburgh's Golden Age during the reign of George III. Even more important, offers of period furniture, paintings and domestic utensils flowed in – a very useful aspect of the appeal, because absolutely nothing from the original house interior had survived the many changes of ownership and taste.

In the spring of 1974 the lease of number 7 expired, and Whytock & Reid moved to handsome new custom-built premises on land in the Dean Village in Edinburgh where the firm had had a cabinet-making factory since 1884.

The man in charge of the transformation of number 7 from a furnishings saleroom and showroom into an elegant Georgian family town house was the Trust's curator, David Learmont, who is responsible for the plenishings of all the Trust's properties. It was a daunting task, a matter of making do, of learning as he went along, of getting a 'feel' for a house whose original physical characteristics had long since disappeared. The result, as 50,000 visitors a year will testify, is a triumphant success. The work was all completed in one hectic year, and the Georgian house opened its doors to the public in August 1975.

Just imagine the problems involved and the questions that had to be answered. What sort of colour schemes had Lamont favoured? How had he furnished his new house (bearing in mind that he was under financial stress at the time)? What kind of lifestyle did the eighteenth chief of Clan Lamont feel he could afford, having bought an expensive address in Edinburgh, to cut a dash in Edinburgh society? For David Learmont, curator for the Trust since 1970 when a life-long obsession with furniture and *objets d'art* became a professional career, the rebirth of the Georgian house became a matter of biographical research as much as anything else.

David Learmont started at the heart of the house, the first-floor drawing-room overlooking the square, which Dr Whyte had used as a study and Whytock & Reid had used as a saleroom. This was clearly the showpiece room, to be used for 'promenading' and for important entertaining. Mr Learmont already had at his disposal a large set of seat furniture, carved in gilt-wood and comprising a sofa and twelve armchairs. These had been on loan from the Trust at Yester House in East Lothian for a number of years. He decided that they should be the key to the room, and therefore to the whole building. They were re-covered in a striped silk taffeta, and were then disposed around the sides of the room as they would have been in the eighteenth century, when the centre of rooms was always kept clear. The ceiling was left plain, as Lamont would probably have had it, but a splendid eighteenth-century crystal chandelier was specially purchased for the room. The Victorian cornice around the top of the walls was removed and replaced by an Adamesque frieze, painted in the 'Adam green' colour that had been identified in the old eating-room at Culzean Castle.

The elaborate curtain cornice-boxes over the three commanding windows were given to the Trust, and came from Croome Court in Worcestershire, a house on which Robert Adam had worked in the early 1760s; they were made by a celebrated cabinet-maker of his time, William Linnell. From these pelmet cornices Mr Learmont hung festoon curtains of dark green silk taffeta which he had specially woven. The fireplace, which had been vandalized, was replaced by a fine Sienna marble chimneypiece of the Adam period that was 'borrowed' from number 5. The pier-walls between the windows presented a problem, which Mr Learmont solved by transferring a pair of pier-tables from Hill of Tarvit in Fife (another Trust property); they fitted to within an inch. Above the tables he installed a pair of pier-glasses; the one on the right-hand side is an original which came from Leith Hall, the other is a replica he had specially made. It is what John Lamont himself, on a tight budget, might well have done. The furnishing was completed by a collection of the sort of pictures fashionable at the time, including a couple of landscapes attributed to Alexander Nasmyth (1758-1840) and a portrait by Allan Ramsay (1713-84), and an Edinburgh-made square piano dating from around 1805.

above The ground floor bedchamber in the Georgian House, 7 Charlotte Square, Edinburgh. The four-poster bed came from Newliston in West Lothian, and retains most of its original late eighteenth-century embroidered moreen hangings.

left The kitchen of the Georgian House. The tall cone of sugar was a familiar sight in nineteenth-century kitchens. In front of it is a lacquer tray with two silver dish covers, in the background the typical Scottish dresser and press and a fine collection of copper utensils.

above Crathes Castle, bastion of the Burnetts.

left The queen's room on the third floor of Craigievar Castle, so named by 'Danzig Willie' Forbes, apparently in the hope that King James VI and I and his queen might one day stay there – but they never did. The canopy bed is Flemish and dates from the end of the seventeenth century; it was brought in by Red Sir John Forbes.

above The long gallery at the top of Crathes Castle. The ceiling is splendidly panelled in oak, which makes it unique in Scotland. The room was sometimes used for holding barony courts, and the furniture is set for such an occasion.

right Part of the richly painted ceiling of the room of the Nine Worthies, featuring Julius Caesar, Joshua 'Chieftain of Israel', and King David.

With the drawing-room settled as the keynote of the composition of the house, the other rooms fell naturally into place. The parlour, or back drawing-room, on the same floor, is furnished less formally as the forerunner of our modern sitting-rooms, with a centre table, bookshelves and Edinburgh-made 'Raeburn chairs' (which are really the same as 'Gainsborough chairs', since both of these famous artists tended to use characteristic chairs for their sittings). There are two writing-desks, to emphasize the growing interest in *belles lettres,* and a delightful Edinburgh-made chamber barrel-organ which plays thirty different tunes ranging from *Rule Britannia* to *Adeste Fideles.*

The upstairs floors are not open to the public, for they are now the official residence of the Moderator of the General Assembly of the Church of Scotland (most appropriately, in the house which the moderate Free Church leader Dr Alexander Whyte once owned). The ground floor, however, has also been restored for public display, with a dining-room at the front and the main bedroom at the back, as was the Edinburgh practice of the time.

The contents of the dining-room and the bedchamber, with its magnificent four-poster bed and moreen hangings from Newliston House in West Lothian, are carefully listed in the guidebook prepared by David Learmont. But for many visitors it is the more intimate items that attract most interest: the portable early nineteenth-century mahogany water closet which has been installed in the little passageway between the two rooms, for instance, known as a 'receiver' and looking rather like a ship's lavatory of the 1930s; the portable medicine chest in the bedchamber made by Messrs James Robertson and Company of George Street, Edinburgh, stacked with bottles of rather ominous-looking patent remedies, like laudanum ('Poison'), pure chloroform ('Poison'), and essence of camphor ('In the incipient or earliest stage of Cholera, it is especially useful'); or the delightfully naughty lustreware chamber-pot, with a figure of a mulatto inside saying, 'Oh dear me, what do I see', and the legend 'Keep me clean and use me well, and what I see I will not tell'. It goes on (I cannot resist quoting it in full):

Marriage, this pot it is a Present sent, some mirth to make is only Meant. We hope the same will not Refuse, but keep it safe and oft it Use.

The most popular feature of the house for visitors has proved to be the kitchen in the basement, where the curator allowed his specialist enthusiasm full rein (he once trained at the Professional School of the Swiss Hotel-Keepers' Association in Lausanne). It had been used latterly as Whytock & Reid's staffroom for their meal-breaks; but David Learmont was able to trace the position of the original cooking-range and baking-oven. The open fire-range he installed came about as a stroke of pure luck; Mr Learmont was walking along India Street one day, past a house that was being renovated, when he spotted a splendid eighteenth-century range going into the debris skip, and nipped in to save it!

As the fame and popularity of the Georgian House grew, so more and more items of this kind were brought to the curator's attention or given to the Trust as presents. Perhaps the most bizarre of these was the case of the little old Edinburgh lady, soon after the Georgian House was opened to the public, who arrived carrying a capacious carrier-bag and was observed eyeing, rather suspiciously, the five glasses on the mahogany sideboard in the dining-room. The guide on duty was on the point of blowing her whistle to raise the alarm when the lady (she was in her late seventies) started rummaging in her bag, from which she produced a matching glass and placed it on the sideboard beside the others. It was a kind of shop-lifting in reverse.

Thus was the Georgian House at 7 Charlotte Square reborn; but like all youngsters, it is still growing up, year by year.

Craigievar Castle, 'quite perfect . . . it is the apotheosis of its type'.

CRAIGIEVAR CASTLE
Grampian

CRAIGIEVAR IS the epitome of the classic, quintessential castle of fairy-tale, all turrets and witch-hat roofs: a Walt Disney castle, a pink Gibbs Dentrifice castle of ivory towers for ivory teeth (Giant Decay and all, remember?), a castle straight out of Ruritania and romance. Yet it is utterly Scottish and perfectly of its time. It stands on a mellow and fruitful hillside in central Grampian, twenty-six miles west of Aberdeen and six miles south of Alford. It soars like some massive pine tree, six storeys high, as solid and down-to-earth as the granite rubble from which it was built, yet looking as light as the sugar-icing harling that coats its walls.

It has been hailed as the finest tower house of its kind, the culmination of Scotland's vernacular architectural achievement early in the seventeeth century, when James VI of Scotland was also James I of England (1603-25):

As a testimony of taste, Craigievar ranks with any representative building in Britain. As a work of art, it claims a Scottish place in the front rank of European architecture . . . It has a sort of sublimity . . . a serene assurance not communicated by any other tower house however pleasing. Quite perfect, lightly poised upon the ground, it is the apotheosis of its type. (Stewart Cruden)

It was built at the moment of perfect equipoise between medieval and Renaissance, between Scottish and European, between the indigenous and the foreign.

It was the house that Willie built.

The story of its building has a fairy-tale quality, too, for it was brought into being by a younger son of landed gentry who was absolutely determined to make good in his own right: a man called William Forbes – a self-made man if ever there was one.

William Forbes (pronounced as two syllables, in the old Aberdeenshire style) was born in 1566, the second son of the laird of Corse in Aberdeenshire. His was a cadet family descended from the second Lord Forbes, who had been standard-bearer to King James III of Scotland. He was brought up in the now-ruined Corse Castle, which his father had built. William Forbes was born with a tinge of blue blood in his veins, but without a silver spoon in his mouth. As a younger son he could have little hope of inheriting the castle of Corse – that would automatically go to his elder brother, that celebrated and saintly pastor, Bishop Patrick Forbes of Aberdeen. So William Forbes had to make his own way in the world. And he did.

We don't know precisely *how* he did it. All we know is that he eventually made a fortune as a merchant, exporting from Aberdeen wares like salted salmon, knitted woollens and hides to the main Baltic seaport of Danzig, and importing in exchange the much-prized building-timber that Scotland then lacked – Sweden board (Suadin Burd, as it was called), and the richly glowing Memel pine from the old town of Memel (now Klaipeda) in Lithuania. So successful did he become in this hazardous but potentially profitable Baltic trade that he earned the nickname of 'Willie the Merchant' or, more significantly, 'Danzig Willie'.

View from the roof of Craigievar over the mellow landscape of central Grampian.

But one traditional story, recorded in Alexander Laing's *Donean Tourist* (1828), suggests that his path to prosperity was by no means easy – and tells us a great deal about the two brothers from Corse, Willie the entrepreneur and Patrick the prelate. It seems that the good Patrick often had to give his younger brother financial help when his business ventures failed, but at last got tired of bailing him out and told him that no more money would be forthcoming. When his next cash crisis loomed, however, Willie the Merchant once again appealed to Patrick for an urgent loan of a thousand Scottish merks; and to obviate the expected refusal, he told his brother that he would find a sufficient security bond for it. Patrick thereupon agreed to lend the money. On the appointed day, William turned up to collect it and Patrick asked for the promised surety – to which William said that the only guarantor he had to offer was God Almighty! Patrick replied, no doubt with a resigned smile, that since it was the first time that He had been offered as surety, He could not be rejected; and as he handed over the money to his ingenious brother, he uttered the pious hope that God Almighty, William's bondsman, would prosper him and do him good.

There is no way of telling whether or not the story is apocryphal, but it carries an interesting moral for all budding businessmen – and bank managers.

There is also a strong tradition that Danzig Willie studied and graduated Master of Arts at Edinburgh University, which opened its doors under royal charter as the 'Tounis College' (Town's College) in 1583. The university itself has no record of him ever having been a student there; but in his later years William Forbes would decorate the dream castle he built at Craigievar with the initials M W F – 'Master William Forbes' – which hints, at least, at a Master of Arts degree of which, like many a self-made businessman, he was extremely proud.

Anyway, he was clearly a man of some substance in Edinburgh at the turn of the century, either as what we now call a 'mature student' or, more probably, as a merchant adventurer who may even have had some association with the town council. In 1603, in his late thirties, he married, and married well. His bride was the daughter of a former provost of Edinburgh, Nicholas Woodward or Edward or Udward (spellings were a little haphazard in those days). The provost was a wealthy citizen 'of old descent in the burgh', and had distinguished himself by building a palatial residence which later came to be known as Lockhart's Court in what used to be Niddry's Wynd before it was demolished to allow the construction of South Bridge. Here, Provost Woodward entertained nobility and even royalty (King James VI and his queen stayed there for a short time in 1591, the year he was provost); and here William Forbes, '*magister* and burgher of Edinburgh' wooed and won the provost's daughter, Margaret Woodward.

This good marriage seems to have put the seal on Danzig Willie's success. A few years later he and his wife started acquiring estates up and down the east coast of Scotland: Menie in the parish of Belhelvie in Aberdeenshire in 1607, the mansion-place and rectory of Kincardine and its adjacent lands in 1608, the lands and barony of Auchtertane in Fife in 1617, the lands and barony of Finhaven and Carreston in Forfarshire in 1619. It was in the middle of this land-purchase spree that William Forbes made his most significant and enduring acquisition – 'the lands and barony of Craigievar, February 16, 1610'.

The lands of Craigievar (the name, an old Celtic word, apparently means 'rock of Mar') had long been in the possession of the Mortimer family; in the long room at the top of Craigievar Castle, we can see the charter by James II with the Great Seal of Scotland attached, confirming the lands of Craigievar to Edward Mortimer in 1457. According to Alexander Laing's *Donean Tourist*, the family's fortune, like that of Danzig Willie, had been founded on commerce; the founding father, one Bernard Mortimer, 'made a traffic of eggs to Aberdeen' in the late fourteenth century. The Mortimers flourished as lairds of Craigievar to such an extent that around 1600 they felt able to start the building of a new home, Craigievar Castle, on their estate. But something seems to have gone wrong; they must have overstretched themselves financially; and another document upstairs in the long room at Craigievar, dated 1610, records the transfer of the property by John Mortimer to William Forbes.

The purchase of Craigievar must have given Danzig Willie particular pleasure, because the estate was right next door to the Corse estate where his brother, the future Bishop Patrick Forbes, was now the laird. He must have relished the prospect of building himself an even more imposing castle than the one in which he had grown up. It would show the world – and his brother – that Danzig Willie had really made it to the top. The young scion of an old landed family had become one of the new plutocrats of the north-east. Craigievar Castle would be a fitting monument to his achievements.

It was a good time for building in Scotland. With James VI on the throne in London as James I, the country was enjoying an unprecedented period of peace and growing prosperity which would last until the outbreak of the Civil War in 1639. There was money around, there were highly skilled craftsmen available – in particular, a family of Aberdeen master masons called Bell who were almost certainly involved in the building of Craigievar – and journeymen plasterers and decorators who specialized in the new Italianate Renaissance style of elaborately moulded plasterwork.

It was also a good time for architecture in Scotland. Castles like Craigievar are not really castles at all, but fortified tower houses. At the time that Craigievar was built these were no longer primarily military in purpose, no longer essentially places of defence against assault or siege by turbulent neighbours or invading armies. Instead they were expected to express the idea of authority, the authority of the laird and the law he administered in the king's name as a Crown vassal, and also to provide a sophisticated and elegant home consonant with his prestige and wealth. The basic structure remained the same, solid and formidable; but the battlements at the top from which the defenders could enfilade an approaching enemy had become decorative. One of the many striking features of the exterior of Craigievar is the way in which stone projections that look like cannons have been stuck on at intervals around the corbel-belt or cornice that crowns the top of the tower. They look as if they might be gargoyles to get rid of rainwater, or even spouts through which boiling oil or molten lead could be poured on attackers. In point of fact they are simply imitation cannons now transformed into a purely ornamental device.

When Danzig Willie Forbes bought the lands of Craigievar in 1610, the castle that the Mortimers had started lay unfinished. We don't know precisely how far it had advanced, or how much Danzig Willie altered the original plans; but during reharling operations by the National Trust for Scotland in 1973, the architects found that in the hall there was a window that had been blocked up. It was a little off-centre, and would have spoiled the symmetry of the room. It suggests that the Mortimers had at least completed the walls of the hall on the first floor, and that Danzig Willie had ordered a considerable readjustment of the design to suit his own more grandiose plans for his family seat.

In plan, the house that Willie built was in the classic L-shaped Scottish mode – a rectangular tower house with a wing to form the lower part of the L, and a square tower set into the elbow, or 're-entrant angle' as architects call it. This kind of building, as the late W. Douglas Simpson points out in his splendid *Guide to Craigievar Castle*, is really a medieval hall-house built vertically instead of horizontally. In such a building the spiral stairs that lead from storey to storey are vertical corridors.

Today, the pride and joy of Craigievar Castle is the hall that Danzig Willie redesigned on the first floor. What a glorious chamber it is. One of its virtues, to the historian of architecture, is that it has remained practically unchanged since it was originally built; the only major modification has been to the two windows on the west side, whose sills were lowered by three feet during alterations carried out in 1825, which also involved the lowering of the top of the beautifully carved wooden panelling on that wall. Apart from that, the hall is as Danzig Willie envisaged it.

opposite The spacious blue room. The plaster ceiling is dated 1626 and incorporates an English armorial tablet.

One wall is dominated by a massive representation in modelled stucco of the Royal Arms of the United Kingdom above the fireplace, with telamones and caryatids on either side. As a tenant-in-chief of the Crown, holding his lands directly from the king, Danzig Willie was entitled to display the Royal Arms – and he did so with all the zest and zeal of a loyalist who could afford to trumpet his allegiance and his status. The huge armorial tablet in Craigievar is arguably the finest surviving achievement of its kind in Britain, in plaster or any other medium. It is also, from the Scottish point of view, impeccably correct: Scotland is accorded two of the quarters, England and Ireland one each; and the Order of the Thistle, with its badge of St Andrew, takes heraldic precedence over the Order of the Garter with its badge of St George. Originally it may have been painted with the full colours of heraldry; today, in stark white, it is overwhelming and magnificent in its effect.

The other major feature of the hall is the ceiling, with its moulded plasterwork, unchanged since it was made some 350 years ago. In technical terminology it is 'a quadripartite groined vault', in which the vaults intersect and support each other; but such a dry description beggars the glory of this superb ceiling, a rich and dazzling array of raised panels, heraldry, foliage, elaborate decorative pendants, and medallion portraits of eminent worthies from biblical or classical times – Joshua and David, Hector of Troy, Tarquin, Lucretia, Alexander the Great, and so on.

We don't know the names of the men who made this ceiling. It used to be thought they must have been itinerant Italian craftsmen. These craftsmen worked in the library of Kellie Castle in 1617, at Glamis Castle in 1620, at Muchalls Castle in Kincardineshire in 1624, and at Craigievar in 1625-6. But it is now believed that they were British craftsmen, probably Englishmen from Yorkshire, who may have learned their skills from Italians one or two generations earlier.

Whoever they were, one of the last tasks they completed for the ceiling of Craigievar was to add the coat of arms and initials of Danzig Willie – Master William Forbes – and those of his wife, Margaret Woodward, and the date 1626, the year in which the embellishment of the hall was completed.

It was in this hall, or upstairs in the long room right at the top of the house, that the barony courts would be held, at which the laird dished out summary and often home-spun justice in the king's name. It must have made an imposing courtroom, with the miscreant standing trembling under the intimidating Royal Arms. But Danzig Willie didn't have long to enjoy his decorated hall or his role of judge and jury in his barony court, for he died in 1627, the year after the handsome ceiling was completed. He had been, in every sense, the true Beginner in the dynastic history of Craigievar (in Sir Richard Bulstrode's terms); and his portrait by George Jamesone in an upstairs room shows us a cultured man of very determined features with an astute look that reflects his entrepreneurial ingenuity.

Danzig Willie was commemorated in an elegant Latin elegy by another cultured laird of the time, Arthur Johnston of Caskieben. In English it reads:

The tomb of a noble Forbes you now behold; hear now as to his character and mind. The toil of others to obtain wealth was, while he lived, to him a pastime. When called upon to depart this life, he said with a smile, 'Farewell, earth; my possession is now in Heaven'. His wealth, his acres, let not any man admire; it was better to be lord of himself than of his lands.

In 1630, Danzig Willie's eldest son, also called William Forbes, was created a baronet of Nova Scotia by King Charles I, thereby crowning the achievement that Danzig Willie the merchant had wrought by his business acumen. His portrait, also by George Jamesone, displays what would become distinctive family characteristics – a firmness of jaw, a somewhat pallid complexion, a hard mouth, a very definite 'Forbes nose'. As the king's man, Sir William Forbes exercised his authority with considerable vigour. The

opposite The ladies' withdrawing-room in Craigievar Castle, on the other side of the stair landing from the hall; it is panelled in Memel pine from the Baltic and the ornate plaster ceiling is decorated with medallions of St Margaret of Scotland, Lucresia Roma and Tarquin.

above left and right Sir William Forbes,
the fifth baronet, and his wife Sarah,
daughter of the thirteenth Baron
Sempill, painted by the young Henry
Raeburn in 1788.

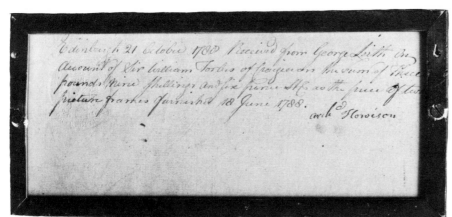

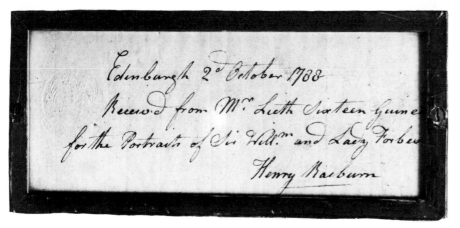

left The receipts for the two portraits:
above £3 9s 6d for the picture frames;
below Raeburn's receipt for sixteen
guineas for both portraits.

highlands to the west were infested by cattle-rustlers and crop-stealers led by a certain Gilderoy, 'notorious limmers' (rascals) who committed 'great oppressions' on the Craigievar lands and neighbouring Corse. Sir William Forbes was not a man to put up with that sort of thing, and in February 1636 seven of them were captured in Atholl and duly hanged at the Mercat Cross in Edinburgh. In the summer of that year, Gilderoy himself and another five of his band were accorded the same fate, their heads cut off and 'set up in exemplary places'.

He seems to have been an impetuous, dashing fellow, this second Forbes laird of Craigievar. During the Civil War he sided with the Covenanters and raised a troop of horse. He captured Harthill Castle in 1640; he was himself captured at the Battle of Aberdeen in 1644, but broke parole and escaped – only to be captured again at the second Battle of Aberdeen in 1646. He and Craigievar seemed to bear charmed lives, however. Even after the Marquess of Montrose had defeated the Covenanters at nearby Alford during his *annus mirabilis* of battles (1644-5), he forebore to plunder Craigievar though the house lay at his mercy. And so a marvellous part of Scotland's heritage was miraculously saved for posterity.

Sir William, the first baronet, died in 1648, to be succeeded by his son, the second baronet, Red Sir John, who was laird of Craigievar for fifty-five years. The origin of the nickname is obvious when you see his two portraits, for his hair was strikingly red. He was brutal at barony courts, and he treated his mother extremely badly. In short, he was a thoroughly wicked baronet. On the arch of the main stairs leading to the hall he added, in 1668, a plaster cartouche displaying his arms and initials and a menacing new personal motto: *Doe not vaiken sleiping dogs*. In the eulogistic epitaph even the most scoundrelly of people were accorded in those days, one couplet stands out for its daring honesty in the midst of all the conventional flattery:

> Although he was to all both just and fair,
> Yet would by none be combed against the hair.

A memory, at least, of his ill-doings lingers on in another handsome chamber in Craigievar, the blue room on the fourth floor. This, too, has a magnificently plastered ceiling dated 1626 and commissioned by Danzig Willie. Legend has it that Red Sir John was asleep in the blue room one night when his slumber was disturbed by an intruder. This intruder is said to have been a Gordon, traditional foes to the Forbes clan. Sir John certainly wasn't going to be 'combed against the hair' by a Gordon of all people. He sprang out of bed and threw the hapless fellow out of the window – four storeys up. Ever since then the blue room has been haunted by a chill 'presence', and no house-guests are asked to sleep there in case the Gordon shade disturbs their slumbers.

Since Danzig Willie's time, the family name of the Craigievar lairds was uncompromisingly Forbes. But in the eighteenth century another name came to the fore, when the fifth baronet (another Sir William Forbes) married Sarah, daughter of the thirteenth Baron Sempill. It was an ancient and noble title which passed through the female line, and in 1884 the eighth baronet (yet another Sir William, known to one and all as 'Auld Sir Wullie') became the seventeenth Lord Sempill on the death of his cousin, Baroness Maria Janet. And thus the illustrious name of Sempill came to Craigievar – but only the title, not the lands. With the title came the oldest relic on display in the hall at Craigievar, a pair of iron gauntlets said to have been worn by the first Lord Sempill when he fell at the disastrous Battle of Flodden in 1513 with the flower of the rest of Scotland's nobility.

In the queen's room on the third floor (so called because Danzig Willie apparently hoped that King James and his queen *would* stay at Craigievar sometime), we can see portraits of the fifth baronet and his wife, Sarah Sempill. They were by a promising young Edinburgh painter called Henry Raeburn. Alongside them hangs the original

above The hall today. In the ceiling are the coat of arms and initials of Danzig Willie – Master William Forbes – and his wife, Margaret Woodward, and the date 1626.

left The magnificent hall of Craigievar Castle with its vaulted ceiling of moulded plasterwork and, over the fireplace, the massive representation of the Royal Arms of the United Kingdom. This was how the hall looked in 1852.

receipt, dated 1788. They certainly got a bargain; Raeburn was newly returned from his studies in Italy, and all he charged for the *two* portraits was sixteen guineas (plus £3 9s 6d for the frames).

The seventh baronet, Sir John Forbes, inherited the title and castle in 1823. He was a younger brother who had made his own way in the world, just as Danzig Willie had done before him. He had made money in India as a judge in the service of the Honourable East India Company. He was the first laird of Craigievar since Danzig Willie who actually brought money to Craigievar. And he saved the place.

It was just as well he had money. When he inherited Craigievar the castle was in a sad state of neglect, for the Forbes family had another estate at Fintray on the lower Don in which they preferred to live. The roof of the castle was leaking badly. Sir John called in a leading Aberdeen architect, John Smith, to report on the damage and offer an estimate for the cost of repairing it. In a charming report, Smith showed that he knew what he was talking about:

I beg leave to add that the castle is well worth being preserved, as it is one of the finest specimens of architecture in this country of the age and style in which it was built, and is finely situated.

His estimate for repairs was 'about £680'. John Smith got the job, Sir John Forbes paid up, and Craigievar was rescued from seemingly inevitable dereliction. It was also rescued from the nineteenth-century obsession for building wings and annexes that marred so many of Scotland's architectural gems. After Sir John had reroofed Craigievar (and lowered the window sills in the hall), he built himself a new mansion-house at Fintray instead of building on to Craigievar itself. So Craigievar remained unchanged and unspoilt, Danzig Willie's dream castle, uniquely Scottish, uniquely beautiful.

The story of Craigievar as the Forbes family home began with a great shipping pioneer, Danzig Willie; it ended with another great pioneer, not of the sea but of the air, Commander William Francis Forbes, tenth Baronet of Craigievar and nineteenth Baron Sempill, formerly known as 'The Master of Sempill', who succeeded to the title in 1934 and died in 1965. He was one of the great aviators of the early days of flying, and one of nature's daredevils; as a boy he used to run along the balustrade of the battlements of Craigievar, to the horror of anyone watching from the ground, six storeys below. He served his apprenticeship with Rolls-Royce from 1910 to 1913, and when war broke out in 1914 he joined the Royal Flying Corps. At that time he had flown only once, as a passenger, but the RFC assumed that all volunteers knew how to fly. When his name was called he took off, but soon discovered that his machine veered like a sliced golf ball to one side. Somehow or other he got the hang of the controls, and three-quarters of an hour later he managed to land the machine safely. From then on he never looked back, and before long he was selected to fly all new planes which required testing.

In all, he flew some 150 types of aircraft. He flew a Puss Moth solo to Australia, he took part in the King's Cup Air Race around Britain throughout the 1920s, and he was sent on advisory missions all around the world to countries wanting to join the aviation era.

Shortly before his death, the trustees of the eighteenth Baron Sempill allowed Craigievar Castle and some thirty acres of land to be purchased in 1963 by a local consortium on condition that it was presented to the National Trust for Scotland. The total sum required to cover the purchase price and the provision of visitor reception facilities was £30,000 – and it was raised within a matter of weeks. Since then an additional sixty-five acres of farmland have been bought to provide a safeguard for its amenity.

Today it is an enchanting place to visit, superintended by Miss Raeburn Murray, an Edinburgh-born nurse who served in the Queen Elizabeth's Overseas Nursing Service in Uganda; she has been the Trust representative at Craigievar since 1970. The number of visitors each year has grown steadily, from 4000 in 1965 to 20,000 today. This in itself creates problems; the precious plastered ceilings must be protected at all times, so no more than twelve visitors can be allowed on any one floor at the same time. Some days this constitutes no problems at all; but on busy days, when the visitors can number five hundred or more, they have to be gathered in groups of twelve which set off every seven minutes for a forty-five minute tour of the house conducted by one of Miss Murray's knowledgeable and enthusiastic local guides. The tour begins and ends in Danzig Willie's hall – a very homely place still, richly carpeted in Forbes tartan, full of family keepsakes that have acquired the patina of historical and national importance.

One little souvenir is particularly charming. On the mantelpiece below the great stucco cornice of the Royal Arms there stands an invitation to a wedding. It was issued for the last occasion when Craigievar was used as a purely family house, for the wedding of the late Lord Sempill's daughter, Kirstine, in 1968. It is addressed, simply, to 'The Craigievar Ghosts': not the chilly shade of the unfortunate Gordon who was killed by Red Sir John, but the friendly ghosts of all the ancestors who made Craigievar what it is today.

There is no record of whether or not they attended the wedding reception. But I reckon Danzig Willie was there, all right. He wouldn't have missed it for anything.

Crathes Castle on Deeside, home of the Burnetts for four hundred years.

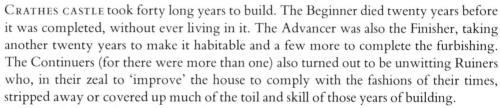

CRATHES CASTLE
Grampian

CRATHES CASTLE took forty long years to build. The Beginner died twenty years before it was completed, without ever living in it. The Advancer was also the Finisher, taking another twenty years to make it habitable and a few more to complete the furbishing. The Continuers (for there were more than one) also turned out to be unwitting Ruiners who, in their zeal to 'improve' the house to comply with the fashions of their times, stripped away or covered up much of the toil and skill of those years of building.

The real Ruiner, however, was fire. In January 1966 a devastating fire razed much of the structure to the ground, but mercifully it spared the original sixteenth-century tower, thus leaving intact for posterity the glories within: the priceless painted ceilings, the unique oak-lined long gallery, and Crathes' most prized family possession – the ancient Horn of Leys, said to have been a gift from King Robert the Bruce himself. By an ironic twist of fate, the fire that destroyed the adjacent buildings thereby restored something of the proper dominance of the tower itself.

Today, some 430 years after the first stone was laid, Crathes stands four-square and solid, a granite monolith much as it was planned in 1553, on a pleasant south-facing slope on Deeside some three miles to the east of Banchory in Grampian. Its proud eminence is marvellously embellished by its grounds; ancient sculpted yew hedges and avenues of lime trees from the early eighteenth century shelter a succession of beautiful gardens, lovingly laid out in the first decades of the twentieth century. It is little wonder that this spectacular combination of castle and garden, abetted by ease of access, has made Crathes the most visited showpiece of the National Trust for Scotland in the north-east, with a stream of some 60,000 visitors a year.

And then, of course, there is the 'inside' story, too – the story of the Burnetts of Leys, lairds of Crathes and baronets of Nova Scotia, that reaches deep into the roots of our social history.

They weren't always called Burnett, and their native soil wasn't Deeside. The family name was originally Burnard, and they had been established in the south, in Bedfordshire, in Anglo-Saxon times.

The man who tempted the Burnards north across the border was King David I of Scotland. David, youngest son of King Malcolm Canmore and an Anglo-Saxon princess, St Margaret, had spent many years at the English court. He made many friends among the Norman-Saxon nobility, married a Norman-Saxon wife, and greatly admired the feudal system that the Normans had imposed on Anglo-Saxon England. He saw clearly the advantages to the Crown of vassal lords who owned land through the king and thus owed him their allegiance; so when he became King of Scotland in 1124 he offered grants of lands to friends from the south who could be relied upon to support him. Thus it was that the Burnards moved north to settle in the Borders.

Their loyalty to the Scottish Crown never wavered for the next two centuries. When King Edward I of England, the 'Hammer of the Scots', tried to enforce his overlordship

The high hall as it was, stripped of its sixteenth-century painted plasterwork. The plaster finish has now been replaced.

on Scotland, the Burnards sided with their own beleaguered king, Robert the Bruce. Their reward came after the Battle of Bannockburn in 1314: Alexander Burnard was given grants of parts of the Royal Forest of Drum on Deeside, as well as neighbouring forfeited lands.

The grant was made in 1323, and from then on a hunting-horn was added to the holly leaves on the family coat of arms as a symbol of authority over the royal hunting-forest. But according to family tradition, it was not just a symbol that Robert the Bruce bestowed. In pride of place over the fireplace in the high hall of Crathes there is displayed in a glass case an ancient hunting-horn of fluted ivory, mounted with bands of gilt metal and set with semi-precious stones and three crystals. It is called the Horn of Leys; and whether or not it was handed over in person by Robert the Bruce (there is no documentary evidence to support the belief), it was the first thing the family rushed to rescue from the fire of 1966.

The name 'Leys' (pronounced *lays*) comes from the Loch of Leys, which was a stretch of shallow water just to the north of Banchory when the Burnards first came to Deeside early in the fourteenth century. In the middle of the loch there was a crannog (man-made island), which had been a place of refuge since prehistoric times. For more than two hundred years the Burnards made their home there in a wooden stronghold. Nothing remains there today except for the outline of the drained loch and the artificial mound; but a collection of large bronze cooking-pots excavated from the mound is on display in a recess in one of the corkscrew stone stairways in Crathes. The name of the loch survives, however; 'Burnard' changed through several spellings down the years to become 'Burnett', and the head of the family is still known to this day as 'Burnett of Leys'.

Living on an island can provoke a certain protective isolationism. There is no indication that the Burnards ever got embroiled in the political turmoils and armed conflicts of those far-off turbulent times. On the contrary, they seem to have developed a positive aptitude for keeping out of trouble, an enviable capacity for staying on the right side of *everybody*, which would stand their successors in good stead in later centuries. Amid all the alarums and excursions of history the Burnards went about their business quietly and peacefully, adding to their extensive lands by judicious marriages, until by the middle of the sixteenth century they felt secure and prosperous enough to leave their stronghold on the crannog and venture on to dry land. And with that we come to the Beginner, the ninth laird of Leys, Alexander Burnet (a second *t* would be added to the name in later years).

Traditionally, the year 1553 is the accepted date for the start of Alexander Burnet's design for a grand new mansion at Crathes, two miles east of Leys. But now the luck of Leys seemed to desert the Burnard/Burnets. Not that any of the violence or sudden disaster disturbed the even tenor of their lives – but Alexander Burnet simply could not get his castle finished. It was a vast undertaking to manhandle the huge boulders of granite rubble from the fields and hillsides and fashion them into the mighty tower that his wealth and prestige as tenant-in-chief to the king warranted; but others had done the same, and in a shorter time.

Did he lack labour? Did he have difficulty finding masons skilled in dressing the granite and fitting the great vaulted ceilings? Was work held up by the struggles and skirmishes that raged almost at his doorstep? That may have been it. In 1562, for instance, the Earl of Huntly with a force of a thousand supporters fought a pitched battle with the queen's troops under the Earl of Moray at the Hill of Fare, just three miles north of the Crathes building site. Whether or not the masons fled the district on that occasion and refused to return we do not know, but the building of the castle must have come to a virtual standstill at some time.

The castle was still unfinished when Alexander Burnet died in 1574, and his son and grandson, the tenth and eleventh lairds of Leys, died within four years of him. Thus it was that it fell to his great-grandson, Alexander Burnett, the twelfth laird of Leys, to finish the task.

Alexander Burnett took over his inheritance in 1578. He was a well-educated and cultivated man, with a wide knowledge of literature, philosophy, science, religion and art; all this he was to apply to the design and decoration of Crathes, particularly the magnificent painted ceilings in the Nine Worthies' room, the Muses' room and the Green Lady's room, with their elaborate literary allusions. And what splendid creations they are – a riot of gaily painted allegories of cardinal virtues and classical muses and worthies like Hector, Alexander, Charlemagne, Joshua, Arthur and David, all interspersed with copious biblical quotations, moral maxims and descriptive jingles.

It was not until 1594 that Alexander Burnett considered the work on the castle far enough advanced for him to move in with his wife, Katherine Gordon. The painters were still at work – indeed, they were to be around for another eight years, painting their rich and colourful designs directly on to the underside of the boards and joists that formed the flooring of the upper rooms, as well as on to the vaulted stone ceiling of the high hall. It must have been exhausting work; the paint was only applied after the ceilings were in position, with the artist working above his head, like Michelangelo painting the Sistine Chapel. First the whole ceiling was painted white with a mixture of chalk and size (made by boiling down scraps of animal skin); then the design would be drawn in strong black outline, and afterwards filled in with colour – perhaps by apprentices. The painters were probably Scottish, but they seem to have worked from pattern-books of engravings published on the Continent.

As they painted, there was a constant coming and going of other workmen in and around the house. Any family that has moved into an unfinished house will appreciate what Katherine Burnett had to put up with in those first years of occupation. As well as the painters and carpenters inside, there were masons outside, finishing off the harling of the walls. It was 1596 before the monogram of the initials of Alexander Burnett and Katherine Gordon were carved on a stone above the main entrance; nearby is another carved stone panel dated 1553, with the coat of arms of the ninth laird and his wife – 'Aleand Burnet Ianet Hameltoun'.

It was 1597 before the great four-poster bed was ready to be moved into the laird's bedroom. This is a magnificent piece of furniture, carved all over with family heraldic devices, holly leaves, the Horn of Leys, boars' heads and strange beasts. On each side of the centrepiece under the canopy (tester) we come face to face with the first occupants of Crathes Castle – a pair of carved and very life-like portraits. The twelfth laird of Leys was a bluff-looking man, with the high cheekbones characteristic of later Burnetts, a luxuriant moustache and a small beard. And even in bed, it seems, he wore a black bowler hat! They had their portraits carved, too, on their oak marriage chest that now stands in the high hall, and their initials and arms incised on their individual chairs, also dated 1597, which now stand in the Nine Worthies' room. It is as if they were so proud of their castle that they wanted to put their mark on it everywhere – as they most certainly did.

According to the masterly account of Crathes Castle by the architectural historian Schomberg Scott, it was probably the Aberdeenshire master mason John Bell who completed the work on Crathes. The Bell family were involved in the building of several of the great tower houses of the north-east, including Castle Fraser and very probably Craigievar; and it may have been the father of the Bell family, George, who started the work at Crathes for the ninth laird of Leys.

What they did, according to Schomberg Scott, was to take the features of military defence of earlier castles and transform them to serve purely aesthetic ends. So where the old fortress builders of the past had used rounded corners instead of sharp squared angles on the outer walls to prevent attackers with battering-rams knocking out a corner-stone and bringing the whole corner down, the Crathes builders used the same rounded corners for most of the height of the tower to give an *impression* of strength – 'like a massive tree trunk, which would have to be pushed over as it stands to make any impression'.

Similarly, the tower at Crathes tapers towards the top. The original idea of this had been to prevent an attacker getting protection from the overhang of the battlements above while he was up to no good below, undermining the walls or tossing fireballs through the arrow-slits. The Burnetts built no battlements in anticipation of attack, but they kept the tapering style to enhance the impression of height and slenderness. The appurtenances of military architecture became pure decoration, like the stone cannons projecting under the castle turrets. The iron yett, or cross-barred gate, which hung behind the massive oak door, obviously gave the entrance greater protection; but it may have been installed because its intricate system of interlocking bars had become a tradition, a status symbol almost, of the great northern laird – even a work of art in its own right.

But there is one defensive feature at Crathes which is anything but decorative – the Tripping Step. Behind the barred yett there is a clockwise spiral staircase of stone. The eleventh step is perceptibly higher than the rest, and as Mrs Anne Murray, the Trust representative at Crathes, says: 'It's impossible to run up that stair without tripping at the eleventh. It breaks your stride as you round the first spiral, and would undoubtedly have put any attacker at a distinct disadvantage'. Luckily, Crathes never had any attackers; but the Tripping Step can take its toll of barked shins from friend as well as foe.

Crathes Castle was eventually completed in 1602, and Alexander and Katherine were able to settle down at last in their handsome fifteen-roomed home. Life went on mainly in one large room on each floor: the kitchen area at ground level; the first-floor high hall, which was living-room and dining-room for the whole household, and also the place where the barony court was usually held; the private floor above, divided into the laird's room and the laird's bedroom; and on the top floor, away from the hurly-burly of the rest of the house, the oak-lined long gallery, the show-room with its delicately carved heraldic shields, where the finest furniture was kept, where formal parties were held, and where the laird sometimes held a baron court as an alternative to the high hall downstairs.

By now, Alexander Burnett had got the building bug. Not content with more than twenty years of building, decorating and furnishing Crathes Castle, he now spent a great deal of money building, repairing and decorating Banchory Church. Finally, in 1619, he started to build Muchalls Castle, near Stonehaven, to a design that was as futuristic as the design of Crathes had been rooted in the past. But he died only a few months after building began, leaving his son Thomas the same legacy that he had inherited – a half-built castle.

Thomas Burnett, the thirteenth laird and future first baronet, tackled the task with as much enthusiasm as his father had done, and Muchalls was completed by 1627. But he seems to have had a greater interest in local and national political affairs than his predecessors of Leys had shown. In 1618 King James VI of Scotland and I of England had appointed him to a committee to investigate the mismanagement of Aberdeen University. He was knighted in 1620, became an honorary Burgess of Aberdeen, and was the Member for Kincardineshire in the Scottish Parliament of 1621; and in 1626, soon after the coronation of Charles I, he was made a baronet of Nova Scotia.

His portrait hangs to the left of the door leading to the high hall from the stairs. It was painted by George Jamesone, the 'father of Scottish portraiture', as were those of four other members of his family. It depicts a man of firm features and resolve, a man of integrity and principle – and he needed all of these qualities to steer the Leys estates through the religious disputes and Civil War that raged during Charles I's reign.

In 1638 Sir Thomas Burnett subscribed to the National Covenant, and was one of those who brought it to Aberdeen to gather signatures and support. It was the first anti-royalist act that any Burnard or Burnett had ever committed; and it was an unpopular act

right The haunted Green Lady's room. The painted ceiling is busy with inscriptions of a religious and edifying nature.

below The room of the Nine Worthies. The four-poster bed, on loan from the National Museum of Antiquities in Edinburgh, is dated 1641 and is thought to have been made in the Orkneys.

in a region that was predominantly conservative and Episcopalian. Even so, such was his known integrity that he kept the friendship and respect of the Marquess of Huntly, the leader of the Royalists. At the same time he kept the friendship of the great Marquess of Montrose, even after that erstwhile Covenanter had become an ardent military campaigner for the Royalist cause. Sir Thomas never wavered in his loyalty to the National Covenant, yet twice in 1644 Montrose stayed at Crathes while his army camped nearby, and he left specific instructions that the lands of Leys were to be spared from the ruinous plundering suffered by the other Covenanter lairds, such as the Irvines of Drum.

Sir Thomas's fraternizing with the enemy, under whatever guise of impartiality or expediency, made him less than popular with some of his Covenanter neighbours but earned his monarch's gratitude: in 1851 King Charles II wrote personally to Sir Thomas (the original letter is on display in the muniments room) exempting his land from the quartering of Royalist soldiers. And believe it or not, in December of that same year, with Charles defeated at Worcester and the Commonwealth established, Cromwell's General Monk wrote to give him precisely the same exemption!

above The ivory Horn of Leys. The sash dates from the late seventeenth century.

Because his lands were never plundered, Sir Thomas was able to leave Crathes and the Leys estates intact to his heir when he died in 1653. His heir was his grandson Alexander, the second baronet, who was then a sixteen-year-old student at King's College, Aberdeen – 'profane, dissolute and naughty', according to the diary of a neighbour. Whatever his follies, he did not have long to indulge them, because he died in 1663 at the age of twenty-six.

If the second baronet brought no distinction to Crathes or the Burnett family, his kinsman Gilbert Burnett, nephew of the first baronet, more than made up for it. There are two portraits of him at Crathes (and none of the second baronet!) – one, attributed to Sir Peter Lely, in a place of honour opposite the fireplace in the high hall, and one over the fireplace in the laird's room. He became a brilliant and controversial churchman, offending both king and Parliament in turn with his tracts and preachings, thus displaying a lack of tact quite uncharacteristic of the Burnetts. Eventually he landed on the right side – with Prince William of Orange at The Hague. William found him a 'tedious busybody', but a very useful one, and took Gilbert back to England with him in 1688. In the following year, with William on the throne after the Glorious Revolution, Gilbert was appointed Bishop of Salisbury. He wrote an enormous number of books, of which the most notable was *History of My Own Time*, published posthumously in ten volumes (1724-34).

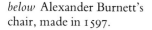

below Alexander Burnett's chair, made in 1597.

By this time, important changes were taking place at Crathes, where Sir Thomas Burnett, the third baronet, was enjoying a long and fruitful (in every sense) lairdship, from 1663 to 1714. He was MP for Kincardineshire in the Scottish Parliament, and after the Treaty of Union of 1707 he was elected to the new Parliament of Great Britain. There is no record of his ever having taken his seat, however; and little wonder. He and his wife Margaret Arbuthnott produced no fewer than twenty-one children in twenty-three years, of whom fourteen survived childhood.

By 1702, when Queen Anne came to the throne, Crathes was starting to burst at the seams, and Sir Thomas decided to extend and partly remodel the castle accommodation. He built a third storey on top of the range of buildings to the east of the tower and converted the range from a service wing to an elegant family residence in the new Queen Anne style (it was this 'Queen Anne wing' that was destroyed in the fire of 1966). That was all very well, but Sir Thomas was also anxious to modernize the decoration in the rooms of the tower itself. It looks as if he started by covering over the painted ceilings upstairs with lathe and plaster, seriously damaging the undersides of the beams (though unwittingly preserving the main boards from the ravages of later redecorators). In the high hall he obliterated the painting on the vaulted ceiling with coats of whitewash.

Sir Thomas no doubt meant well in his efforts to make his castle a home, and to him goes the credit of planting, in 1708, the fine yew hedge and lime walk that now protect and enhance Crathes' magnificent gardens. But the cost of it all, added to the expense of supporting his enormous family, broke the estate.

When the third baronet died in 1714 his son Alexander, the fourth baronet, had to sell off large parts of his inheritance, including Muchalls Castle. In a way, his straitened circumstances must have been almost a relief to the sixteenth laird of Leys. He was a gentle, rather simple man who disliked change of any kind. An oval portrait of him in the stone hall, the ante-room to the high hall, shows that he had a face both melancholy and anxious. He had an abnormal dread of ghosts (known in the region as 'boodie fear') – perhaps with good reason; for it was during his time that the first reports were recorded of the apparition of a young lady dressed in green with a baby in her arms. She was always seen in a chamber opening off the Nine Worthies' room, that has been known as the Green Lady's room ever since. She was said to be a young girl under the protection of the laird; she had had a baby by one of the estate workers, and both mother and child had then died in mysterious circumstances.

Was it a glimpse of the Green Lady that started the fourth baronet's 'boodie fear'? Or did some knowledge of the fate that befell his young charges haunt his mind and unbalance him? It might have been just another castle ghost story were it not for one rather odd circumstance: when the Green Lady's room was being renovated in Victorian times, a small recess was uncovered under the hearthstone. In it was the skeleton of a baby.

It was the eleventh baronet who was to make alterations to Crathes, as the third baronet had done before him. Sir Robert Burnett, eleventh baronet and twenty-third laird of Leys, was born in 1833 and emigrated to America after studying at Oxford. In the United States he bought in 1860 a 25,000-acre ranch near Los Angeles in Southern California for $3000 and started sheep-farming on a large scale. When he sold it twenty-five years later, it fetched $140,000. Today it would be worth literally millions of dollars as real estate, accommodating as it does several towns, a racetrack, oilfields, industrial plants, a university, and Los Angeles Municipal Airport.

When the eleventh baronet inherited the title and lands of Leys he returned to Scotland and proceeded to give Crathes a facelift. To his credit he did his best to restore some of the painted ceilings damaged by the third baronet. In 1877 he removed the lathe and plaster which had been fixed to the beams, and had the damaged lower edges pared off and the beams repainted; and he had the good sense to leave untouched the main boards with their original sixteenth-century paintings – the first time they had seen the light of day for more than 150 years.

But any pretentions to being a conservationist deserted him when he came to the high hall. Here he bricked up the old fireplace in the far wall and built a new one in the central window recess in the west wall. Then he covered the walls with pine panelling and Spanish leather in the Victorian style of the day. When a later laird decided to strip all this off in 1920, the pine and leather came away with all the original plasterwork and whatever decoration may have covered it.

The last baronet to live in Crathes Castle was the thirteenth, Major General Sir James Burnett, twenty-fifth laird of Leys and nephew of the eleventh baronet. Sir James had a deep interest in trees and shrubs, while Lady Burnett had a great affection for herbaceous plants and a natural flair for design. Between them they were responsible for creating Crathes' remarkable gardens, each one with a different theme, a different colour-scheme and a different mood, from the serene to the exuberant.

Perhaps the thirteenth baronet did more than any previous laird to show his affection for the old castle by making it over, in 1952, to the National Trust for Scotland. The Trust embarked on a complete conservation programme for the painted ceilings, with financial help from the Historic Buildings Council. The three precious ceilings were completely dismantled and taken to Edinburgh, where they were treated against woodworm and fungus and had the adhesive properties of the paint restored. Then the ceilings were returned to Crathes and carefully replaced exactly as they had been when Alexander and Katherine Burnett moved into their new castle in 1594.

The great gale of 1953 that blew down hundreds of acres of valuable forests like matchwood, and the great fire of 1966 that so nearly destroyed Crathes for ever, were terrible hammer-blows. But the Burnetts had taught themselves to be survivors in difficult times; and Crathes Castle itself is a marvellous story of continuity and survival.

Culzean Castle, on the coast of Strathclyde: Robert Adam's dream castle.

CULZEAN CASTLE
Strathclyde

SOME TWO CENTURIES AGO, the most celebrated architect in Britain was called to the most dramatically appealing building site in Scotland. The architect was Robert Adam, Scots-born and Italian-trained, whose fashionable London practice had come to grief over the disastrous riverside Adelphi project, which had forced him to return to his native Scotland. The place was Culzean (pronounced Kullane) on the fretted Ayrshire coast on the lower Firth of Clyde, five miles west of Maybole, one of the ancestral fastnesses of the Kennedys of Carrick. The outcome was a dream castle in a dream setting, one of the premier jewels in the treasury of the National Trust for Scotland.

The Adam brothers were not unacquainted with the family, for their niece was married to a Kennedy of nearby Dunure; but they probably knew no more about the origins of the family than modern historians do. These origins reach so far back in time and legend that one writer, James Allan Rennie (in *The Scottish People*), has even made the serious suggestion that they were descended from that merry and musical monarch of fable, Old King Cole. He identified him as a King Coel (meaning 'melody') who ruled the Celtic kingdom of Strathclyde in south-west Scotland in early Roman times. This man allegedly had a son called Cunnedda (Kennedy), meaning 'ugly-headed' or 'grim-headed' in Gaelic. There is every possibility, says Rennie, that this Prince Cunnedda of Strathclyde was the progenitor of the Kennedys, the powerful and prolific family which for centuries held sway in Carrick, the southernmost division of Ayrshire.

It's a pleasant fancy, and no less plausible than the more common identification of the nursery rhyme king with the ancient British tribal leader Cunobelin, founder of Colchester and the original of Shakespeare's Cymbeline. What is beyond dispute is that the history of that part of Ayrshire was very largely the story of the Kennedys. They had been a power in the province long before Robert the Bruce became second Earl of Carrick in 1304. During the disastrous reign of Bruce's son, King David II, John Kennedy of Dunure was recorded as Steward of Carrick in 1367; and about the same time he acquired the lands of Cassillis (pronounced Kassels), which was to remain the chief family seat of the Kennedys for four centuries until the transformation of Culzean Castle as Robert Adam's romantic masterpiece.

Not that the Kennedys had it all their own way. Carrick was royal Stewart stamping-ground as well, and King Robert II, Bruce's grandson and founder of the Stewart dynasty, had a score of children, most of them illegitimate but nonetheless jostling for power and privilege. Through the marriages of Robert's multitude of offspring the whole nobility of Scotland became rapidly 'Stewartized'; and the Kennedys were no exception.

In 1407 Kennedy of Dunure's grandson, James Kennedy, married Princess Mary, the daughter of King Robert III and sister of the future King James I. This encouraged James Kennedy's five brothers to flex their muscles even more, and their descendants alone would own no fewer than forty-three homes and castles spread over south-west

Scotland. It was to lead to endless and vicious family feuding, for there simply wasn't enough room in Carrick for all these ambitious Kennedys.

One man stayed above it all, however: James Kennedy, Princess Mary's son, who played a central and saving role in national affairs as Bishop of St Andrews, first as trusted counsellor to his cousin King James II and then as a guardian of the young King James III. He was the outstanding prelate of his age. He founded and endowed St Salvator's College at the University of St Andrews, and is still remembered by the students there in the annual Kate Kennedy procession. He also built an enormous ship, and an elaborate tomb for himself, each of which is said to have cost even more than St Salvator's.

The head of the family was recognized during the reign of King James IV, when a great-grandson of James Kennedy and Princess Mary was created Earl of Cassillis. At about the same time he acquired the lands of Culzean in 1505 from another branch of the family. Then in 1513 he fell at the Battle of Flodden with his king and the flower of Scotland's nobility. It was the ominous opening to a desperate century of strife for Scotland – and for the Kennedys.

The second Earl of Cassillis was murdered. The third earl helped to negotiate the betrothal of the young Mary Queen of Scots to the dauphin of France – and seems to have been murdered for his pains as well, for he died in Dieppe of suspected poisoning. The fourth earl fared better, even though he was also a supporter of Queen Mary. He entertained her at Cassillis House in 1563 soon after her return to Scotland from her sojourn in France, and he is said to have escorted her from Kirk o' Field in Edinburgh on the fateful night of Darnley's murder in February 1567. Despite the scandal of the queen's marriage to Darnley's presumed murderer, the Earl of Bothwell, only three months later, he rallied to her standard for a showdown with her affronted nobles at Carberry in June 1567; but when the queen's army melted away without striking a blow, the Earl of Cassillis melted away too, leaving his queen helpless to avoid the enforced abdication that followed. He knew when to change sides, all right, and later became a Protestant. But he is perhaps best remembered for roasting alive the commendator of nearby Crossraguel Abbey in the dungeons of Dunure in an attempt to force him to hand over abbey lands to the Kennedys.

And all the time the Kennedys were fighting and feuding among themselves. The family had split into two main factions, the Cassillis Kennedys to the north and the Bargany Kennedys to the south, and the constant rivalry kept the countryside in fear for generations. Between them the feuding families could muster a thousand fighting men. The culmination of their murderous enmity came in December 1601, when the laird of Bargany was ambushed and killed after a pitched battle near Maybole. The leader of the Cassillis Kennedys on that occasion was Sir Thomas Kennedy, uncle and guardian of the young earl and therefore known as 'The Tutor of Cassillis'. His splendidly restored portrait, painted by an unknown artist when he was forty-three, now hangs in the saloon ante-room: a man not to be trifled with, hard faced, cold eyed, cruel mouthed, and dressed to kill. Exactly five months after the battle near Maybole he received his due when he was murdered in revenge on the sands of Ayr. He was forty-six years old.

This was going too far, even for the Kennedys of Carrick. Under threat of the direst royal displeasure, things quietened down for a while. During the first four decades of the seventeenth century after the Union of the Crowns, while Scotland enjoyed unprecedented peace, the Kennedy family was in eclipse. But no sooner had the strife of the Covenanting era broken out than the Kennedys were in the field again, as pugnacious and contentious as ever.

John, the sixth Earl of Cassillis, was a leading Covenanter who signed the National Covenant of 1638 and the more radical Solemn League and Covenant of 1643 which allied Scotland with the English Parliament against King Charles I. On the other hand, Sir Alexander Kennedy of Culzean remained a keen Royalist and Episcopalian, and

The picturesque north front of Culzean on its rocky cliff-edge, as envisaged by Robert Adam.

became so hated for his persecution of Presbyterian Covenanters that he earned the nickname of 'Kennedy the Wicked'. His funeral, after a lingering death from fever, was said to have been attended by the devil in the shape of a cow, and his corpse carried off to hell during a thunderstorm by a posse of fiends.

The sixth earl rose to be one of the most powerful men in Scotland, one of the four Lords of the Treasury and Lord Justice General, the chief judge in Scotland after the king. But he almost ruined the family fortunes with his Covenanting zeal. A minister had told him, 'Blessed shall your Lordship be of the Lord, and blessed shall your honour be, if ye empawned and lay in Christ's hand the earldom of Cassillis.' He almost did. He loaned over £6000 (in Scots money) of estate funds towards the maintenance of a Protestant army in Ireland, and also had to meet the cost of running his own regiment. (A portrait of the sixth earl's second wife hangs in the first drawing-room.)

The sixth earl's enthusiasm for the cause meant that the seventh earl, whose portrait hangs in the picture room, had a hard time trying to meet the debts on the family estates. He was forced to sell off a lot of property, and by 1700 the Cassillis Kennedys had no lands left in Wigtownshire. They still had a powerful base in Carrick, but, as a contemporary wrote, the Kennedy name at that time was 'under great decay in comparison of what it was ane age agoe'.

The eighth Earl of Cassillis died childless in 1759, and once again the Kennedys fell to feuding among themselves about the succession; but this time they confined their quarrel to the courts. After three years of legal wrangling it was decided that the earldom, along with Cassillis House, should go to the Culzean Kennedys, a minor branch directly descended from the sixteenth-century third earl. With that legal ruling, the 'great decay' of the Kennedy name was arrested and reversed; the malevolent feuding of previous centuries was at an end, and a brilliant new era dawned. Culzean Castle as we know it today was conceived and born.

The man who inherited in 1762 as the ninth earl of Cassillis was a thirty-six-year-old bachelor, Sir Thomas Kennedy, who had come into Culzean eighteen years earlier. He decided to go on living at Culzean instead of moving into the much grander family seat of Cassillis House. This crucial decision would have momentous results, for the ninth earl and his bachelor brother, David, who succeeded him as tenth earl in 1775, were to revolutionize the Culzean estates and transform Culzean Castle itself.

They were cultured men, these brothers, born into a huge family of nearly a score of children, of whom twelve died in infancy. Their father, Sir John Kennedy, had attended Glasgow University and was a firm believer in sound education. Thomas and David both went to Maybole School, then one of the most progressive in the country, where they studied classics as well as newer subjects like geography and mathematics. David, the younger brother, went on to study law at Glasgow University and become an Edinburgh lawyer; there he made friends with James Boswell of Auchinleck (the future biographer of Dr Johnson), who described him as 'a good, honest, merry fellow indeed'. Thomas went on the fashionable Grand Tour of Europe, and pursued his studies at the Royal Academy at Caen and at the Turin Academy. Letters of recommendation from a friend at Caen described him as a 'good-humoured, well-mannered young gentleman' who played the violin. The portrait of Thomas, the ninth earl, looking pale and earnest and with a book in his hand, hangs between the windows of the first drawing-room; the tenth earl's much more florid portrait by Pompeo Batoni hangs above the centre door of the picture room.

The eighteenth century, particularly the second half, was the Age of Improvement in Scotland, and certainly there was ample scope for it. When Sir Thomas Kennedy inherited Culzean Castle it was a gaunt and gloomy medieval tower house, a fortified keep, built primarily for defence and sited for that purpose on an impregnable rock plateau on a clifftop overlooking the sea, and guarded on the landward side by a deep

opposite The first drawing-room, the walls re-covered with specially woven blue damask. The ceiling roundel, painted by Antonio Zucchi, was almost ruined by suspending a gasolier from it in the nineteenth century, but it has now been restored.

gully and escarpment that served as a dry moat. It had been built in the typical L-shape of its time, with vaulted service quarters on the ground floor, a single great hall occupying the first floor, and a cluster of small private rooms on the floors above. It was draughty, uncomfortable, and hopelessly out of date; yet this was the house he preferred to the mansion of Cassillis.

The estate was in no better shape. An estate map dating from 1750 gives a bleak picture of almost featureless heathland. Vegetation was severely restricted by the prevailing south-westerly winds and salty spray from the sea. Agriculture was poor, and living conditions for the peasants even worse. A contemporary commentator wrote:

The farm-houses were mere hovels, with an open hearth for a fireplace in the middle, the dung-hill at the door, the cattle starving and the people wretched. The ditches which existed were ill-constructed and the hedges worse preserved, the land overrun with reeds and rushes.

To improve the domestic amenities of his house and bring them up to Georgian standards of comfort, Sir Thomas carried out extensive repairs to the fabric, and during the 1760s he added a long and narrow wing on the edge of the cliff between the castle and the sea.

He also introduced radical agricultural improvements on his estates. He had several distinguished land improvers as near neighbours – his cousin the Earl of Eglinton, for instance, and Sir Adam Fergusson of Kilkerran; everyone was talking about land improvement, and there was a host of books and pamphlets and learned discourses available on the subject. Sir Thomas introduced crop-rotation and the more scientific use of fertilizer. In the 1750s he carried out major enclosure projects to increase the size of the farms. This meant uprooting the small tenants and sub-tenants who were scratching a meagre living under the old system, so Sir Thomas built for them a new model village at Straiton with the idea of starting new industries and providing a market for the surplus food the improved estates were producing. Thirty years later Straiton had a population of two hundred, mainly engaged in weaving; today it is a charming rural village on the edge of the hill country fifteen miles south-east of Ayr. He planted a great number of trees to provide both shelter belts and forestry. He also built rudimentary roads to link up his estates and facilitate access to the market-towns. It is a happy coincidence that John Loudon McAdam, who invented the 'macadamizing' system of road-making, was a fellow Ayrshireman and younger contemporary of the improver lairds of Culzean; his first experimental road was built on his estate at Sauchrie, five miles from Culzean across the Carrick hills.

All these improvements were costly undertakings, and the Earl of Cassillis, as he was by then, had to borrow heavily in the 1760s. Even so, by the time he died in 1775, Culzean was in very much better shape and heart than it had been only thirty years earlier.

It still wasn't good enough for his brother David, however. As a fashionable lawyer and former MP for Ayrshire and now the tenth Earl of Cassillis, he wanted a much more elegant and refined country seat in which to entertain his friends from Edinburgh and London during 'the season'. To this end he lost no time in calling in his famous contemporary, Robert Adam, who had by then returned to Scotland from London. They were to work together on the Culzean project over the next fifteen years.

Most of Adam's work had been done in England. But he knew Scottish castles and the national preference for living in them long after they had ceased to be necessary as a means of defence. When he was a youth he had been given the Castle of Dowhill as a gift by his father, and he had worked with his father on the modernization of Inveraray Castle, one of the first successful attempts at combining the traditional prestige of living in a castle with contemporary standards of living.

Before tackling Culzean Castle, however, Adam turned his attention to the more

above The magnificent
circular saloon in the drum
tower of Culzean Castle,
overlooking the Firth of
Clyde. The ceiling has been
painted in the delicate hues of
Adam's original design,
reproduced from a signed
watercolour drawing of his
proposed colour scheme that
came to light a few years ago.

left Culzean Castle from the
south-west: one of two major
paintings in the picture room
by Alexander Nasmyth, 'the
father of Scottish landscape
art'.

right Sir Thomas Kennedy, ninth Earl of Cassillis, who started the radical improvement of Culzean Castle and its estates in the 1760s.

far right David Kennedy, tenth Earl of Cassillis, the man who commissioned Robert Adams to rebuild Culzean Castle in the 1770s.

pressing task of designing an efficient complex of buildings for the home farm. In 1775 the farm manager, John Bulley, wrote:

My chief design at present is only to put the land into proper condition for a more perfect system of husbandry. But several things are wanted before that can be completely carried on. I have not a proper farmyard, nor a house or shed for feeding cattle, or for the convenience of raising near so much dung as might be made; but these things will come in due course. Lord Cassillis has an extensive and very commodious plan of offices, which he intends to build soon.

This 'extensive and very commodious plan of offices', which was completed by 1777, in fact turned out to be one of Adam's most brilliant but least-sung creations. It was a complex of stables, byres and barns forming a hollow square, each side a T-shaped building with the stem of the T on the outside of the square. There was a turreted arched entrance at each corner where the Ts nearly joined. It must surely be the most elegant steading in Scotland. To heighten the effect, Adam sited it not in the heart of the farm fields but right on the clifftop about a quarter of a mile north of the castle itself, where the two buildings complement one another and the rugged landscape with striking effect. Today the home farm, superbly restored by the National Trust for Scotland at a cost of some £230,000, has been adapted for use as a park centre for the 300,000 visitors a year who come to enjoy Culzean Country Park (the first to be established in Scotland).

With the home farm completed, Robert Adam now tackled Culzean Castle itself; and the old castle, perched on its rocky clifftop with the sea thundering below, inspired him to produce a perfect blend of dramatic exterior and elegant interior such as had never been achieved before.

His work at Culzean Castle was planned and carried out in three distinct stages. The first, begun in 1777, was to build up the massive south front overlooking the terraced gardens in the landward gully. It involved a virtual rebuilding of the old tower, burying it in a new sham fortress enclosed by two lesser wings, also with battlements and turrets. Later, a kitchen wing was added to the east and a rounded tower wing to the west to accommodate a brew-house. Internally, the entire ground floor of the old tower was converted into a single splendid room with curved end walls and curved Adam doors, which he planned as the dining-room. This old eating-room, as it is now called, was decorated with restrained plasterwork typical of Adam's mature years; appropriately it features swags, urns, vine leaves and grapes. Three roundels in the ceiling were painted by Antonio Zucchi, who did a great deal of work for Adam. The old-fashioned small private apartments were replaced by gracefully decorated salons.

The second stage, which was begun in 1785, was the building of a great drum tower on the north side, on the very edge of the cliff. Inside it he created a breathtakingly beautiful, perfectly circular saloon for promenading, with six tall windows looking out over the untamed sea and the rugged island scenery across the Firth of Clyde. It is this remarkable contrast between the restrained eighteenth-century elegance within and the wildness without that gives the saloon its unique impact.

The remodelling of the southern part and the addition of the drum tower to the north left an empty space in between, a small and sunless courtyard which Adam planned to fill with a new staircase. Here, in 1787, he created the celebrated oval staircase with brilliant theatrical effect. The skylit cupola flooded the heart of the castle with light; and to exaggerate the perspective and therefore the height of the stairwell (it is actually forty-seven feet high), he reversed the orthodox architectural pattern by placing a major order of ornate Corinthian columns on the principal floor and a simpler order of much slimmer Ionic columns on the floor above. Both from below and above it is an exquisitely graceful work of art.

Both inside and out, Adam planned every detail himself. He designed the furniture and fittings, the fireplaces, the tables, the mirrors and the sconces. He chose the wall

opposite, above Drum Castle, Grampian: the north front, with the handsome modern entrance arch.

opposite, below Falkland Palace: the south range containing the chapel royal.

The dining-room, originally Adam's Library.

coverings, and prepared all the colour schemes. Outside he landscaped the policies; he turned the dry moat into a sunken garden, and established the utilitarian walled garden at a discreet remove. Finally he designed a romantically ruined archway and viaduct over the gully to add dignity to the castle and to frame the view of his masterpiece.

It was a massive achievement, a marvellous monument to the romantic inspiration of Scotland's greatest architect. It was fittingly caught in two major paintings of the castle and its sea setting by Alexander Nasmyth, 'the father of Scottish landscape art', which now hang on each side of the centre door of the picture room.

The work was barely completed when the tenth earl died, still a bachelor, in 1792 (the same year as Robert Adam). The title passed to a distant cousin, Captain Archibald Kennedy RN, who had been born and brought up in the United States. Up to the American War of Independence he had had some regard for the 'rebels', but later he found it prudent to move to London, abandoning his substantial properties in and around New York. The windfall of the Culzean inheritance must have come as a godsend. Portraits of him and his American wife, Ann Watts, both by Mather Brown, hang in the picture room on the wall opposite the fireplace.

Two years after inheriting the title and property he died, and his twenty-five-year-old American-born son Archibald became the twelfth earl in 1794. In his long tenure he proved himself a vigorous and progressive laird, just as interested in developing the estate as his predecessors had been. He planted more than five million seedling trees to lay the foundations of a forestry industry. During the Napoleonic Wars he raised an independent company of foot and had gun emplacements built along the clifftop to the west of the castle. The weapons of his West Lowland Fencible Regiment provide a most impressive display of arms covering the walls of Adam's former entrance hall, now known as the armoury.

He took easily and eagerly to every aspect of Scottish life. He was a Knight of the Thistle, and in 1802 was one of the sixteen peers chosen to represent Scotland in Parliament. He became a close friend of the Duke of Clarence, son of King George III; and when Clarence succeeded to the throne as King William IV in 1830, he created his friend Archibald Cassillis the first Marquess of Ailsa. The name came, appropriately, from the thousand-foot-high core of volcanic rock called Ailsa Craig in the lower Firth of Clyde so starkly visible from Culzean Castle.

A portrait of him by Ben Marshall over the fireplace of the dining-room shows him as a young man of thirty, riding a horse at full tilt; it represents a hard gallop he made for a wager on how fast he could ride from Culzean to Glasgow. There are also two enormous portraits in the dressing-room of him and his handsome wife Margaret Erskine of Dun. He lived to be seventy-seven, by which time both his sons were dead (there is an equestrian portrait of his elder son by John Ferneley between the windows of the dining-room). So in 1846 he was succeeded as second Marquess of Ailsa by his grandson, also called Archibald, whose portrait on horseback in the uniform of the Ayrshire Yeomanry, by Charles Lutyens, hangs behind the pillars of the dining-room. The second marquess died in a hunting accident in 1870, and was succeeded as third Marquess of Ailsa by his twenty-two-year-old son, Archibald. This laird would enjoy even greater longevity than his great-grandfather, the first marquess; he lived to be ninety years old, and during his sixty-six years as patriarch of Culzean the old castle took its final form.

To accommodate his growing family of six children and the extra household staff required, in 1879 he built a new west wing over Adam's brew-house. He also added a new front hall and morning-room at the east side. Internally he made a large number of alterations to suit Victorian tastes. The old eating-room was converted into a library and lined with dwarf-oak bookcases with curved backs to fit the end walls, and an unnecessary marble top was added to the graceful Adam chimneypiece. Next door, Adam's original library, which had had a plain ceiling, and a dressing-room beyond,

The breathtaking oval staircase: a brilliant *coup de theatre*.

were knocked into one and given an Adam Revival ceiling, and furbished as a big family dining-room with false pillars at the far end.

Fortunately, there were no major structural changes to the main rooms, but things were changed around a bit – a fireplace moved from here to there – and most of Adam's carefully chosen colour schemes were changed. The major aberration was the installation of acetylene gas-lit chandeliers. In the first drawing-room and elsewhere the gasoliers were suspended from the ceiling roundels painted by Antonio Zucchi, and the damage they did was considerable.

Outside in the grounds, however, his influence was entirely benign. He was a noted horticulturalist; it was he who gave the fountain court, the formal garden at the south front of the castle, its essential character, and he added a fine botanical collection on the landward side of the walled garden. He was also an enthusiastic sailor and designer of racing yachts; the ship model room in the castle contains half-hull models and pictures of some of his boats. He had a boatyard at the home farm, the forerunner of the Ailsa shipbuilding yard at Troon.

His portrait, venerable and white-bearded, hangs in the dining-room; it was painted by Fiddes Watt. After his death in 1938 the marquessate was inherited by his three sons in turn – Archibald, Charles and Angus. Archibald, the fourth marquess, hardly had time to enjoy the title; he continued to be known as 'Cassillis' because he had been the fifteenth earl for so long. His portrait by W. E. Miller as a young man in a kilt hangs over the sideboard in the dining-room.

The fourth marquess died in 1943. With two crippling death duties on the estate, and others inevitable, the fifth marquess in 1945 offered the castle and more than five hundred acres of the policies to the National Trust for Scotland. It was a terribly difficult decision for the Trust, for there was no endowment to go with the property; but because of Culzean's outstanding national importance, it was accepted in a moment of heroic optimism.

So began a new chapter in the life of the old house, less violent but every bit as exciting as any other in its long history. In the past thirty-five years something in the region of a million pounds has been expended on restoration, conservation and maintenance to transform it back to Adam's romantic masterpiece.

Part of the original gift was the proposal that Dwight D. Eisenhower, then Supreme Commander of the triumphant Allied Forces in Europe, should be given life tenure of the top floor of Culzean Castle as a tribute from the Scottish people to a great warrior. Within months the Trust had converted that top floor into a National Guest Flat, whose use Eisenhower gracefully accepted. It is a splendidly appointed place with four twin-bedded rooms and a circular drawing-room that almost matches the matchless saloon below; it had originally been two semi-circular bedrooms. Eisenhower stayed there on several occasions, once as president of the United States, and frequently granted the use of it to friends. There is now a very effective Eisenhower Presentation on the floor below, telling the story of his life and great achievements. Since Ike's death in 1969, the National Guest Flat has been used for government hospitality and important visitors concerned with the social and economic improvement of Scotland and especially the aims of the National Trust for Scotland.

The last few years have been a story of constant, patient renovation and restoration. Work began in 1966 on renovating the outside stonework, where the local sandstone had become badly eroded. The roof too required extensive repair and replacement. The year 1972 saw the start of a full restoration scheme for the interior of the castle, which involved the most meticulous historical and scientific research. Adam's original designs for Culzean, some held by the Trust and some by the Sir John Soane Museum, London, were carefully studied, as well as the methods and materials in use in the eighteenth century. Paint scrapings were taken from ceilings and walls and then chemically analysed to try to establish the original colour schemes.

The armoury in what was Adam's original entrance hall.

Sometimes pure luck helped. In 1968 Adam's original watercolour drawing of the great saloon, dated 1790, was discovered in an antique-shop in Edinburgh and given to the Trust. It showed the subtle and delicate hues of the design he had had in mind. The ceiling had been white for many years, but after the acquisition of the drawing (which now hangs on the landing outside the main door), the Trust took tests of all the paintwork in the room, and today the original eighteenth-century colour scheme has been restored.

The other ceilings that had been ravaged by the use of gas chandeliers were skilfully restored. Another retransformation took place in the picture room overlooking the fountain court, which had originally been the high hall of the old tower house before Adam's day. The walls had been hung with a Victorian embossed wallpaper but, when this was stripped off, the Trust restorers found underneath it battens complete with tacks for fixing fabrics, together with the signature of Charles Boyd, Upholsterer, of Edinburgh, 1795. As a result the walls have been hung with specially woven damask. The superb oval staircase and landings were carpeted in 1973 as a gift from a British carpet firm, thus advertising the fact that its carpeting is tramped on by 100,000 pairs of feet and still looks as good as new.

But perhaps the most significant moment in the post-war story of Culzean came in 1969. In that year its 565 acres of woodlands, fields, gardens, cliffs and seashore became Scotland's first Country Park under the Countryside (Scotland) Act of 1967. It involved a unique and highly successful partnership in management; the Trust still owned the park, and provided the management team for a joint committee with the local planning authorities. A ranger naturalist service was inaugurated, with the twin function of conserving and wardening the natural amenities of Culzean and providing an information and educational service for the public. Adam's clifftop home farm, by now quite inadequate for modern farming demands, was restored between 1971 and 1973 as a park centre to provide a base for the ranger service and for a visitor service, including an auditorium for lectures and audio-visual presentations.

This pioneering creation lifted a heavy financial millstone from the Trust's neck, for the Countryside Act enabled public funds to be channelled into new country parks. Much more important, it helped to restore Culzean as an integral whole, of woods, gardens and buildings of great distinction, just as its eighteenth-century creators had envisaged it. It has enabled the Trust to concentrate its resources on the castle itself; and it has enabled millions of visitors of all ages to enjoy to the full this great heritage of castle and countryside.

Drum Castle, showing the stately south front of the Jacobean house.

DRUM CASTLE
Grampian

IF A SCOTSMAN'S HOME is his castle, then Drum Castle in Grampian is the absolute prototype of the Scottish home. One of Scotland's oldest inhabited castles, if not the oldest one of all, it was occupied by the same family, the Irvines of Drum, for no fewer than 653 years, twenty-four generations of them in almost unbroken succession. Yet it exudes an extraordinary warmth and homeliness, and visitors to Drum Castle, from King Robert the Bruce onwards, have always delighted in its welcoming atmosphere. Today Drum is one of the treasures of the National Trust for Scotland, and the 20,000 pilgrims who go there every year call it 'The Happy House'. It doesn't even have a ghost.

Drum Castle manages to look both compact and straggling. Basically it is a medieval tower house, built just before or after 1300, which is now linked to an elegant Jacobean mansion with dormer windows and crow-stepped gables which was built with Renaissance bravura in 1619. It cannot boast great gardens, like so many National Trust properties, but it has marvellous grounds and woodland walks covering four hundred acres.

The name Drum is an old Celtic word meaning 'high ridge'. Drum Castle lies ten miles west of Aberdeen in the parish of Drumoak, set back from the road in parkland dotted with fine old trees that are all that remain of the ancient Royal Forest of Drum. Strategically, it has always been an important site, for it commands two important fords over the River Dee about a mile to the south – Dalmaik and Tilbouries. In Roman times the ford at Tilbouries was superintended by the legionary camp of Normandykes at what is now Peterculter; and in medieval times Scottish kings were no less aware of Drum's significance as a royal redoubt.

The earliest history of Drum Castle is obscure. Scholars assume that there was probably a timber hunting-lodge on the site, where Scottish kings would come to hunt the deer and wild boar among the royal oaks of Drumoak. It seems likely, however, from recent historical research, that the great granite tower, the heart and core of Drum Castle, was built during the reign of King Alexander III (1249-86), that energetic and charismatic king who died tragically young – he was only forty-five – when his horse stumbled over a cliff in pitch darkness near Kinghorn in Fife. The size and solidity of the tower of Drum – seventy feet high with walls twelve feet thick at the base – suggest a royal fortress rather than a mere hunting-lodge: King Alexander would have been looking to Drum as a stronghold from which to help control the north-east.

If it *was* built during Alexander's reign, then it is equally probable that the builder was a certain Richard Cementarius (what a marvellously appropriate name for a master mason), the first recorded provost of Aberdeen. He is credited with designing the ancient Bridge of Don, the 'Brig o' Balgownie', at Aberdeen; the high pointed arch of the Brig is so similar in shape to the pointed barrel vaulting in the upper hall of Drum tower that the building of the tower is now generally attributed to him.

The tower is a simple, solid, functional structure, sturdy and square with rounded corners and those immensely thick walls to withstand the shock of battering-rams. The main entrance was set high in the wall at first-floor level and could be reached only by a retractable wooden ladder – a drawbridge, in effect, without the moat. Today there is a new approach, a flight of stone steps dating from the Regency period; in medieval times access would have been much less comfortable – and much more difficult for would-be attackers.

From the troubled decades that followed the death of Alexander III, Robert the Bruce eventually emerged as undisputed King of Scotland. With the triumph of Bannockburn in 1314 behind him, it became possible for him to reward the most faithful of his supporters for the risks they had taken on his behalf. Thus it was that on 1 February 1323 Robert the Bruce signed a charter (still preserved in the charter chest in Drum Castle) that passed to his trusty armour-bearer and clerk-register, William de Irwin of the Bonshaw family of Woodhouse in Dumfriesshire, the Royal Forest of Drum.

And so the de Irwins came to Drum Castle (the spelling of their name adopted in the locality soon became Irvine) to start their remarkable record of six-and-a-half centuries of family occupation. It can't have been a very comfortable home – but then, what was in those days? The first-floor entrance led from the wooden ladder straight into the common hall through a doorway that is now blocked up; a stone staircase plunged down into the vaulted basement, where scullions laboured in the gloom; upwards, a newel (spiral) staircase led giddily to the upper hall, which formed the private apartments of the old keep.

The common hall on the first floor was converted into a library in the nineteenth century, and was also used as a billiard room. It is still very impressive, a great barrel-vaulted chamber occupying an entire storey of the keep, its ceiling adorned with the heraldic shields of families linked to the Irvines. This was where the whole household would eat. It was divided half-way up by a wooden floor, which provided a sort of attic in which the servants slept.

Above the common hall was the old upper hall, another prodigiously tall room, also divided into two floors. It used to have a flagstone floor, but the flagstones have long since gone. This was the private 'solar' drawing-room of the castle's owner. The windows on either side are flanked by stone seats, there is a capacious stone wardrobe cut into one wall, and the fireplace is wide and welcoming. The upper floor would have contained the private bedrooms.

Above the private apartments, right on the roof, lived the soldiery who guarded the castle and its environs. They lived in what is called a 'cap-house', ready to tumble out of their beds to take their turn patrolling the battlements. But at least they had one modern amenity – recesses in the walls which were actually stone lavatories, where they could relieve themselves without the danger of being shot at when they were at their most vulnerable!

It is in the upper hall that one really senses the authentic whiff of history, as redolent as the lingering scent of peat-smoke. It is very easy to imagine Robert the Bruce staying here, mixing politics with pleasure in the form of hunting, feasting on venison with his subjects in the common hall downstairs, taking counsel with his courtiers in the private apartments of the upper hall, gazing out through the deep windows as he sat on the stone benches of the embrasure. Although there is no record of Robert the Bruce ever visiting his Royal Forester, William de Irwin, first Irvine laird of Drum, the splendid upper hall, so reminiscent of the work of Richard Cementarius, positively shouts his presence.

The Irvines were always fiercely loyal to the Crown. Under the Bruce and Stewart dynasties their power and prosperity flourished exceedingly, nurtured by royal patronage and periodically reinvigorated by judiciously chosen marriages, until their estates were so extensive that it was said that an Irvine could ride all the way from Drum to Dundee without ever stepping off his own land. But as well as basking in royal favour,

opposite The courtyard on the north side of Drum Castle, with the modern additions of 1875, including the new front door (centre).

above The restored chapel. On the right is the Gothic stone canopy from the altar tomb of Sir Alexander Irwin, the fourth laird of Drum, salvaged from St Nicholas Church in Aberdeen.

right The library in what was originally the common hall of the old tower. Above the chimneypiece hangs a huge self-portrait of Hugh Irvine as the Archangel Gabriel.

the Irvines of Drum often had to pay dearly for their Royalist allegiance.

In 1411, for instance, the third laird, Sir Alexander de Irwin, paid with his life at the Battle of Harlaw, near Aberdeen, which has been described as the bloodiest battle ever fought in Scotland. Here a marauding army from the Hebrides, led by Donald of the Isles, was met by a determined force of north-eastern gentry and their tenants under the command of the Earl of Mar. The Aberdeenshire men were outnumbered by ten to one, but they fought like tigers; and none fought better than Sir Alexander de Irwin. He took on the most formidable of the Islesmen, the Chief of the Macleans of Duart in Mull, known as Red Hector of the Battles. It was a ferocious encounter, which ended with both men lying dead on the field after a notable and noble combat. Tradition insists that their heirs – the new Maclean of Duart and the next Sir Alexander de Irwin, the fourth laird – exchanged swords as a sign that no feud existed between the families, and in mutual recognition of the heroism of that epic battle.

It was this fourth laird, great-grandson of William de Irwin, armour-bearer to Robert the Bruce, who brought the political fortunes of the Irvine family to new heights. There had long been enmity between the Irvine family and the Keiths (one place-name by the River Dee, 'Keith's Pot', commemorates an incident when a group of Keiths was assailed by Irvines and driven to death in the river); but the fourth laird ended this by marrying Elizabeth de Keith, daughter of Sir Robert de Keith, Marischal of Scotland and one of the most powerful men in the country. This had been his father's last wish before his death at the Battle of Harlaw.

In 1423, newly knighted in his own right, he was employed as an ambassador to negotiate the release of Scotland's king, James I, who had been captured by English pirates in 1406 and detained by Henry IV of England for eighteen long years. The mission was successful, at the cost of a ransom of £40,000, and King James never forgot it: during the thirteen years of his reign after he returned to Scotland, while he tried to curb the power of his nobles with harsh and often savage measures, there is no record that the Irvines ever suffered royal displeasure. After the murder of King James in 1437, and during the troubled times of James II's minority (he was only six years old when his father was assassinated), Sir Alexander de Irwin was chosen captain and governor of the town of Aberdeen in 1439 and again in 1440.

In his latter years, having retired from active affairs, he founded in St Nicholas Church in Aberdeen the chantry of St Ninian-the-Confessor; in the south transept, known since then as Drum's Aisle, he provided a monument for himself and his wife, Lady Elizabeth de Keith, with their stone effigies recumbent on an altar-tomb surmounted by a pointed Gothic stone canopy. He died the following year, in 1457, after a long and full life, at peace with both man and God.

It is not unlikely that the tower was added to around this time to provide more spacious living, for taste in domestic standards was changing. But it wasn't until the time of the ninth laird that Drum Castle blossomed into a full-scale Jacobean great house with the addition of the handsome Renaissance mansion adjoining the tower. This was the creation of Alexander Irvine, ninth laird of Drum, who rejoiced in the nickname of 'Little Breeches', or 'Wee Breeks', apparently because of a predilection for wearing short trousers – a habit he had adopted after a tour of the Continent. He was described by a descendant, a century later, as 'a plain man' who 'lived decently', and was remembered with affection for his 'benignity and ample bounty'.

Unfortunately there is no extant portrait of 'Little Breeches'. He may well have looked rather ordinary and plain, even quaint, but there was nothing ordinary or plain about his career and achievements. He was appointed Sheriff-principal of Aberdeen, and was also one of the powerful 'Lords of the Articles', the committee of the Scottish Parliament which was responsible for drafting new laws. He inherited Drum in 1603, in the same year that King James VI of Scotland inherited the English throne; and in the brief burgeoning of Scottish prosperity that followed the Union of the Crowns, the laird of Drum ensured that the Irvine fortunes flourished as well. He increased the Irvine estates by purchasing Kellie Castle in Angus; and in 1619, at the height of the Renaissance building boom in Scotland, he completed the Jacobean extension to Drum.

The new mansion, which may well have incorporated earlier rooms or structures, consists basically of a long tenement flanked by a square tower at either end, abutting on but not surrounding the old keep. Its chief domestic characteristic was the provision not only of architectural pomp but privacy as well; separate areas for dining, withdrawing, and sleeping, away from the hurly-burly of the communal great hall. It had its own high hall, which is now a superbly appointed and panelled drawing-room; earlier, in Georgian times, it had been the dining-room, complete with chamber-pot in a little cupboard at the window so that the gentlemen could carry on their post-prandial conversation with the minimum of interruption. The mansion also had an equally impressive 'withdrawing-room' for the ladies (now the dining-room). It had a special business room, or laird's room, where the laird conducted the affairs of the estate; in it today you can see an easy chair in which Mary Queen of Scots is alleged to have held informal court – even though it dates from the end of the seventeenth century, a hundred years after the poor lass had been beheaded in England! It also had another cunning little room below it, with an outside door, known as the 'speak-a-word' room; here the laird could meet estate workmen in private – and also, if he so desired, slip out of the house unnoticed.

Alexander Irvine's original conception for the Jacobean mansion has been much praised by architectural historians. Only one tiny detail marred its execution, although it is the sort of flaw to be remembered with affection, not irritation: the stone on which his initials and those of his wife, Lady Marion Douglas, had been carved, with the date 1619, was set in upside down, and reads to this day – 6191!

Like the fourth laird before him, the ninth laird was also a notable benefactor. When he died in 1630 he willed £10,000 in Scottish money to endow six scholarships at Marischal College in Aberdeen (which had been founded in 1593 by his kinsman by marriage, the fifth Earl Marshall of Scotland) and four grants for the Grammar School of Aberdeen. His widow, Marion, who survived him for nearly twenty years, endowed Lady Drum's Hospital for the care of needy widows and spinsters; the hospital is no longer there, but a street, Drum's Lane, runs through its former grounds, commemorating the 'benignity and ample bounty' of the ninth laird and his good lady.

These halcyon days for the Irvine family were to come to an abrupt and brutal end in the Civil War of the Covenanting period that broke out in 1638; the next laird and his family, as staunchly Royalist as the Irvines had always been, were to pay a heavy price for their unwavering allegiance to King Charles I, and Drum Castle with its beautiful Jacobean mansion would suffer worst of all.

From 1639 until the Royalists laid down their arms in 1646, Drum suffered constant harassment. It was plundered by Covenanter troops in April 1639, again in June 1640, and yet again in May 1644. The tenth laird, Sir Alexander Irvine, was driven into exile for a while, imprisoned time and again, fined, persecuted, and excommunicated for his total opposition to Presbyterianism. His sons were imprisoned with him, one of them dying in captivity. Lady Irvine and her household were evicted. All the traditional ties of alliance through kinship were riven during those bitter years. It was the Earl Marshal who ordered the sack of Drum Castle in 1640; in 1644, when the Covenanting leader, the Marquess of Argyll, evicted Lady Irvine and plundered the castle, one of the gentlewomen who was driven out with Lady Irvine was her daughter-in-law – Argyll's own neice.

At long last the protracted agony of the Civil War in Scotland came to an end, and Drum Castle, despite having been condemned to total destruction by the Scottish

right The drawing-room, originally the high hall of the Jacobean house. The sash windows are Georgian. The panelled ceiling is nineteenth century.

right The dining-room, formerly the withdrawing-room of the Jacobean house. The table, dating from the late eighteenth century, is actually 'a set of tables' which can be enlarged or reduced at will, or even made into two tables, one round and the other rectangular.

Parliament in 1642, was left in peace. The tenth laird, despite all his appalling trials and tribulations, survived until 1658; but the estate of Drum was now sadly depleted, the great house half wrecked, the Irvine fortunes gone. The new laird, inheriting a mountain of debts, had to sell off much of the family lands. As often happens when a family is in a period of decline, there were disputes over inheritance. Elaborate efforts were made to cut some people out of wills, or to stop unwelcome marriages, and even – so it was whispered – to prevent the birth of a potential heir. The line of succession veered away from the direct line of male heirs, and did not revert until 1737. It was a bad, bad hundred years for the Irvines of Drum.

Yet such are the ironies of history that the century of troubles left the Irvines better equipped to face the challenge of the nineteenth century; the slimmed-down estate of Drum was actually more easily manageable now, more amenable to the agricultural improvements that would help to restore the Irvine fortunes.

The portraits in the dining-room and the drawing-room chart the course of the nineteenth century as it affected Drum, as do the various building changes that were made. In the drawing-room hangs the portrait of the eighteenth laird, Alexander Irvine (again!), who was laird for eighty-three years. He succeeded as a minor in 1761, and died at an exasperatingly old age, in his nineties, in 1844 – exasperating anyway for his son, the nineteenth laird, who had been hanging about as the heir-apparent for years. His portrait on the wall of the drawing-room looks positively sour, which is no doubt why he is known familiarly as the 'Disgruntled Laird'.

His brother, on the other hand, positively glows: Hugh Irvine, younger son of the eighteenth laird, and therefore released from the burden of anticipated inheritance, was an artist of considerable quality, a friend of Lord Byron. A very 'Byronic' portrait of him by Henry Howard hangs in the dining-room, above what is probably Hugh Irvine's most celebrated work – his view of Castlegate, Aberdeen, done in 1812. Above the chimneypiece in the library (the former common hall of the old tower) hangs another painting by Hugh Irvine – a self-portrait as the Archangel Gabriel, painted while he was studying in Rome.

It was the nineteenth laird – the Disgruntled Laird – who converted the common hall into a library and billiard room, slapping a huge new window through the thick east wall of the tower and giving the chamber a timber barrel vault to form a new false ceiling. This was the penultimate major alteration to Drum Castle.

The last alterations were made in the 1870s, under the patronage of the twentieth laird, Alexander Forbes Irvine, laird from 1861 to 1892. He was a very distinguished man in his own right, a lawyer of considerable repute who was Sheriff of Argyll for seventeen years and vice-Dean of the Faculty of Advocates. Perhaps the most striking portrait in Drum Castle is that of his wife, Anna Margaretta, by Graham Gilbert, which hangs above the fireplace of the drawing-room. What an exceptionally beautiful woman she was! The Drum tenantry seem to have appreciated the fact, too, for their wedding present to their future laird and the lovely Anna was the ornate chimneypiece, which replaced the original Adam fireplace that used to stand there.

In 1875 the twentieth laird decided on some Victorian improvements to ensure that Upstairs should never need to meet Downstairs when servants were going about their business; he also wanted a formal entrance hall for receiving guests. He commissioned David Bryce, a noted Edinburgh architect, to prepare plans for these projected extensions. Bryce died the following year, after the plans had been drawn up, but they were executed over the next few years by his brother, John Bryce.

It was Bryce who designed the hall and front door as additions to the north front of the Jacobean house, where today's visitors enter; and to enhance it he rebuilt the courtyard leading to it, including an exceptionally fine entrance arch. Above the new hall a spacious corridor was added, running the full length of the house and opening into the drawing-

The drawing-room of Haddo House: the largest room in the house, it is frequently used for chamber concerts. Above the fireplace hangs a painting of David and Goliath by Domenichino. The top portrait to the right of the door is of the Prime Minister Earl's second wife, Lady Harriet Douglas.

The high hall at The Binns, now furnished as a drawing-room with Hepplewhite open armchairs. The plaster ceiling is dated 1630. The Royal Coat of Arms above the fireplace (the Dalyells hoped that King Charles I would visit The Binns in 1630), is flanked by the Prince of Wales' plumes, a compliment to Charles I's son who was born that year.

The laigh hall at The Binns: originally two rooms, it was remodelled as one in the eigtheenth century and given an arcade. The carved stone chimneypiece is late seventeenth-century.

Leith Hall, Grampian, from the west. In the centre is the ornate archway into the courtyard, and above it the four tall windows of the music room.

room and dining-room, and an oak stairway was inserted that led up to the bedrooms on the second floor.

Drum Castle was now a proper Victorian residence. But one more major work of reconstruction was undertaken in the nineteenth century – the restoration of the chapel. For a family that had paid so dearly for its Episcopalian traditions, it was almost a debt of honour to the past. The chapel stands in a little copse not far from the house. It is very old, and was probably rather larger originally than it is now. After it had fallen into disuse, its restoration was begun by the nineteenth laird – the Disgruntled – in 1857, and continued by the twentieth laird. It now contains all sorts of historical treasures, including a huge solid silver figurine from Augsburg of the Blessed Virgin – no one realized it was silver until it was cleaned recently.

And then, in 1951, the history of Drum came almost full circle. In 1875, 'Drum's Aisle' in St Nicholas Church in Aberdeen was renovated. The Gothic stone canopy over the effigies of the fourth laird and his wife was removed and laid in the churchyard. But it was never replaced. Eventually the lovely Anna, wife of the twentieth laird, lost patience and installed it in Drum Castle. There it remained until 1951, when the last resident laird, the twenty-fourth, Henry Quentin Forbes Irvine, re-erected it in the restored chapel.

And so the great fourth laird came home again, you might say. But by then the long years of Drum Castle as a private family home of the Irvines were numbered.

The twenty-second laird of Drum died in 1922 and was succeeded by his eldest son, Alexander, who subsequently died without issue. Drum was then inherited by his brother, Henry Quentin Forbes Irvine, who had worked for some years on coffee estates in Kenya and served during the Second World War in the King's African Rifles, and who returned home in 1945 to take up the responsibility of running the estate.

The new laird was very conscious of the historic importance of the heritage of 'Grampian, the Castle Country', as the Trust's President, the Earl of Wemyss and March, has termed it; and for many years before his death in 1975, members of the public enjoyed the privilege of seeing over Drum's tower, castle and chapel on Sunday afternoons throughout the summer, under the guidance of Mrs Irvine. In 1964 he entered into an agreement whereby he would bequeath to the National Trust for Scotland the property of Drum Castle and over three hundred acres of land, together with an endowment to secure its future maintenance. He died in November 1975, and the castle was opened to the public in July 1976.

It's a very special place. Under the supervision of the Trust's representative, Mrs Alison van de Scheur, it retains all its intensely homely qualities, as the thousands of visitors would attest.

But there was one very special visitor recently, an anonymous one, who epitomizes this quality. She was observed kneeling on the lawn and kissing the grass. It turned out that she was on holiday in Scotland from New Zealand, and that she had been a housemaid at Drum for nine years during the 1920s. Her hours had been long and arduous – up at 4 a.m. to blacklead the grates, hot water ready for the cook at 6 a.m., and then an endless round of tasks until she was off at 10 p.m. Even after that she was young and spry enough to go to a local dance whenever there was one on.

She had actually never seen the rest of the castle – she had been strictly Downstairs; Upstairs was out of bounds. She was seeing it now for the first time. And she kissed the grass. It must have been a happy house indeed to inspire that kind of affection.

The fortified gatehouse of Falkland Palace.

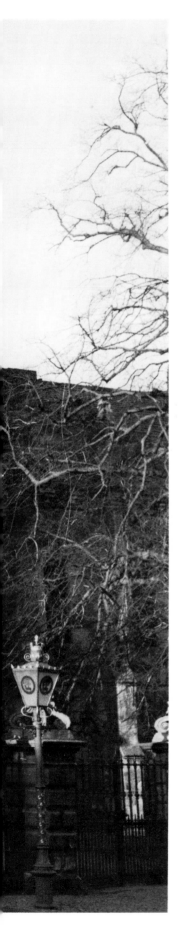

FALKLAND PALACE
Fife

ONCE UPON A TIME, Falkland Palace in the heart of the ancient kingdom of Fife was the holiday retreat of royalty. For centuries it was the happy haunt of the romantic, doom-ridden Stuart dynasty of Scotland, and it remains to this day the property of the sovereign. This alone makes it the principal 'historic' building in the care of the National Trust for Scotland.

Once upon an even earlier time there had been a stout fortress at Falkland, dating as far back as the early twelfth century; references have been found to a certain 'Macbeath Thaynetus de Falkland' (Macbeth, Thane of Falkland) having a stronghold there at that time. By the thirteenth century the castle of Falkland was the stronghold of the Macduffs, earls of Fife.

Today there is almost nothing to be seen of the ancient fortress, apart from the base of the round great tower, more than fifty feet in diameter, which breaks through the grass to the north of the palace rose garden.

Of the great palace that grew as an adjunct of the castle, sadly little remains. It had been a complex of three ranges, built on the north, east and south sides of a square courtyard bounded on the west side by a high wall and entered by means of an imposing twin-towered gatehouse in the south range. What we are left with is the stump of history, what Thomas Carlyle once called 'a black old bit of coffin or protrusive shin-bone striking through the soil of the dead past', but now lovingly restored to something at least of its former glory.

The whole of the north range, which was probably the oldest section of the palace, built as a royal great hall by James II in the fifteenth century, has gone, accidentally burned down in 1654 while it was occupied by a garrison of Cromwell's troops. Today its position and outlines, including the siting of the two large oriel windows which lit the high table on its dais at the east end of the hall, are marked by the paving of the rose-garden that encloses the north side of the present courtyard. Here, each summer, red and yellow roses flaunt the royal livery colours of Scotland, to symbolize the times when kings and queens feasted and made music in the Lyon Chamber, as it came to be called.

The east range, rebuilt by James IV early in the sixteenth century and embellished by his son James V, is today a roofless ruin. Only the vaulted cellars remain, and above them the long open expanse of what was once the king's guard hall, and the presence (audience) chamber and the privy dining-room beyond. At the far end, where the east range met the north range, the round dovecote tower in the angle between the two blocks contained a spiral stone staircase that led from the royal kitchens in the basement to the privy dining-room and from there up to the queen's apartments above. None of this remains today, alas; the effect of the fire in 1654, followed by two centuries of neglect, reduced the whole building to ruin. On the other hand, the east range now features a totally reconstructed and refurbished king's bedchamber in the 'cross-house' that projected from the outside wall. It was in this room that the dying King James V heard of the birth of his baby daughter, Mary, the future Queen of Scots, in December 1542, and greeted the news with a despairing prophecy: 'The De'il gang wi' it. It will end as it began. It cam' wi' a lass, and will gang wi' a lass.' He was referring to the Stuart royal line, which had come into being through Robert the Bruce's daughter Marjorie when she married Walter the Steward. But he was wrong about the second lass; Mary Queen of Scots was destined to marry another Stuart (Lord Darnley) and have a son by him, and so keep the throne in the House of Stuart until 1714.

The only major part of the palace complex still in a good state of preservation is the south range, whose façade dominates the High Street of the tiny former Royal Burgh of Falkland (it lost its regal title during the sweeping local government reorganization of 1975). It was built by James IV at the same time as he rebuilt the east range, but its magnificent facing of dressed stone was added by James V to celebrate his second French marriage, and remains to this day the earliest display of French Renaissance architectural design in Britain; indeed it has been called 'the finest monument to the Auld Alliance' – the long and lingering alliance between Scotland and France against their powerful neighbour, England. The south range contains the magnificent chapel royal, which boasts the only original interior still surviving at Falkland – rescued in the nick of time by dedicated restoration work started in 1887 by a Stuart descendant, John Patrick Crichton Stuart, the third Marquess of Bute. It is now in regular use for public worship as a Roman Catholic chapel, and is the centrepiece of any visit to Falkland Palace. Beyond it, at the western end, is the twin-towered gatehouse which contains the living-quarters of the captain, or keeper, of Falkland Palace; these are not, of course, open to the public.

Apart from the chapel royal and the king's bedchamber, the other attractions for the visitor are the palace garden, all lawns and colourful flower borders, which was laid out in its present form after the Second World War; and the real (royal) tennis court. This was built by James V in 1539, eight years after King Henry VIII had constructed his own tennis court at the riverside palace of Hampton Court. Recent research has revealed that Henry's tennis court was totally rebuilt at some later time; so the Falkland tennis court can claim to be not only the sole real tennis court in Scotland to survive from the Stuart period, but also the oldest *original* court in Britain. It was a hard game, undoubtedly, which monarchs would share with their domestic servants on occasion, a mixture of tennis and fives, for it was originally played by hand, not with a racquet. The hard ball was played over a fringed or tasselled rope across the court (later replaced by a net), and could be bounced off the sloping wooden roof of the spectators' gallery on one side of the court – to the occasional peril of the spectators. Today, after restoration first by the third Marquess of Bute and more recently by the Trust, the court is once more available for contests in this most royal and ancient game.

So what does Falkland Palace today have to offer the 50,000 visitors who flock there every year? It is not an inhabited and complete royal palace like Holyroodhouse in Edinburgh, which was begun by James IV around 1500 and is still the residence of the sovereign when visiting Scotland. It is nothing like as grand as the sumptuous palace of Hampton Court on the Thames, begun by Cardinal Wolsey in 1514 and taken over by the autocratic, ever-greedy Henry VIII. Falkland Palace has a different appeal; it has the genuine echo of royal Stuart panoply sighing in the wind, the very stuff of Scotland's turbulent history – for the story of the ill-fated Stuarts *is* the story of Scotland, from the accession in 1371 of Robert II, grandson of Robert the Bruce, to the start of the Hanovarian dynasty with George I in 1714. The visitors to Falkland are, in effect, pilgrims to Scotland's history.

Falkland Palace now is largely a matter of image and imagination. The image is supplied by a splendid painting of Falkland by the seventeenth-century Dutch artist Alexander Keirincx (called 'Carings' in contemporary English sources), a copy of which has recently been put on display in the museum room, once the barrel-vaulted brewhouse in the cellars of the east range just inside the east port. It had been known for a long time that Keirincx/Carings had been commissioned by Charles I to make several paintings of the royal properties in Scotland, but soon after the start of the Commonwealth they had all been dispersed. In 1977 the Falkland painting 'emerged' in Copenhagen, and was bought by the Scottish National Portrait Gallery. It adds a vivid new dimension to our perception of Falkland at its heyday, the Falkland of James V when it was the favourite hunting-lodge of the Stuarts.

But it is the imagination that reigns supreme at Falkland now; and how richly it can exercise itself as it wanders through the vanished precincts of the old palace. This was where the Stuarts came to try to escape from the cares of monarchy, to feast and sing and dance, to play tennis and chess, to hunt deer and boar in the oaks of Falkland forest – and, sometimes, to be hunted themselves.

The way in which Falkland came into the possession of the Stuarts was itself an ominous prelude to the sad Stuart centuries, in which every single monarch from James I to James VI – all seven of them – came to the throne as a minor. Mary Queen of Scots set the record for minority accession by inheriting the crown when she was less than a week old. Apart from the seventh and last of the exclusively Scottish sovereigns, James VI of Scotland and I of England, all of them died violently or grievously after troubled minorities. Even some of the architects employed by the Stuarts at Falkland died sudden and unpleasant deaths.

Falkland Castle had been the home of the Macduffs, earls of Fife, until 1371. In that year Isabel, Countess of Fife in her own right, finding herself widowed and childless after no fewer than four marriages, granted the castle of Falkland, and the earldom, to her brother-in-law the Duke of Albany, youngest son of King Robert II (1371-90). Albany was one of the most charismatic men in Scotland at the time, and it is surely no coincidence that Isabel gave him Falkland in the year that his father was crowned king. He was tall and handsome and extremely popular, especially in the Highlands.

Robert II was a good-natured, middle-aged man of fifty-five when he ascended the throne, with eyes so bloodshot that he earned the nickname of 'King Blearie'. On his death in 1390 he was succeeded by his eldest son Robert III, who had been crippled and half-paralyzed by an injury received in a tournament. As a result the real government of the country fell into the hands of his younger brother, the Duke of Albany, who acted as Guardian of Scotland for the first nine years of his brother's reign; but in 1399 the Guardianship was passed to the king's elder son, the Duke of Rothesay, Albany's nephew, when he reached the age of twenty-one. It was this that sowed the seeds of disaster.

After three years, Rothesay's Guardianship was revoked in 1402, and the Duke of Albany was appointed Guardian again. Clearly there was little love lost between the two, uncle and nephew. Young Rothesay, 'a brilliant but licentious youth' as historians put it, was arrested by Albany and conveyed to Falkland Castle, where he was imprisoned in a 'befitting chamber' in the great tower. A strange fiery comet appeared in the sky, which was interpreted by popular superstition as a death omen for princes; sure enough, at Easter 1402 as the comet waned, Rothesay, heir to the new Stuart throne, died in Falkland Castle. It was given out that he had died of dysentery, but suspicion and rumour had it that he had been deliberately starved to death by his uncle, the Duke of Albany.

This seems to have been the story believed by Rothesay's younger brother, the future King James I, who succeeded to the throne on his father's death in 1406. He was in no position to assume the crown at the time, for he was then a prisoner of Henry IV in England, having been captured by an English privateer at the age of twelve while on his way to hoped-for safety in France – anything to get away from the deadly influence of Albany. His father, Robert III, died soon after hearing the news of his capture, and it would be eighteen years before James was allowed to return to Scotland, with the payment of a ransom of £40,000, to assume his kingship. In the meantime the Duke of

right The rebuilt 'cross-house' of Falkland Palace. On either side are the ruined reaches of the east range. To the right is the Dovecote tower in the angle between the east range and the ruined great hall of the north range.

right A painting of Falkland Palace by the Dutch artist Alexander Keirincx (1640) – a recent discovery now on display in the museum room in the cellarage of the east range.

Albany ruled the country as governor until his death in 1420, to be succeeded by his son Murdoch, the second Duke of Albany. When King James I was finally freed in 1424 he took savage revenge on the Albanys who had allegedly murdered his elder brother: Murdoch, second Duke of Albany, along with his two sons and his father-in-law, the Earl of Lennox, were beheaded on Heading Hill at Stirling Castle in 1425. Thereafter, Falkland passed to Albany's uncle, Walter Stuart, Earl of Atholl. But in 1437 Atholl was involved in the brutal midnight assassination of James I at Blackfriars' Monastery in Perth; for this he was beheaded after suffering excruciating public torture – three endless days of being flogged and forced to wear a red-hot iron crown inscribed 'The King of Traitors'. It was in this awful fashion that the forfeited estate of Falkland came to the Stuart crown.

James I is now seen as one of Scotland's ablest and most cultured kings, author of that tender and passionate collection of poems, the *Kingis Quair* (King's Book), which tells of his love for the wife he married in England, Jane Beaufort, daughter of the Earl of Somerset. All the Stuarts that followed him were cultivated people who patronized the arts of poetry and music, to the detriment of politics perhaps; and it is as if a curse descended on them with the acquisition of Falkland Palace.

James II, nicknamed 'Fiery Face' because of the large red birthmark that disfigured his cheek, inherited the throne and Falkland Castle when he was only six years old. When he came of age and took over the reins of government he proved himself a shrewd and vigorous ruler. In 1449 he married Mary, daughter of the Duke of Gueldres (Gilderland), niece of the Duke of Burgundy, and as part of her marriage settlement he gave her the castle of Falkland; to improve it he built the great hall of the vanished north range so that they could entertain on a grand scale, and it seems likely that he also built the east range. It was now that Falkland became a palace and a royal residence of note; and in 1458 he honoured the little town that had grown up around the castle by making it a royal burgh, in recognition of 'the frequent residence of the royal family at Falkland, and the damage and inconvenience sustained by the many prelates, peers, nobles and others' who attended court. Today, the 'little houses' of Falkland are almost as important as the palace itself; they tell the story of the courtiers who served the Stuart court through good times and bad. These 'little houses', sixty-eight of which are now listed as being of special architectural and historic interest, help to make Falkland a much larger experience than a mere visit to a palace; many of them have now been salvaged and restored, and form a happy complement to the palace itself.

James II was accidentally killed during a Scottish siege of Roxburgh Castle in 1460; he was so interested in the new cannons he had brought that he was standing beside one of them while the gunner was firing, and it burst.

James II's widow, Mary of Gueldres, not yet thirty, was left with five young children and the responsibility of acting as Regent for the new king, James III, who was then only nine years old. She had a new chamber built for herself at Falkland with a special door leading down to her private garden. She is still remembered in the so-called 'Gilderland walk' through what is left of the Falkland woods, a path that leads between two clumps of trees known as the 'Queen's quarrels'; Sir Iain Moncreiffe of that Ilk, Albany Herald and formerly Falkland Pursuivant-Extraordinary, who has written a most lively and evocative guidebook to Falkland, suggests that the name may have arisen because the trees were hardwoods used for making crossbow arrows, or 'quarrels' as they were called in the Middle Ages.

James III had a refined and cultivated mind, filling Falkland Palace with artists, musicians and architects, but he never managed to impose his authority on Scotland's turbulent nobles, as his father had done. Indeed, in 1482 he had to endure the humiliation of seeing one of his favourites, the architect Thomas Cochrane, being lynched before his very eyes at Lauder by his disaffected nobles; Cochrane, who is thought to have built the great hall at Stirling Castle for James III, may well have been responsible for remodelling the great hall at Falkland, for the similarity between the two designs is very striking.

James III's reign ended as dismally as it had begun: in 1488 the Lowland nobles rose in open rebellion, nominally headed by the king's fifteen-year-old son, the future James IV. There was a pitched battle at Sauchieburn, about a mile from historic Bannockburn, and the king's army was defeated. As James III galloped from the field he was thrown from his horse, and was stabbed to death by a pursuer in the hovel where he had taken refuge.

James IV was undoubtedly the most brilliant of all the Stuart sovereigns. He so repented of his part (albeit enforced) in the rebellion that led to his father's death that he always wore a heavy iron belt, to which he added a new link every year. Like his forefathers he was intensely artistic and loved music and poetry; he was also an outstanding linguist who spoke seven languages in addition to his native English and Scots – Latin, French, German, Flemish, Italian, Spanish and Gaelic. He was amorous, energetic, intelligent; and his people loved him. Above all he was much more of a diplomat than his predecessors, and had the gift of carrying people with his decisions: the Spanish ambassador reported in a cipher dispatch to Madrid, 'He lends a willing ear to his counsellors, and decides nothing without asking them, but in great matters he acts according to his own judgement, and in my opinion he generally makes the right decision.'

This was the man who extended Falkland Palace considerably by adding to the great hall of the north range the cross-house of the now-ruined east range and the chapel royal of the south range. This new palace he filled with colour and music and gifted friends, including the poet William Dunbar. It seems as if there was no limit to what this gifted king could have done for Scotland, until he threw it all away with one disastrously ill-judged action – an invasion of England in 1513 on behalf of the Auld Alliance with France. As every Scottish schoolchild knows, that incursion came to terrible grief a few miles inside the English border at Flodden, where James IV fell with a large number of his nobility: 'The flowers of the forest are a' wede awa''.

His son, James V, was only a year old when his father fell at Flodden. His widowed mother, Margaret Tudor, sister of Henry VIII, was appointed Regent at first, but after a time the Regency came to her second husband, the Earl of Angus, who kept young James a virtual prisoner in Falkland Palace. But eventually, in 1528, at the age of sixteen, he escaped one night disguised as a groom and ensconced himself in the security of Stirling Castle. When he took over the reins of government he also took revenge on the Douglas family of which the Earl of Angus was head; the Douglases were executed or exiled and their estates forfeited to the Crown, and the Earl of Angus's sister, Lady Glamis, was burned at the stake as a witch.

Despite the fact that his mother was Henry VIII's sister, James V plumped solidly for the Auld Alliance with France. In 1537 he married Princess Madeleine, daughter of Francis I, King of France, and set about beautifying Falkland Palace for his bride; a painter was engaged for eleven weeks redecorating the ceilings of the royal apartments with 'azure and vermilion and rose of Paris, with white lead and verdigris and indigo of Badeas, and with much fine gold' (Moncreiffe). He also completed the two galleried walks on the east side of the east range which gave a magnificent view out over the forest of Falkland and the Howe of Fife.

Madeleine was very delicate in health, alas, and died soon after arriving in Scotland. Nothing daunted, James V returned to France to find another bride; this time he married, in 1538, the vigorous Mary of Lorraine (Mary of Guise, as some historians call her), who had been adopted by Francis I. To mark this second nuptial occasion James used French and, later, Scottish masons to embellish the external walls of the east range and the south range, and thus created the very first true Renaissance façade to be built in Britain.

To the east range they added ornamental pilaster buttresses and also created windows

opposite The reconstructed king's bedchamber in the 'cross-house' at Falkland Palace. The 'Golden Bed of Brahan' which forms the centrepiece dates from the early seventeenth century, and was brought from abroad as a sumptuous gift to the Earl of Seaforth from a clansman.

with Tudor head-moulds, which are unusual in Scotland. But it was the south range, with its chapel royal, that was and remains his *pièce de résistance* and a triumph for this new masonic alliance. The street front, as built by James IV, is a fine example of Scottish Gothic architecture with its five massive buttresses linking up with the twin-towered gatehouse; but the five holy statues in the niches of these buttresses, now badly eroded, were carved in 1538 by a foreign craftsman called Peter the Flemish-man.

It was on the inner façade that the French masons were given their head to transform Gothic into Renaissance. In 1538 Nicholas Roy, a French master mason who had been recommended by Mary of Lorraine's father, the Duc de Guise, arrived at Falkland to carve the round medallions that flank in pairs the five great windows overlooking the courtyard. These traditionally represented heroes and heroines of classical mythology, but local tradition has it that in fact they were carved in the likeness of the king's most intimate circle – his parents, his two French wives, his friends and advisers, and a trio of royal mistresses from his younger days, by each of whom he had already fathered sons. The courtyard buttresses bear the date 1539, the Scots thistle and the French fleur-de-lys, and the initials of James and his second queen: IRSDG for *Iacobus Rex Scotorum Dei Gratia* and MARIA RDG for *Maria Regina Dei Gratia*.

James V's architect in charge of the work at Falkland was his cousin, Sir James Hamilton of Finnart, bastard son of the Earl of Arran. He was a wild and adventurous character with a knack of making enemies; in 1540 he was framed by those enemies on a charge of treason, and beheaded after being defeated in a trial by combat. It is said that his ghost returned to haunt his old friend the king, and foretold his early death and the death of his two sons by Mary of Lorraine.

Foretold or not, James's two baby sons did die; not long afterwards, in 1542, James V himself died in the king's bedchamber at Falkland Palace. No one knows the cause; some say it was of hepatitis, some of melancholia, others of a broken heart following the news of Scotland's humiliating defeat by the English at Solway Moss. He was only thirty years old.

His baby daughter, then only a few days old, was to become the enigmatic Mary Queen of Scots: tall, imperious, beautiful, passionate, infinitely alluring and infinitely unhappy. Yet some of her happiest days were spent at Falkland Palace. When she returned to Scotland after her sojourn in the French court and her brief marriage to the dauphin of France, she came to Falkland every summer between 1561 and 1565 to enjoy country pursuits as a respite from her calamitous affairs of state and heart. But trouble followed her even to Falkland; in 1562 James Hepburn, fourth Earl of Bothwell, that 'glorious, rash and hazardous young man' as the English ambassador, Sir Nicholas Throckmorton, described him, who was to marry her in 1567, was so enamoured of her that he was arrested at the palace on a charge of trying to abduct her.

Mary's son by Darnley, James VI, was proclaimed king when only a year old after his mother's enforced abdication in 1567. He too loved Falkland as a holiday retreat and a hunting-lodge, to such an extent that he gave it to his bride, Princess Anne of Denmark, as a 'morrowing gift' on the day after their wedding in 1589. But he too had his moments of drama there. In 1582, at the age of sixteen, he was confined there by the Earl of Gowrie for a time before he contrived to escape to friends in St Andrews. Ten years later, in 1592, the unstable Francis Stuart, fifth Earl of Bothwell, attacked the palace with a force of three hundred horsemen in a wild attempt to abduct his cousin the king. The attempt failed, but the flanking towers of the gatehouse which face the High Street have the bullet marks in them to this day.

After James VI's accession to the English throne in 1603, Scotland saw very little of him. He paid his last visit to Falkland Palace in 1617, but he always remembered it with affection; in 1620 one of his English courtiers, Sir Henry Cary, was created a Scottish peer as Viscount Falkland (the Falkland Islands were later to be named after this family), and

opposite The chapel royal – the only surviving original interior of the palace. On the left are some of the hand-turned pillars of the oak entrance screen; farther in, the old royal pew and pulpit, restored with the help of fragments found by Lord Bute; and, behind the altar, the restored panelled oak screen.

above King James v of Scotland and his queen, Mary of Lorraine.
James v died in the king's bedchamber at Falkland Palace a few days
after hearing of the birth of his daughter, the future Mary Queen of
Scots.

right The turnpike stair to the long gallery that leads to the chapel
royal. A series of magnificent seventeenth-century Flemish tapestries
cover the length of the wall on the right; they were presented by
Lord Ninian Crichton Stuart, Hereditary Keeper in succession to his
father, the third Marquess of Bute.

one of the royal officers of arms in Scotland is still called Falkland Pursuivant-Extraordinary.

King Charles I visited Scotland briefly to be crowned in 1633, and stayed for a while at Falkland. For that notable occasion the splendid chapel royal was redecorated. Along the whole length of the north wall a painted wooden freeze was installed, depicting latticed windows opposite the real ones, and the ceiling was repainted with Scottish renaissance strapwork displaying various Stuart and Tudor royal badges, together with the initials of King Charles, his queen and his son, the Prince of Wales.

A year after Charles I died on the scaffold, that same Prince of Wales, now Charles II, visited Falkland when he returned to Scotland to be crowned in 1650, and stayed there again in 1651. On his first visit he ordered colours to be presented to the veteran Scottish troops who had been specially chosen to guard him, the Scots Guards; and in 1950, to commemorate the tercentenary of the presentation of the first colours, a special detachment of the regiment laid their tattered colours of 1886-91 to rest in the palace, where they are now enshrined in the chapel royal.

In the following summer Charles II was once again at Falkland, but not in any holiday mood. Cromwell was in Scotland, his army in command of the Lowlands south of the Forth after the Battle of Dunbar. It was at Falkland that Charles II decided on the desperate gamble of a counter-invasion of England behind Cromwell's back – an invasion that came to grief at the Battle of Worcester when Cromwell caught up with the Scots army.

Charles II was the last Stuart to stay in Falkland Palace, indeed the last sovereign to visit Scotland until George IV's celebrated descent on Edinburgh in 1822. In that intervening period, the palace crumbled into a ruinous state of neglect. Cromwell's troops felled the forest of Falkland to build a fort at Perth, and with that the hunting days were over; they accidentally burned down the great hall, so the feasting days were over as well. Sir Iain Moncreiffe of that Ilk felicitously cites the words of Sir David Lindsay of the Mount, Lord Lyon King of Arms, poet and playwright and boyhood friend of King James V:

> Fare weill Faulkland, the forteress of Fyfe,
> Thy polite park under the Lowmound law,
> Sum tyme in thee I led ane lustie lyfe,
> The fallow deir to see them raike in row.

The fact that there is anything at all left of Falkland Palace for us to enjoy today is entirely due to the generous initiative and historical enthusiasm of one remarkable man, John Patrick Crichton Stuart, third Marquess of Bute, who bought the estate of Falkland in 1887. This purchase brought him the custody of Falkland Palace itself as Hereditary Constable, Captain and Keeper on the sovereign's behalf. In the next thirteen years, until his death in 1900, he quite literally saved Falkland from total dereliction.

Lord Bute had inherited his title, and the vast family wealth and estates in Scotland and Wales, in 1848 at the age of six months; he was seventeenth in line of direct descent from King Robert II through one of his illegitimate sons, Sir John Stuart, hereditary sheriff of Bute, Arran and Cumbrae. As an undergraduate at Oxford Lord Bute had become a convert to Roman Catholicism, and he was deeply interested in history and architecture. He restored and partially rebuilt Cardiff Castle and Castell Coch, a thirteenth-century fortress five miles north of Cardiff, as well as Pluscarden Priory in Grampian, but he had a special interest in Falkland. He had already given a lecture to the Associated Societies of Edinburgh University, of which he was honorary president, on the subject of the Duke of Rothesay, son of Robert III, who died so mysteriously at Falkland in 1402. Now, at the age of forty, he had the opportunity of doing something more tangible to disinter a significant feature of Scotland's – and his own – royal heritage. His biographer, Sir David Hunter Blair (*The Marquess of Bute*, 1921), wrote:

He spared neither time nor money in his work of restoring the historic pile to something of its ancient grandeur; and it was said that for a number of years he devoted the whole available income of the estate to his building operations at the palace.

Firstly he restored and panelled the old gatehouse, traditionally the private quarters of the Keeper, whose duty it was to maintain the palace. He rescued the chapel royal, which still had its original sixteenth-century carved oak entrance screen with its slender hand-turned pillars. He reconstructed the old royal pew and the pulpit from fragments he found, dark with age but still showing the red and gold paint of the royal livery of Scotland. He restored the great panelled oak screen behind the altar, the so-called 'chancellory wall' of 1540, and was enchanted when his craftsmen found the name 'Marie Stuart' cut into the reveal of the easternmost window. He rebuilt the cross-house containing the king's bedchamber, recreating all the old walls that determined its original position and proportions. He restored the vaulted cellars and kitchen of the east range. Indeed he wanted to rebuild the whole of the east range with its king's guard hall, presence chamber, privy dining-room, and queen's apartments above – a task that finally daunted even him.

But the third marquess wasn't finished yet. He excavated the foundations of the ruined north range and the original thirteenth-century castle, levelled and terraced the ridge on which they had been built, and constructed containing walls on the remains. He restored the real tennis court. He found an eighteenth-century map showing an orchard north-west of the palace, and promptly planted one there. In the royal burgh itself he restored Brunton House, once the Hereditary Falconer's home, as a local school (it is now in private ownership). And all this work he did with a scrupulous attention to detail and authenticity that was far, far ahead of its time.

His great labour of love was continued by his successor as Hereditary Keeper, his second son, Lord Ninian Crichton Stuart, who furnished the chapel gallery with a set of magnificent seventeenth-century Flemish 'verdure' tapestries, and opened the chapel itself to public worship. Sadly he was killed in action in 1915 in the First World War, and was succeeded by his six-month-old son, Michael – yet another Stuart minority.

As Major Michael Crichton Stuart of the Scots Guards he earned fame during the Second World War with the Long Range Desert Patrol, leading the longest patrol in the recorded history of warfare – more than 4000 miles of enemy territory in forty-five days – and wrote a book about it all called *G Patrol*. Back home after recovering from severe wounds received at the Salerno landing he became the first Keeper for centuries actually to live in the gatehouse of Falkland Palace, where he and his wife raised a family of four children. He died early in January 1981, aged sixty-five.

His contribution to Falkland was no less significant than that of his grandfather, the third marquess. He had the main gardens restored to a layout based on a seventeenth-century engraving of the palace. He renewed the roof over the south range with its precious chapel royal. But he also took particular interest in the 'little houses' around the palace, which are just as steeped in history as the palace itself. He restored, quite superlatively, Moncreif House, immediately facing the palace, which dates from 1610 and is the last surviving thatched house in Falkland. The inscribed 'marriage lintel' over the door was installed on the occasion of the marriage of Nicholl Moncreif, a member of James VI's household who became an important court official as the king's averiman (equerry). The celebrated Praise and Thanks Stone above the door records his gratitude to his king:

All praise to God and thankis to the most excellent monarche of Great Britane of whose princelie liberalitie this is my portioune. Deo laus. Esto fidus. Adest Merces. Nicoll Moncreif. 1610.

Major Crichton Stuart also restored another courtier's dwelling, St Andrew's House, a two-storeyed, harled building of the mid-seventeenth century, on the same side of the street, beside the palace gates, and Key House (dated 1713 on its marriage lintel) which was once the palace inn.

In 1952 the Keeper, in order to ensure the safety and preservation of the palace, appointed the National Trust for Scotland to be Deputy Keeper, and made a substantial endowment for the maintenance of the palace and royal garden 'in all time coming'. One of the Trust's first tasks was to complere the third Marquess of Bute's plan for the interior decoration of the reconstructed king's bedchamber. The designs were done by the Trust's eminent architectural historian Schomberg Scott, and carried out by the Scottish artist David McLure. A timber ceiling was installed once again, and traditional windows with the upper part of leaded glass fixed into the stonework for light, while the lower part was left unglazed, with wooden shutters that open for ventilation.

The ceiling and shutters were painted in the rich colours that all the Stuarts loved, to create what Schomberg Scott called 'what King James v would have recognized and accepted as a royal bedroom for the King of Scots'.

The most striking feature of the room is the magnificent bed, known as the 'golden bed of Brahan', which dates from the early seventeenth century. It is certainly not the bed in which the dying King James v launched his famous last words: 'It cam' wi' a lass, and will gang wi' a lass.' But the bed is eminently fit for a king.

And so, once again, is Falkland Palace.

The sweeping approach to the entrance porch of Haddo House.

HADDO HOUSE
Grampian

THERE IS A DOOR that metaphorically separates the stately grandeur of the public rooms of Haddo House from the small private south wing at present occupied by June, Lady Aberdeen, widow of David, the fourth marquess, tenth earl and last laird of Haddo. On one side of the door everything is serene and elegant, filled with lovingly preserved furnishings, fabrics and portraits: history embalmed. On the other side of the door there is a kind of cheerful bedlam, all dogs and grandchildren and scattered toys; there is shouting, laughing and barking, and a crowded breakfast-room where Lady Aberdeen serves gargantuan meals to three tables of family, friends, visiting musicians and actors, house-guests and unexpected callers.

This is the real Haddo – Home, Sweet Home to a remarkable line of Haddo lairds (including a Prime Minister of Britain, the fourth Earl of Aberdeen), and to the thousands of people who have stayed there down the years. To this day it is the most lived-in of all the National Trust for Scotland properties in the north-east.

When Bruce Millan, then Secretary of State for Scotland, announced the acquisition of Haddo House for the nation in March 1978, he described it as 'one of the grandest mansion houses in Scotland'; and indeed it is. It was designed in 1731 by the architect William Adam (father of even more famous architect sons) and remodelled and refurbished in 1880 in the 'Adam revival' style then fashionable in Victorian circles. Part of the 'grand' house is now used for giving stately home bed-and-breakfasts to shooting-parties and visiting VIPs (what June Aberdeen, with a bubbling sense of humour not always apparent among the aristocracy, wickedly calls 'rent-a-marchioness'); she cooks the meals in her pinny and then appears for dinner in a tiara. But the *real* life of Haddo goes on behind that dividing door and constantly spills out through it – a controlled uproar of family warmth, friendliness and artistic creativity which has made Haddo a major cultural and social centre, and given it a very special place in the hearts of Aberdeenshire folk. Paradoxically, perhaps, it is this essential homeliness that inspires the professionalism of Lady Aberdeen's musical and dramatic productions with the Haddo House Choral and Dramatic Society, that great cultural beacon of the north.

The recorded history of Haddo starts way back in 1469, when the lands were acquired by the Gordons of Methlick (Gordon is still the family name of the marquesses of Aberdeen). They built themselves a residence called the House of Kellie, of which no trace remains. This building was destroyed, or severely damaged, during the turbulent Covenanting era of the Civil Wars of the seventeenth century. The incumbent laird, Sir John Gordon, was a staunch Royalist who was created a baronet of Nova Scotia in 1642 by King Charles I as a reward for his services. Two years later the Covenanters, under the Marquess of Argyll, laid siege to the House of Kellie; it was vigorously defended and surrendered only because of a shortage of food and water. Despite a promise of safe conduct, Sir John was taken prisoner to Edinburgh, where he was incarcerated in a dungeon in the Tolbooth prison adjacent to St Giles High Kirk – 'Haddo's Hole', as the cell came to be known, now commemorated by a plaque in St Giles. After summary trial he was beheaded at Mercat Cross. On the scaffold his last words were: 'I recommend my soul to God, and my six children to His Majesty's care, for whose sake I die this day.' The day was 19 July 1644. Meanwhile, Argyll had garrisoned his troops in Haddo House, and what they could not plunder they destroyed, leaving house and lands in ruins.

After the restoration of the monarchy in 1660 the Gordon title and estates were also restored by a grateful Charles II. They were inherited by the late Sir John's eldest son, another Sir John, who was succeeded in turn by his brother, Sir George Gordon, in 1665. He was a lawyer of outstanding ability who rose to become a Lord of Session in 1680, with the title Lord Haddo. In 1662 he was appointed Lord Chancellor of Scotland, and was made first Earl of Aberdeen in recognition of his own services and his father's devotion to the Stuart cause.

The first earl died in 1720 at the age of eighty-three, rich in years and honours and material things. The eighteenth century was a time of growing prosperity for Scotland after the Union of the Parliaments in 1707, and the Gordon estates blossomed as well. It was his son, William, the second Earl of Aberdeen, who was the true Beginner of Haddo House, for it was he who commissioned William Adam to build it in 1731, either on or near the site of the old House of Kellie, some twenty miles north-west of Aberdeen.

William Adam had been the pupil of Sir William Bruce of Kinross, Surveyor of the Royal Works, an exponent of the neo-classical style, who had rebuilt Holyroodhouse Palace in the 1670s. This became the standard for all types of houses in Scotland, and Adam's drawings in his book *Vitruvius Scoticus* show what he intended for Haddo: a three-storeyed main block, advanced and pedimented in the centre, with a double flight of stairs leading to a main entrance at the first-floor level. On either side were two-storeyed wings linked to the main block by curving colonnades of arches.

It was elegant, it was Italianate, and it would have been great for the Mediterranean. In Aberdeenshire, with its brisk climate, external stairs to a main door opening directly into a sitting-room, and wings without corridors, made for difficulties to say the least. It was like building a Californian swimming-pool in the Arctic. And yet it was a bold and emphatic statement of economic confidence. As Cosmo Gordon of Ellon wrote in his *Souvenir of Haddo*:

Haddo belongs to the time when men recognized with relief that even in Scotland they could live safely in houses with large windows and airy rooms and could forget the tall fortress-like towers many of which had been built in Aberdeenshire less than a century before. It is a house, not a castle, but when first built the new Haddo must have looked as modern to some of the neighbours as constructions of glass and steel look to us today.

opposite, above The design for Haddo House as envisaged by William Adam in 1731. The original entrance was on the first floor, approached by two curving flights of steps.

opposite, below The morning room of Haddo House, formerly the library and study of the Prime Minister Earl of Aberdeen, has an air of relaxed informality. Between the windows is an eighteenth-century Irish bookcase of light wood, painted to represent inlay.

It is arguably the most elegant house in the north-east, a classic English stately home transplanted straight to Scotland.

If the second earl was the Beginner of Haddo, then the third earl was almost the Ruiner. The third earl was George, known to all as the 'wicked earl'.

As far as wicked earls go, the third Earl of Aberdeen was very wicked indeed. He was also extremely competent. He inherited an estate that was already wealthy, and by shrewd management and business acumen he increased his large patrimony immensely. He used the profits to purchase three other great houses – the fortress of Cairnbulg in Buchan, Ellon Castle near Haddo, and Wiscombe Park in Devon. In each of these he installed a mistress (they all had brown eyes, apparently), and with each he raised a flourishing family of children who would later raise a third-generation crop of brown-eyed generals and admirals. If nothing else, one can only admire the stamina of the man!

It was all done at terrible cost to Haddo and his own family. He was an inordinately vain and self-centred man who always referred to himself as 'us' (not even 'we'). To stock his new homes, 'us' plundered Haddo of its furnishings; to conserve his energies, he

abandoned his wife and five children entirely; to pay for his lifestyle, he pillaged Haddo of its income.

At least he had done something to provide for his eldest son and heir, Lord Haddo; he had bought for him the neighbouring estate of Gight (pronounced Gecht) from Mrs Byron, the mother of Lord Byron, last of a dozen violent generations of Gordons of Gight. But now tragedy struck. At the age of twenty-seven, Lord Haddo was killed when his horse threw him, startled by the sudden emergence of a servant-girl from the well. Although so young, he had already had six sons and a daughter by his wife. Lady Haddo had apparently been outspoken in her condemnation of her father-in-law's activities, and after her husband's death the wicked earl cut her off without a shilling, as they used to say. She left Gight, which then fell into decay, and went with her large family to England.

From the entrance hall we can see the portrait of this promising but ill-fated young man dominating the half-landing of the main staircase: a handsome man in a red coat, leaning nonchalantly against a classical balustrade. It was done by Pompeo Batoni, a painter much in fashion among aristocrats making the European Grand Tour.

The accident occurred in 1791. At the time, Lord Haddo's eldest son and heir (and now, as a result, heir to the wicked earl's earldom as well) was a boy of seven: George Gordon, destined to become the most famous member of the family as the fourth Earl of Aberdeen, Prime Minister of Great Britain from 1852 to 1855. He also turned out to be the Salvager of Haddo.

As the fatherless heir to a great earldom, the new Lord Haddo was brought up with great care in the magic circle of people in high places. His joint guardians were William Pitt the Younger and the first Viscount Melville, the 'Iron Man' of Scottish politics in the late eighteenth century. A career in politics for the fledgling Lord Haddo was almost a foregone conclusion, especially when he proved himself to be a young man of much brilliance and ability.

The wicked earl (the third) died in 1801, and Lord Haddo succeeded his grandfather as fourth Earl of Aberdeen at the age of seventeen. In 1805 he paid his first visit to Haddo House to inspect his patrimony. What he saw came as a profound shock to him. The great forests and parklands had been denuded of trees. There was a a carpet of peat-moss threatening to drown the house and grounds. The house itself, long abandoned, was practically derelict, and the interior, as he wrote to a friend, was 'of appalling badness'. He almost threw in his hand there and then, we are told; but instead he set himself the task of restoring the house to its former glory. He had the peat-moss removed and drained; he planted no fewer than fourteen million trees; he commissioned James Giles, the noted Scottish artist, to landscape the policies into what Cosmo Gordon has called its present 'ordered beauty'. He improved the estate greatly and built new farmhouses. He turned the restoration of Haddo into a lifelong personal crusade.

All this he had to do during brief vacation visits in summer, for he was already getting involved in political life. He was elected to Parliament as a Scottish representative peer in 1806; by 1813 he was the British Ambassador in Vienna, charged with the delicate and difficult task of arranging the terms on which the Great Powers of Russia, Prussia, Austria and Britain would join forces to defeat Napoleon. He was only twenty-nine years old.

There is a portrait of him in his twenties, by Sir Thomas Lawrence, hanging on the wall opposite the fireplace in the ante-room that adjoins the drawing-room. It is painted in the 'Byronic' style fashionable at the time, and shows a dashing young man, dramatically handsome, with the looks of a matinée idol – and that is precisely what he might have become. As an undergraduate at St John's College, Cambridge, he was a leading figure in amateur theatricals. The story is told that when one of the actors in the local repertory company was taken ill, the young earl applied to fill the part under an assumed name, and got it. After the performance the manager said, 'Look here, Mr So-

and-So, you've evidently got the right notion of acting, and if you'll join my company I'll help you to a career on the stage.' Mr So-and-So declined, on the ground of other and more pressing engagements. But he never lost his interest in acting, and enjoyed a long friendship with the actor John Philip Kemble, who often stayed at Haddo to recuperate from his celebrated bouts of dissipation. There is a portrait of him, also by Sir Thomas Lawrence, in the dining-room.

The ante-room is what one might loosely call the 'political room' at Haddo, dedicated to memories of the fourth earl's career. The rather funereal marble bust of Queen Victoria above the Adam chimneypiece was presented to him by the queen herself in 1855 when he resigned as Prime Minister. There are portraits of many of Lord Aberdeen's political mentors and colleagues – William Pitt the Younger, the Duke of Wellington, Lord Castlereagh, Sir Robert Peel, the Marquess of Londonderry, Lord Bathurst; there is also a portrait of the French Minister of State, M. Guizot, painted by Paul de la Roche and presented to Guizot himself. It was with Guizot that Lord Aberdeen, as Foreign Secretary, worked hard to establish an accord with France; and it was during their talks at Haddo that Lord Aberdeen is said to have coined the felicitous phrase *entente cordiale*.

He was Foreign Secretary twice, first under Wellington (1828–30) and then under Peel (1841-8). In 1852 he was 'called' to the post of Prime Minister of a coalition government after the resignation of Lord Derby. His ministry was immensely successful and popular at first; but then came the Crimean War of 1853-6. After much heart-searching, Lord Aberdeen committed Britain to an alliance with France and Turkey against Russia, and joined the war in 1854. The gross military mismanagement of the war forced Lord Aberdeen's resignation from office in February 1855; the trauma of the decision to declare war left terrible scars, and it is said that after it he never smiled for the rest of his life (he died five years later, in 1860).

Not that he had very much to smile about by this time, anyway. The golden promise of his youth never materialized in his personal life. He married twice; his first wife, Catherine, daughter of the first Marquess of Abercorn, bore him three beautiful daughters, on whom he doted – there is an enchanting portrait of them by George Hayter on the inner wall of the main staircase. But tuberculosis carried off first his wife and then all his children, one by one. His second marriage, through a bewildering skein of kinships, was to the Marquess of Abercorn's widowed daughter-in-law; but his new wife, Harriet, refused to live at Haddo House. It must have been a dreadful disappointment to the laird who had lavished so much love and hard work on rescuing Haddo from dereliction.

Another portrait of him, painted while he was in office by Graham Watson, hangs in the dining-room, which is very much the family portrait gallery. The change in him from that handsome Byronic youth is most striking and curiously moving. Here we see a man of stern, austere, unsmiling mien, a man of unbending will as the public saw him; but behind the mask there was a man capable of great passion and great affection whose life became unbearably shadowed with sorrow.

After Lord Aberdeen's death in 1860 there came a strange and even bizarre hiatus in the family fortunes of the Gordons of Haddo. The fifth earl, George, eldest son of that unsatisfactory second marriage, had poor health and died at the age of forty-seven only three years after he succeeded to the title. He and his wife Mary, on whom the Prime Minister Earl had bestowed all his love and affection in his later years (the elegant Broadwood piano in the drawing-room was one of his gifts to her), had three sons – George, James and John; and it was their remarkable and totally diverse lives (and deaths) that were to have a decisive and lasting effect on the Haddo story. This was the major watershed.

They were all high-spirited and adventurous lads. George, the eldest, and James, the

above The curving corridor of Haddo House.

above right The grand staircase. On the half-landing is a large portrait of the young Lord Haddo, killed in a riding accident in 1791 at the age of twenty-seven.

right Queen Victoria slept here, in the room now known as the queen's bedroom.

middle brother, were both mad about guns and boats – twin obsessions that would eventually prove the tragic undoing of each of them. George's idea of fun was firing a pistol from his bed at a mark on an envelope held by his brother James (William Tell brought up-to-date). They both shot for Scotland, and James rowed for Cambridge in the 1867 Boat Race. One summer during a family holiday at St Leonard's-on-Sea the two boys hired a rowing-boat and disappeared until the afternoon of the following day; they had been to Boulogne and back!

When George succeeded his father as the sixth Earl of Aberdeen, he was on his way home from Canada, where he had been working as a lumberjack after completing his first year at St Andrew's University. He stayed at Haddo for a year, and built the present church at Methlick; then in 1866 he disappeared to America – for good. He had a craving that would not be denied for a life at sea, and a life of anonymity. He discarded his title, and under the alias of George H. Osborne he signed on as an ordinary seaman in Boston and worked his way in small cargo ships for four years before taking his master's certificate. He wrote long and affectionate letters to his family, but never revealed his alias to them.

Then, in 1870, the letters stopped abruptly. His mother, Lady Mary, became so worried at this silence that she sent an agent across to America to try to trace him. After a long search it transpired that a certain 'Captain G. H. Osborne' was in fact the missing Sailor Earl – but that he was not only missing, but dead. He had been washed overboard and drowned while sailing as first mate on a three-masted Boston schooner, the *Hera*, en route to Melbourne, in January 1870. He was only twenty-eight years old.

It was a second cruel blow for Lady Aberdeen. Two years earlier her second son, blond and handsome James, who would now have become the seventh earl, had been killed at Cambridge – in a shooting accident, of course. And so the earldom of Aberdeen descended to the third brother, John – and with that began a remarkable and very long new chapter in the history of Haddo.

John Campbell Gordon, seventh Earl of Aberdeen (and later first Marquess of Aberdeen) was to be laird of Haddo for sixty-four busy and constructive years. He would have a distinguished career of public service, as Viceroy of Ireland twice (in 1886 and from 1905 to 1915) and as Governor-General of Canada (1893–8). And he would marry a determined and forceful wife, Ishbel, daughter of the first Baron Tweedmouth. Their happy fifty-seven year union would become a legend in the north-east; where the wicked earl had referred to himself as 'us', they always called themselves, in broad dialect, 'We twa'' – and that was the title of the engaging joint autobiography they published in 1925.

It was on 1 June 1878 that the seventh earl brought his bride to Haddo House after a honeymoon in Egypt that had been deliberately prolonged so that Ishbel could see her new home in the warmth of summer. In fact the weather was as bleak and forbidding as a day in March, and the new countess had to sit in an open carriage facing a biting north-easterly wind all the way from Aberdeen, her face as blue as her velvet dress.

But what an entrance, nonetheless. The open barouche was drawn by four horses with postillions. Several miles before Haddo they were met by a huge escort of two hundred mounted tenantry, some on the great Clydesdales that pulled the Haddo ploughs, others on tiny Shetland ponies. They all fell in before and behind the carriage and ushered it in triumph the rest of the way to the house, where another huge crowd of tenants waited with their families. When the French Minister, M. Guizot, had visited Haddo as a guest of the fourth earl, he had commented on 'cette grande existence féodal' ('this great feudal life'); it was certainly all of that, and more. The Haddo estates had nearly a thousand tenants.

One of the first major undertakings of their married life was to remodel and modernize Haddo House itself, no doubt at the prompting of the beautiful young wife. Haddo was

The great library of Haddo House, furbished by the seventh earl and Countess Ishbel – 'We twa''.

eminently unsuited to the rigours of the Aberdeenshire climate, thanks to William Adam's Italianate design of having two sweeping stone staircases at the front of the house leading via a narrow main entrance on the first floor directly into the ante-room. Lady Ishbel recalled how this entrance let in a blast of cold air that went right through the house when the door was opened, and 'tended to cause confusion to guests arriving from a distance, who suddenly found themselves ushered into the drawing-room with all their wraps, through what appeared to be a window'. In the new design prepared by Wardrop and Reid of Edinburgh, a new entrance hall was made on the ground floor with a spacious porch, the outside stone stairways were removed and a new internal grand staircase built instead. New wings were built for the servants' quarters and nurseries, for Lady Ishbel had been appalled by the dankness of the atmosphere and the dampness of the curtains in the old Haddo nurseries on the ground floor. The first bathrooms were also installed, and the whole house redecorated from top to bottom.

Not content with this major undertaking, the Aberdeens also built a chapel adjoining the house, designed by Sir George Street (the designer of the Law Courts in London). Haddo chapel, which was completed in 1881, was his last work, a simple but very graceful building. To build a church had been one of the Prime Minister Earl's dearest ambitions; but weighed down with the guilt he felt over the Crimean War, he deemed himself unworthy, like David in the Bible, to build a house for the Lord. His son George, the 'Sailor Earl', had built Methlick Church for him; now 'We twa'' built a non-denominational house of prayer which has been an integral part not just of the architecture of Haddo House but of family life there for precisely a hundred years. It was 'We twa'' who started the tradition, still carried on to this day at Haddo, of Sunday evening services conducted by ministers of different denominations, with music played on the fine Father Willis organ, and bible lessons read by whichever talented actors or musicians happen to be staying at Haddo.

Financially, all this building and rebuilding was a crippling drain on the estate, and eventually, in 1920, 'We twa'' had to sell off 45,000 acres to make ends meet. In their autobiography they wrote, a little ruefully, 'Whether we would have undertaken this vast transformation had we known our future, and the times that were coming, is another matter'.

Despite this huge expenditure on Haddo itself, 'We twa'' never stinted their expenses in filling their grand new-look house with a constant stream of guests. Statesmen, scholars, musicians, actors, evangelists, and representatives of the thousand and one causes that the Aberdeens supported, chaired, patronized or trusteed, all came to stay at Haddo during the long summer months. Gladstone was a frequent visitor. So were Henry Drummond, the evangelist preacher; that great American-Scottish evangelical team of Moody and Sankey; the founder of the Society for the Prevention of Cruelty to Children; the organizer of the White Cross Unions for Men; and representatives of movements ranging from the newly formed Boys' Brigade (Lord Aberdeen was its honorary president) to the Lily Band for Halftime Workers and the Women's Industrial Council, of which Countess Ishbel was president.

All this was in addition to the round of public duties and patronage and entertaining at Dublin Castle during the periods of viceroyship in Ireland, where their genial charm made them amazingly popular at a time when anti-British feeling was running high. There is a delightful painting at the head of the grand staircase at Haddo of the seventh earl's two younger sons, Dudley and Archie, dutifully posed on a wheelbarrow of Irish potatoes and entitled *Two Little Home Rulers*. Of the two little boys, Dudley would eventually inherit Haddo after his elder brother George; Archie was killed in a motoring accident. There is a bust of him in Haddo Chapel, and it is his figure that tops the American War Memorial in Princes Street Gardens in Edinburgh.

But whatever the pomp and circumstance of the Aberdeens' public life, there was always a very special bond between the ordinary folk of Haddo and their most amiable laird and his wife. Apart from some endearing eccentricities of behaviour, this was surely because they shared and showed a very real sense of social concern for the community. That's why, in the 1880s, 'We twa'' organized evening classes to give farm girls some recreation and further education. Committees were formed in all the surrounding districts to give tuition in history, geography, literature, domestic science, needlework and knitting. University examiners were brought in to award marks and certificates. Choirs were formed, plays performed, concerts held. Then came the Household Club for all the Haddo House servants, who paid an annual subscription of a shilling (children free) to join a choir conducted by the head forester, a woodcarving class led by the Haddo governess, a drawing class run by the butler, a sewing class run by the nurse, a reading circle, an ambulance class, or various sports clubs including cricket, football and tennis.

To accommodate all these activities in 1890 'We twa'' built what was in effect a community centre – an enormous wooden shed, Canadian style, which turned out, quite by accident, to be acoustically perfect. It was large enough to house an indoor tennis court and many other activities besides; it was the genesis of the Arts Centre at Haddo that flourishes so bravely to this day.

In 1816 the seventh Earl of Aberdeen was created first Marquess of Aberdeen and Temair (the ancient form of Tara, in Ireland) for his public services. Four years later they sold off the 45,000 acres to raise the capital needed to pay their bills, and retreated to the House of Cromar (now known as Alastrean House, a guest-house for RAF officers) near Tarland, leaving Haddo and a residue of 14,000 acres to their eldest son George, Earl of Haddo. George succeeded to the titles when his father died in 1934 at the age of eighty-seven. The other half of the 'We twa'' partnership, Lady Ishbel, died in 1939, aged eighty-two.

George, the second marquess (and eighth earl), worked hard to rescue the impoverished estate from the effects of his parents' lavish overspending. During the Second World War he turned Haddo House into a wartime maternity home for evacuee mothers, and 1500 babies were born there. He succeeded his father as Lord Lieutenant of Aberdeenshire, and was a kenspeckle figure at all important occasions in the north-east. To the family he was the much-loved 'Uncle Geordie', or 'Uncle Doddie' in the vernacular.

Uncle Doddie had no children, so when he died in 1965 he was succeeded as third marquess (and ninth earl) by his younger brother Dudley, the 'Little Home Ruler'. But long before that, in 1944, he had handed over the estate of Haddo to his nephew, David, Dudley's oldest son; and with that we come to the last great flowering of Haddo as a private house.

David Gordon of Haddo, the last of the old-style lairds of Haddo (he became fourth marquess and tenth earl in 1972 when his father Dudley died) was no less remarkable than any of his ancestors. When he was a seventeen-year-old at Harrow he fell for his housemaster's daughter, Beatrice Mary June Boissier, and there and then determined that one day they would marry. He realized he would have to wait a bit, though – she was only eleven years old at the time!

They married eventually in 1939. June Aberdeen remembers vividly her confused emotions at her first sight of Haddo House in 1938: she was enchanted, overawed – and dismayed. Once again the great house was in disarray, and hopelessly antiquated; nothing had been done in it or for it for years and years. When the Aberdeens moved in, in 1945, their most pressing task was to make the house a proper home again, and revitalize the estate. And yet 'Haddo was still in the Edwardian era, but even then it had a charm that wound itself round my heart, and has persisted ever since'.

It meant an enormous amount of hard work, literally from dawn to dusk, for this latter-day version of 'We twa''. But they did it. David was a fully trained land agent, which stood him in good stead when he came to modernize the whole estate, farm by farm.

When Uncle Doddie died in 1965, David became Lord Haddo. But to one and all he was simply 'the laird'. He was a tremendously affable man, with a twinkling sense of humour and the ability to speak with everyone alike, from ordinary country people to the monarch, a quality that endeared him to all.

David and June also worked hard to make Haddo into a major cultural centre, through the Haddo House Choral and Operatic Society. That had been David's idea from the start, greatly reinforced by the fact that June was a trained musician, educated at the Royal College of Music and a highly proficient conductor. While he was still on active service in the Middle East during the war he had written to his wife about his idea, saying it was to be the first thing they would do when the war was over. And sure enough, it was.

The sound of music and laughter was heard again at Haddo. The expansive Haddo tradition of courtesy, kindness and friendly welcome was rekindled. The grounds and rooms where Kemble had wandered once more played host to visiting players of all kinds. David leaned his powerful bass voice into the choral works, and delighted in taking stage roles; June herself acted, stage-managed and conducted, working tirelessly (as she still does) to attract top artistes to come and perform at Haddo.

The story of that noble and flourishing enterprise can be read in detail in a marvellous little booklet by the late Eric Linklater, entitled *The Music of the North*. And it will surely continue to flourish as a part of Haddo life, even though Haddo House itself is now in the care of the National Trust for Scotland, and even though David Aberdeen is no more. He died in 1974 at the untimely age of sixty-six.

Long before he died, David Aberdeen had realized that it was becoming almost impossible to meet the cost of running the stateliest home in the north-east, and had expressed the wish that Haddo House should be made over to the nation. You have to love a house like Haddo very much indeed to devote your life to running it; but you have to love it even more to give it up.

So while Mrs Iona Lean and her guides escort the thousands of visitors through the public rooms and retell the story of the Gordons of Haddo, June, Marchioness of Aberdeen, continues her labours of love for music and the arts – and for Haddo – on both sides of that dividing door.

And Haddo House sings.

Hill of Tarvit, an Edwardian country house in Fife.

HILL OF TARVIT
Fife

HILL OF TARVIT in the undulating northern reaches of the ancient kingdom of Fife is not a mountain but a modest mansion – though a very special one. It is a relatively modern country house fit for a fortune, indeed a house specifically designed to fit a fortune. That fortune was originally amassed in the nineteenth century by a Dundee jute manufacturer called John Sharp, one of the Victorian magnates who helped to make Dundee a major industrial city (the city of 'jam, jute and journalism' as the old saying has it). It was consolidated by Frederick Bower Sharp, the youngest of his four sons, who devoted much of his own share of the £750,000 Sharp legacy in 1895 to accumulating a splendid new house to accommodate it. That was how Hill of Tarvit, just across the waters of the Firth of Tay, came about.

The Sharps were fond of saying that they 'came out of the mud of the Tay'. Certainly, they were the product of a city that had suffered remarkable ups and downs throughout its long and crowded history. The Romans had been there, and established their forward camps in the district. It always had strategic geographical importance as a point of defence for central Scotland, and this strategic position was to cost it dear during the embattled centuries when kings of Scotland and kings of England would struggle for control of northern Britain. King Edward I, the Hammer of the Scots, sacked the town in 1296. It was sacked again in 1385 when King Richard II invaded Scotland, and yet again in 1547 during the 'Rough Wooing' by King Henry VIII of the infant Mary Queen of Scots on behalf of his young son Edward, the future King Edward VI. The trouble was that Dundee, commanding the Firth of Tay and the hinterland of the Grampians, was a convenient turning-point for invaders, who would wreak havoc on it, time and again, before retracing their steps to England. The final terrible blow came in 1651 when Cromwell's great general, George Monk, savaged the town as an exemplary punishment to Scotland for having dared to proclaim Charles II king.

The cruel destruction and massacre of 1651 virtually destroyed Dundee's economy. It had been based on a tidy combination of fishing by the menfolk and linen-weaving by the womenfolk. While the men were away fishing, or whaling in Icelandic waters, the women employed themselves in spinning locally grown flax and weaving it into linen cloth. After General Monk's visitation, however, Dundee spent the next century in the direst poverty. The fishing went on, but the local flax merchants lacked the capital to restore the weaving industry. They could only import the cheapest Russian flax available for spinning, and then weave it into the poorest grades of coarse sacking.

Nonetheless, this coarse cloth began to find an export market, particularly for the plantations in America, where it was used to clothe the slaves. The American War of Independence of 1775-83 had a catastrophic effect on Scottish trade, particularly the tobacco trade on which Glasgow was waxing fat. But the Dundee coarse cloth trade managed to survive; and then, in the 1820s came the start of the revolutionary new process that was to transform Dundee into a major industrial city – and was also to help the Sharp family emerge 'out of the mud of the Tay'.

In 1824 the Honourable East India Company, ever vigilant for new market outlets, sent to a linen manufacturer in Dundee a few bales of an unfamiliar Indian fibre called jute. It wasn't very successful at first as it was difficult to work, and it was neglected until someone conceived the idea of steeping it in whale oil, an existing by-product of the other main Dundee industry; with that, jute came into its own. The trade statistics tell a vivid story of entrepreneurial expansion: imports of jute from India rose from 4000 bales in 1836 to 289,000 bales in 1850. The late Moray McLaren wrote in his *Shell Guide to Scotland* (1965):

It was this combination of readily supplied whale-oil and the technical skill of weaving coarse cloth cheaply, plus an abundance of skilled female workers, that established Dundee as the world centre of the jute industry.

And Dundee itself grew fast; from a town of 35,000 people it became a city of 130,000 in less than half a century, as people poured in from the countryside and over from Ireland to find work in the new jute mills after the disastrous potato famines of the 1840s.

It is now that the Sharps begin to appear. In 1836 a patent was granted to Mr John Sharp for 'certain machinery for converting ropes into tow, and certain improvements in certain machinery for preparing hemp or flax for spinnning, part of which improvements are also applicable to the preparing of cotton, wool and silk for spinning'. It meant that anyone who installed this improved machinery had to pay Mr John Sharp £100 for the privilege.

Not much is known about this John Sharp, the grandfather of Frederick Bower Sharp, except that he was born in 1788 the eldest son of the seven children of William Sharp and Isabella Kinnear of Fingask, and that he studied at Heidelberg University in Germany. He started spinning on his own account in 1845, but he does not seem to have been a particularly successful businessman; it is noticeable that his new patent in 1836 was for hemp and flax production, not jute. When he died he was hopelessly in debt. It was his son, another John Sharp, born in 1824, who laid the foundations of the Sharp fortunes as jute manufacturers.

He was born at the right time. As he came into manhood the Dundee jute boom was beginning to take off. Jute factories were being built all over the place, and the mill owners were rapidly becoming very rich indeed. Just as Glasgow had had its tobacco lords and now its new cotton lords, so Dundee had its jute princes. And just as in Glasgow, where the rich merchants had moved to the western outskirts to escape from the slum tenements that housed their workers in the crowded factory areas, so the Dundee jute princes moved out into the green fields and salubrious breezes of the Firth of Tay. Some moved across the Firth altogether and built themselves mansions at the original ferry terminal of Tayport. Others, in order to be within reach of their factories, moved no further than Broughty Ferry and its sandy beaches on the Tay to the east of Dundee. By the end of the nineteenth century it was said that the two most wealthy residential areas in Britain were the homes of the cotton kings in Bowden, near Manchester, and the jute princes in Broughty Ferry. Broughty Ferry, 'suburb of Dundee', was believed to contain more wealth than any area of corresponding size in Scotland.

One of the jute merchants who made the prestigious move to Broughty Ferry was John Sharp junior, who had revived his father's business by switching to jute. As the available machinery improved, he found new markets for his sackcloth and bagging; when the American Civil War of 1861 threatened to destroy the market for sacks for the cotton produce of the southern plantations, he ingeniously started a new export line – supplying sandbags for both sides in the war.

John Sharp junior married well, as they say. His bride was Christian Bower, the

opposite Scotstarvit Tower, a sixteenth-century tower house about a mile to the west of Hill of Tarvit. Gaunt and empty now, it can be visited; the key is kept at Hill of Tarvit.

daughter of a wealthy flax merchant in Perth (nothing like keeping the business in the family). It was the sort of dynastic marriage that landed magnates throughout the Middle Ages had always favoured to increase their estates and power, now brought up to date by the changing social conditions of the Industrial Revolution. He built a large Victorian mansion in Broughty Ferry called Fernhall (it was demolished in the 1930s); later he also bought the estate of Balmuir, one of the old Claverhouse estates on the northern outskirts of Dundee, and liked to style himself 'John Sharp of Balmuir'. When he died in 1895 he left some £750,000 – 'a cool three-quarters of a million' as one of his great-grandsons, Stephen Sharp, himself a City man, puts it; 'A huge fortune for those days'. Even so, the Sharps were by no means at the head of the Dundee jute league, which was then dominated by the Coxes, the Grimonds, the Walkers, the Ogilvies, the Gilroys and the Cairds.

Jo Grimond MP, former leader of the Liberal Party, is a product of the jute-making Grimonds of Dundee, and has written about the jute princes of the nineteenth century with characteristic directness in his *Memoirs* (1979):

They built themselves Scots baronial houses in Broughty Ferry or further afield and vied with each other over their carriages, shrubberies and villas. Now they are gone and so are their chimneys and villas. They were a tough lot. They achieved much. But let no one be taken in by nostalgia when considering Scottish cities. They had confidence and capacity but under their reign Dundee was ridden with slums and poverty.

By a curious coincidence, happy or ironic depending on which way you want to look at it, it was to be Jo Grimond who would be instrumental in ensuring that Hill of Tarvit, the Sharp showcase, came to the National Trust for Scotland.

John Sharp junior had four sons and two daughters. The four boys all entered the family business of John Sharp & Sons, Milne Street Mill, Dundee. The eldest, also named John, was born in 1855; he succeeded his father as 'the boss' and also succeeded to the estate at Balmuir. The second son, Robert, who remained a bachelor all his life, worked steadily as a director of the firm. The third son, William, was rather less assiduous: he made his name as a cricketer with Forfarshire, and spent a lot of time playing golf. He travelled a lot in the south of France, where he started a golf club in the village of St Jean de Luz and even had a square named after him, the *Place de W. R Sharp*.

It was the fourth and youngest son, Frederick Bower Sharp, who was to make the most lasting impact. He was born in 1862 and went to school at Clifton College in Bristol, where one of his classmates was later to become Earl Haig, a lifelong friend. He joined his elder brothers in the family firm in due course, but he was essentially a financier rather than a mill-owner. He trained in the City of London in the office of Lord Armitstead. When he came home to Dundee, his interest was mainly in investment trusts. He became chairman of the Alliance Trust Company of Dundee, one of the earliest investment trusts in Scotland, and a director of the Investors' Mortgage Security Company of Edinburgh. His shrewd financier's eye made him invest heavily in the railway boom; he became a director of the Caledonian Railway, and when it was merged with the London-Midland-Scottish he served on the central board for several years. He had a gold pass on his watchchain that from 1915 onwards allowed him free travel by rail anywhere, even as far as Paris. Tragically, it was to be on the railways that his only son, Hugh, was to be killed in the Castlecary disaster in 1937.

Frederick Sharp lived the life that befitted a wealthy Victorian and Edwardian gentleman of finance. He became an avid art collector and connoisseur. He played golf a lot (he was a member of the Royal and Ancient at St Andrews, the golfing capital of the world). He was suitably generous to deserving causes: he and his brother Robert made it possible for Sir James McKenzie to found the McKenzie Institute for Clinical Research in St Andrews, and helped to fund the Maternity Unit at Dundee Royal Infirmary which was opened in 1930. According to his obituary notice in the *Fife Almanac* of 1933, 'Each New Year he provided a treat in the form of a Dinner and Concert for the old folks of Cupar, and many cases of distress throughout the year were anonymously relieved by Mr Sharp.'

Like so many others, he waited until he had established himself before thinking of marriage. He was in his thirties before he chose as his bride Beatrice White of Castle Huntly, a sister of his eldest brother John's wife, Eleanor. He was thirty-five when their first child, Hugh, was born in 1897, and forty-seven when a second child – a daughter, Elizabeth – arrived in 1910.

In 1904 Frederick Sharp decided that his estate was now such as to deserve a more prestigious home in which to house his family and his art collection. He bought an old house called Wemyss Hall, set in five hundred acres of forest and farmland some two miles south of Cupar, the county town of Fife, which was within easy reach of St Andrews and had a good rail service across the Tay Bridge to Dundee.

Wemyss Hall was a modest building originally erected in 1696 and attributed to Sir William Bruce of Balcaskie, Surveyor of the Royal Works, who had rebuilt the Palace of Holyroodhouse in Edinburgh for King Charles II in the 1670s. A large service wing had been added behind it in Victorian times. About a mile to the west across the public road through the estate stood (and still stands) its ancient predecessor, Scotstarvit Tower, a residential tower house built around the middle of the sixteenth century and embellished early in the seventeenth century by Sir John Scot, lawyer and man of letters, author of a series of uninhibited biographical sketches of his countrymen entitled *Scot of Scotstarvet's Staggering State of the Scots Statesmen*. The tower itself is now a gaunt and empty landmark rising for five storeys to a cap-house with an unusual conical stone roof; it is owned by the National Trust for Scotland, under the guardianship of the Scottish Development Department (Ancient Monuments), and the key is available at Hill of Tarvit. An even more notable literary landmark used to be a feature of the area: The Mount, just north of Cupar, which was the home of Sir David Lindsay of The Mount, author of the celebrated *Ane Pleasant Satyre of the Thrie Estates*. An edited version of *The Three Estates* was produced by Tyrone Guthrie and created a sensation at the first Edinburgh Festival in 1947; its very first performance, in the open air (and lasting all of nine hours), had taken place on what is now the playground of Castlehill School in Cupar in 1535. Only a dozen miles to the south-west is Falkland Palace, royal retreat of the Stuarts.

This was the historic area of Fife where Frederick Bower Sharp in 1904 decided to built his home to fit a fortune. According to *Country Life* (28 December 1912) he had to make a conscious choice between the two existing buildings on his land, Wemyss Hall and Scotstarvit Tower, as the nucleus for the new house he wanted. He chose Wemyss Hall:

For modern habitation it seems more reasonable to build in that more humane manner that grew out of the revival of letters and broadening of sympathies which was summed up in the full Renaissance. For this reason, and as well as for the more practical one that an old Keep forms a difficult nucleus for a modern home, the choice of Wemyss Hall rather than Scotstarvit as site and architectural influence for Hill of Tarvit seems altogether wise.

To give shape to his dream house, Frederick Sharp commissioned the Scottish architect Robert Lorimer, then forty years old and soon to be knighted for his work on the Thistle Chapel in St Giles Cathedral in Edinburgh. In their different ways they were both deeply conservative men: Sharp because he was conserving and husbanding a great Victorian legacy of wealth and manners and bringing it into Edwardian times, Lorimer because he was conserving and modernizing a great Scottish architectural tradition he had learned to love at his family home not far away, Kellie Castle.

The remodelling of Wemyss Hall as Hill of Tarvit led to such extensive rebuilding as to

The baronial hall, richly panelled in warm oak.

amount to a virtually new house. The existing structure stood a little way up a slope that faced south across a broad expanse of fields. Lorimer built an entirely new, two-storeyed 'front house', leaving the Victorian extensions behind it for use as service quarters. He put the main entrance on the left (west) side of the house within an arcade of three arches. In the public rooms within he had to provide a baronial hall to house fine Flemish tapestries and Jacobean furniture, a drawing-room to set off an important collection of French furniture, and a dining-room of the Regency period.

The front south-facing rooms were all given elegant French windows opening on to a balustraded terrace. This terrace overlooked terraced gardens, to which Lorimer, with his close interest in garden design, paid a great deal of attention (and for which Frederick Sharp paid a great deal of money). The terrace below, approached through a carefully shaped passage of yews, was a long lawn on which croquet was played on summer evenings. Below that, another terrace provided a grass tennis court, with a hard court beside it. At the foot of the walled garden there was a curling-pond. The fields beyond were converted into a nine-hole golf course (it has now reverted to agricultural use). It all conjures up a marvellously vivid picture of Edwardian life in its heyday, as does the house of Hill of Tarvit itself.

The most striking aspect of the house is undoubtedly the lofty baronial hall, carefully and precisely designed to carry two magnificent sixteenth-century tapestries, one showing Alexander the Great receiving the wife and daughters of the defeated King Darius III of Persia after the Battle of Gaugemala in 331 BC, the other a lively hunting-scene, with a little dog in the bottom right-hand corner cheekily cocking a leg. The warm oak panelling, carved with a motif of vines as in the plaster ceiling of the vine room in Kellie Castle, was executed by William Scott Morton of Edinburgh at a cost of £6000. There are some truly splendid pieces of seventeenth- and eighteenth-century furniture in the hall, some fine Old Masters on the walls, and many good Chinese vases, porcelains and bronzes (including a duck-shaped incense burner that emits smoke both fore and aft). It should be an awesome and overpowering chamber, but surprisingly it isn't. It gives off a remarkably homely feeling, as indeed does the whole house, making visitors feel that if they had the odd bob or two themselves they could easily imagine themselves putting their feet up and settling there comfortably.

Off the baronial hall, the drawing-room provides a startling contrast. It is all in white, for one thing, to provide a cool setting for eighteenth-century French furniture and *objets d'art*. It has an elaborate plaster ceiling, executed by the Edinburgh craftsman Thomas Beattie who did so much notable work for Lorimer. The walls are hung with choice paintings – a Breughel, an Allan Ramsay, a Fantin-Latour and many others – but among them are two rather more intimate and homely pictures: a pastel portrait of Beatrice White Sharp, and another of her son Hugh at the age of seven, in kilt and Eton collar, both done in Florence in 1904 when Frederick Sharp was contemplating and planning his new house.

There is another fine plaster ceiling in the library, this one executed by another of Lorimer's favourite craftsmen, Sam Wilson, and yet another superb collection of paintings: two Raeburns, no fewer than four Allan Ramsays, a Fantin-Latour, a George Morland, an Albert Cuyp, all looking down on a roomful of furniture from the time of George III. The sideboard carries a framed photograph of Hugh Sharp in his thirties, looking extremely personable. It was probably due to him that the room came to be known as the library, for whereas his father had collected antiques and Old Masters, Hugh Sharp built up a collection of rare first editions of books, both British and American, which were presented to the National Library of Scotland after his death.

The dining-room breathes another contrasting atmosphere. It is an elegant room of Chippendale and Regency furniture, with yet another elaborate plaster ceiling, again executed by Thomas Beattie, with an appropriate motif of foliage and acorns and

above left The drawing-room, specially designed to house Frederick Sharp's collection of French furniture. Above the fireplace hangs a pastel portrait of his son, Hugh Sharp, at the age of seven.

above right A portrait of Frederick Sharp in his sixties, by Gordon Shields.

left The table in the dining-room, featur a huge nineteenth-century German silv galleon, can concertina into a small side table.

depicting the initials of Frederick Sharp and his wife Beatrice White, and the date, 1905. The dining-table, which features a huge German silver galleon, is an ingenious contraption patented early in the nineteenth century, which concertinas into a small side-table. The paintings on the wall are few but effective, especially a mouth-watering seventeenth-century still-life of a cold supper – ham, fruit and wine – by William Heda.

Frederick Sharp's old smoking-room, complete with a billiard table, is now furnished as a sitting-room, in which smoking by visitors is strongly discouraged. The ornate stone fireplace came from a garret room in nearby Scotstarvit Tower, with the date 1627 and the initials of Sir John Scot and those of his wife Anne Drummond, sister of the poet William Drummond of Hawthornden. The smoking-room is approached through an alcove, and in this alcove there hangs a portrait in oils, done by Gordon Shields in 1927, of the founder of Hill of Tarvit himself, Frederick Bower Sharp; it shows a dignified silver-haired gentleman in his sixties with a military moustache stiffly brushed and waxed sideways. One of the paintings in the smoking-room – *The Blackheath Golfers* – is a reminder that Frederick Sharp, according to his great-nephew Stephen Sharp, had his interest in art originally fired by collecting pictures of golfing subjects. In the drawing-room there is also a considerable collection of seventeenth-century Dutch scenes of skaters playing golf.

Mr and Mrs Sharp probably used the south-west bedroom and dressing-room upstairs, which are now open to the public. The bedroom has the original 1905 Lorimer fireplace and most of the original electrical fittings, with the exception of the chandelier. The centre of the ceiling forms a deep dome which creates an extraordinary acoustic effect as one walks beneath it, like going through an echo-chamber. Both rooms have been redecorated as closely to the originals as possible; and they, like the gallery landing, are also hung with paintings from the Sharp collection.

In this beautiful house, in these elegant Edwardian surroundings and among all these artistic treasures, Mr and Mrs Frederick Sharp made their home with young Hugh, to be followed by a daughter, Elizabeth, in 1910. She was the apple of her father's eye, a tall, fair-haired child who grew to be nearly six feet in height. She was quiet and retiring, like her mother, and her abiding interest in life was the Girl Guides. Her brother Hugh was talented and charming and a great sportsman. He went to school at Rugby, served with great distinction in the First World War (he was commissioned as a second lieutenant in the Royal Garrison Artillery straight from school at the age of eighteen, and ended the war, laden with British, French and Italian decorations, with the rank of Deputy Assistant Quartermaster General at the age of only twenty-one), studied at Oxford, trained in the City of London, and then came home to help run his father's financial interests while his uncles ran the jute mill.

It was story-book, upper-middle-class life. Frederick Sharp, astute, charming and rather autocratic, would be driven by his chauffeur in his Lagonda or Rolls-Royce to catch the Dundee train at Cupar. There would be a little shooting, a lot of tennis, and some golf with his old friend, Joseph Grimond (Jo Grimond's father), who shared his enthusiasm for collecting antiques. The jute industry was beginning to decline in the face of competition from Calcutta, but Frederick Bower's investment trusts were doing very nicely. Life can only have seemed idyllic.

In August 1932 Frederick Sharp fell ill and died while on holiday in Aviemore. He was in his seventieth year. Hill of Tarvit and the Sharp fortune came to Hugh. He was now thirty-five and unmarried, extremely able and energetic and versatile. He held several directorships in the investment trust world on his own account – not just the Alliance Trust and the Second Alliance Trust of Dundee, but the First and Second Edinburgh and Dundee Investment Company, the Scottish and Canadian General Investment Trust, the Investors' Mortgage Security Company, the Scottish Mortgage and Trust Company . . .

His business affairs took him on travels all over the world. But he still had time for a wide variety of sporting interests. He played a fine game of golf, and was a member of the Rules Committee of the Royal and Ancient at St Andrews. He was president of the Cupar Golf Club and the Cupar Rugby Club (he had been a fine schoolboy player before the war). He was a skilful left-handed exponent of real (royal) tennis, which he had learned to play in London. He was an expert yachtsman, and owned a yacht which he sailed all around Scotland and in the Baltic. He was a fine shot, and hunted with the Duke of Buccleuch's hounds. He was an enthusiastic and expert skier, both on the Continent and in the Highlands of Scotland, where he was one of the pioneers of skiing as a holiday sport.

Socially, he achieved the ultimate accolade when he was appointed a member of the exclusive and prestigious Royal Company of Archers, the monarch's personal bodyguard in Scotland.

And then, in 1937, came tragedy: sudden and shattering tragedy. Hugh Sharp had never had time to get married; but in October 1937 he announced his engagement. His fiancée was Mabel Margaret Hogarth, the daughter of a shipping family from Cardross, near Helensburgh on the Clyde coast. Everyone was delighted. Hugh made plans for a big celebration party for the estate workers and other friends in the hall of the neighbouring village of Ceres, where he was president of the Ceres British Legion and affectionately regarded as the 'honorary laird'. The party was to be held on 16 December, starting with a dinner and followed by a concert given by a musical ensemble that Hugh had arranged to travel from Edinburgh.

On Friday, 10 December, he was due to drive to his fiancée's home in Cardross for the weekend. There was heavy snow in the west of Scotland, and Mabel telephoned to suggest that he should travel by train instead. Hugh Sharp duly caught the 2pm train from Dundee to Glasgow. On the way, it came to a stop about five hundred yards beyond the Castlecary Station, which is six miles south-west of Falkirk. It was there that the 4.30pm express from Edinburgh to Glasgow came thundering through the snow and the dark and crashed into the rear of the stationary Dundee train. So severe was the impact that some carriages were hurled into the air, and wreckage was strewn all over the line and the adjoining fields. There were 179 injured, and thirty-five dead. One of the dead was Hugh Sharp.

All Scotland was stunned by the magnitude of the disaster, and by Hugh Sharp's death. The *Fife Herald* wrote:

It would be impossible to number the households in the counties and cities of Scotland which today have not yet recovered from the terrible shock of Hugh Sharp's death ... In Cupar and district, particularly in Ceres, we thought of him as our own ... In business, or as a 'laird', or in the chair of a club meeting, Hugh Sharp's most endearing qualities were his true modesty, his helpfulness and his humour. He gave the benefit of his worldly goods and of his experience without revealing that he had either ...

The Times of London wrote:

In many homes and offices in America, in many capitals in Europe, there will be sadness today on his account ...

His mother and sister stayed on at Hill of Tarvit, more quietly than before and with a greatly reduced staff. Mrs Sharp had never liked ostentation, and she would only allow herself to be driven in the Rolls-Royce if the mascot on the bonnet had been removed. She continued her unobtrusive good works among the old and unfortunate in the area, and was missed by many when she died in 1946.

Elizabeth Sharp, still unmarried and now living alone in that great house with, latterly, only a housekeeper, became even more retiring and self-effacing. She wrote deeply felt and often moving poetry. And she threw herself completely into her Girl Guides work.

She was Commissioner for Fife, and Scottish Commissioner for Training and Camping and did a great deal to keep the Guide movement going during the Second World War. She was always happiest out of doors, particularly in the hills, and she loved camping. In Guiding circles they still like to tell the story of how, having taught so many Girl Guides to clean their cutlery by digging the knives and forks into the ground, she had once affronted the butler at Hill of Tarvit by absent-mindedly wiping her fork on the carpet!

When she was told, after her mother's death, that she had incurable cancer she just carried on as usual with her Guiding and her committee work, with her gardening and her duties as JP. She made a will leaving £5000 to the Scottish Girl Guides Headquarters in Edinburgh; their bookshop at 16 Coates Crescent is named after her. So is the headquarters of the Fife Girl Guides, to whom she bequeathed £1000, which formed the basis of Guide finances in the county for years afterwards.

She died in 1948 at the age of thirty-eight, having faced her last illness with calm courage. And with her death, the brief and brilliant line of Frederick Bower Sharp, jute magnate of Dundee, came to an end.

But it was certainly not the end for Hill of Tarvit. Elizabeth Sharp had already made careful provision for the Edwardian house her father had built for his art treasures and his little family. It so happened that Jo Grimond, their family friend of long standing, was Secretary of the National Trust for Scotland at the time (1947-9). With his help she had arranged to give Hill of Tarvit to the Trust, along with an endowment to maintain it.

For many years, from 1951 to 1977, the upper floor of the house was used, appropriately, by the Marie Curie Memorial Foundation as a small convalescent home for cancer patients. During that time, only the downstairs rooms were open to the public, and access was rather limited. When the convalescent home closed in 1977, Hill of Tarvit became available for much fuller public use. In 1978 the Victorian wings were converted for use as flats – one on permanent lease, two for holiday lets. Three cottages in the grounds were also refurbished for holiday letting.

In Hill of Tarvit itself, more rooms are being brought into use for public viewing, including the bathroom at the end of the gallery landing. Robert Lorimer had designed a lavatory pedestal for Shanks, and one had probably been installed there but had subsequently been replaced; now the Trust have got hold of a Lorimer model (it was called *Remirol* – Lorimer spelt backwards!) from the convent of St Marie Reparatrice at Elie in Fife, in return for installing a new lavatory for the nuns.

In the grounds outside, the formal Lorimer gardens are being gradually restored to their original pattern of planting. On top of the hill behind the house, a 'topograph', or indicator dial, has just been installed, to enable walkers to put a name to all the topographical features within view.

Hill of Tarvit is much the youngest house in the possession of the National Trust for Scotland. But it's just as much a 'period' house as the more venerable buildings in the Trust's care – a house that only the heyday of the Edwardian era could have produced. It is an integral part of Scotland's industrial and social history, when Tayside was the realm of the jute princes of Dundee. The tragic circumstances that brought Hill of Tarvit to the Trust, scarcely more than forty years after it was built, have provided a marvellous opportunity of preserving a *future* ancient building before it has time to degenerate through neglect – a chance to come in almost at the beginning, and preserve in the amber of time the house that symbolizes the way the Sharps had 'come out of the mud of the Tay'.

The approach to the north front of The Binns, and the present main entrance.

HOUSE OF THE BINNS
Lothian

IN NOVEMBER 1944 The House of The Binns, near Linlithgow, became the first historic house in Scotland to be presented to the National Trust for Scotland under its new country house scheme. This scheme, which had been launched in 1942, made it possible for the owner of a house of historic or architectural importance to transfer it to the Trust, together with its contents and an endowment for its upkeep, in return for which the owners and heirs may continue to live in it. The property is then declared inalienable – i.e. it is to be held by the Trust in perpetuity for the benefit of the nation, for the people to possess, to visit and enjoy.

So it was, on 30 April 1946, that a thirteen-year-old schoolboy called Tam Dalyell (pronounced *Dee-ell*) solemnly handed over to the Earl of Wemyss and March (then deputy chairman of the Trust) a clod of earth from The Binns to symbolize the gift of his birthright to the nation, expressed in the ancient Scots legal ritual of *sasine,* the act of granting possession of feudal property. That lump of earth with its withered grass is now under a glass cloche on the accounts desk in the barrel-vaulted smoking-room at The Binns; and on the wall above the fireplace hangs the signed Charter, complete with the statutory 'blench penny' (symbolizing a nominal quit-rent), whereby his mother, Mrs Eleanor Dalyell, then the owner of The Binns, made it over to the Trust:

Considering that I am in sympathy with the purposes and aims of the National Trust for Scotland ... and that I am desirous that The Binns with its history and legend and the memory of the family of Dalyell of The Binns shall be preserved in all time coming for the benefit and enjoyment of the Nation ... Therefore I do hereby give grant and in free Blench farm Dispone to and in favour of the National Trust for Scotland ... heritably and irredeemably All and Whole ... the lands and estate of The Binns ... Reserving always ... the sole right to use the territorial designation 'of The Binns' and to fly at The Binns, if and when in residence there, the Armorial Banner of Dalyell of The Binns and to hold the Baron Court in the Laigh Hall of The Binns ... and also all right competent ... to the hidden treasure of The Binns should it be recovered ...

The 'hidden treasure' of The Binns is supposed on a somewhat dubious basis to have been a hoard of gold and jewellery concealed in the grounds by or for King James II at the time of his flight to France during the Bloodless Revolution of 1688. No one takes the idea very seriously; nor is there any need to, for The Binns is enough of a treasure in itself – a little gem of early seventeenth-century architecture steeped in story and legend, still lived in and cherished by the Dalyell family that built it 350 years ago. It is positively modest compared with the splendidly palatial Hopetoun House a little further to the east along the shores of the Firth of Forth; but it richly reflects the history of the Dalyells who built it and extended it, and through them the history of Scotland itself.

The name itself is determinedly Scottish: 'Binns' (or 'Bynnis' in some older spellings) is a variant of the more familiar Scots word 'ben', meaning a hill, and The House of The Binns takes its name from the twin hills on whose western slopes it stands. There are indications that the site has been occupied from prehistoric times, with legends to support them; this was where a group of Picts are said to have made a last despairing stand against the Roman invaders, and the ghost of a Pict, a little old man in brownish garb who seems to be gathering firewood, is said to be seen at times on the hillside.

The first documentary record of 'the lands of the Bynnis' occurs in 1335. There was certainly a house there in 1478. In 1599 'the lands of Bynnis and Croceflattis with the manor place thereof', and various other properties in the area, were purchased by Sir William Livingstone of Kilsyth; and in 1612 Livingstone in turn sold them to the man who can truly be called the founder of The Binns – Thomas Dalyell.

Thomas Dalyell was a cadet of the ancient family of Dalzell, later the earls of Carnwath, whose seat was near Motherwell in Lanarkshire. As a member of a junior branch of the family, Thomas Dalyell had to make his own way in the world, which he did by becoming a butter merchant in Edinburgh, importing butter from the Orkneys, where his brother James (who is believed to have been married to the daughter of the Bishop of Orkney), organized its collection from the local farms and shipped it to Leith. Thomas Dalyell did very well as a butter merchant, with a house and warehouse in the High Street, and in 1601, at the age of thirty, he was able to make a 'good' social marriage – to Janet Bruce, the daughter (albeit illegitimate, although she was later legitimized) of Edward Bruce, first Baron Kinloss, the Master of the Rolls to King James VI of Scotland.

The year 1603, the year of the Union of the Crowns, was a turning-point in the fortunes of many a Scotsman on the make. When James VI succeeded Elizabeth on the English throne as James I, a large number of Scots followed him to his court in London. Among them was his Master of the Rolls, Edward Bruce, who in turn took his new son-in-law, Thomas Dalyell, as Deputy Master of the Rolls.

The Scots who went off to make it in London did just that – and earned themselves a bad reputation as the 'hungrie Scottis'. One of them was the celebrated 'Jingling Geordie' – George Heriot, the Edinburgh goldsmith – who went to London as James VI's court jeweller and banker and amassed there a considerable fortune of £25,000. For Thomas Dalyell, former butter merchant of Edinburgh, now Deputy Master of the Rolls, the opportunities were limitless, for his job was not so much that of a legal officer of the Crown, as it is now, as that of a senior member of the king's private Civil Service. As such he had immense powers of patronage, buying and selling offices and no doubt creaming off a good commission for himself in the process. By 1612 he had made enough money to return to Scotland with one overpowering ambition – to become a member of the landed gentry, because land was status, land was power, land was wealth. And so he bought from Sir William Livingstone 'the lands of Bynnis and Croceflattis with the manor place thereof', and settled to a new occupation as a landed laird. It is said that it was now that he changed the spelling of his name from Dalzell to Dalyell, just to show his snooty Lanarkshire cousins that he had made it on his own; it is just as likely, however, spelling being what it was in those days, that it was simply a scribal mistake.

The house that Thomas built at The Binns was in fact a restoration and enlargement of 'the manor place thereof' that was standing there already. There is no record of the original structure, but Thomas seems virtually to have rebuilt it. While the original house as restored by Thomas still forms the nucleus of the present house, not much of it remains to be seen externally today. But it was a tall, grey, three-storeyed building with twin stair turrets at either end topped by pepperpot roofs. Dormer windows in the steep pitched roof gave superb views north over the Firth of Forth and south towards the Pentland Hills (only the row of five dormer windows looking south has survived). At the south-eastern corner there was a service wing, possibly detached from the main building, which incorporated a vaulted kitchen, used as a bakehouse.

Happily, the ornate plaster ceilings and cornices in four of the main rooms have survived unscathed by later 'improvers'; these are still to be seen in the high hall (now the drawing-room), the king's room, the sea room and the vault chamber. They were made in 1630 when King Charles I was expected to come to Scotland to be crowned and the Dalyells, with their court connections earnestly hoped that he would stay at The Binns on his way to Linlithgow Palace. He did not, as it happened (he eventually came to Scotland in 1633 but did not stay at The Binns); but the expectation has left us with some splendid examples of the elaborate plasterwork carried out by the English craftsman Alexander White.

The high hall ceiling has a geometric design with heraldic devices and a splendidly bold central boss that once supported a pendant light. Above the chimneypiece there is the coat of arms of Charles I, flanked by the Prince of Wales' plumes, intended as a compliment to the future Charles II, who was born in May of that year. The date, 1630, is to the right of the huge mirror of greenish Waterford glass that dominates one wall.

The king's room-to-be has the most elaborate of the plaster ceilings. It features a running pattern of thistles and roses (very popular after the Union of the Crowns). We can also see the four royal emblems of thistle, rose, harp and fleur-de-lys (because the Stuarts also claimed to be kings of France). Two of the nine ancient worthies of history appear twice in medallions – Alexander the Great and King David the Psalmist; incidentally, the *n* in Alexander and the *d* in David are the wrong way round. Above the fireplace is another representation of the royal arms, but with a curious difference: although it carries the English motto it is the Scottish coat of arms, with the lion on the right and the unicorn on the left. There is also a heavy frieze of fruits and cherubs signifying a cornucopia of plenty – a sycophantic compliment to the reign of the king who never came.

The sea room (so called because it affords a particularly fine view across the Firth of Forth) has a more intimate wagon-roof ceiling. It carries emblems of the peacocks that still strut the grounds of The Binns and roost in the old plane tree near the entrance to the stable courtyard; and, predictably, there is a traditional family saying to the effect that when the peacocks leave The Binns it will mean the end for the Dalyells. Also on the ceiling there are some charming moulded heads of children, which are thought to be stylized representations of Thomas's brood. The plasterers left behind one of the lead moulds, and it is now on display in the Laigh Hall downstairs.

We don't know how long Thomas Dalyell took to refurbish The House of The Binns between the purchase in 1612 and the decorated ceilings of 1630. To start with, he and his wife lived at nearby Mannerstoun House on the Blackness Road. Their intertwined initials can be seen all over the place at The Binns, both inside and out, over doorways and fireplaces and on ceilings, as well as some dates: 1622 above the fireplace of the laigh hall, 1621 at the window in the sea room.

Anyway, whenever it was that they actually moved in after the last flurry of redecoration in 1630, Thomas Dalyell had another twelve years of life in which to enjoy his role as landed gentry. His portrait above the fireplace in the business room, almost certainly by the Aberdeen-born artist George Jamesone, reflects a canny face, the rosy-cheeked contented face of a shrewd operator who had made good.

The story of The Binns, however, is largely dominated by Thomas's son, another Thomas, who inherited on his father's death in 1642. He is better known to history as the famous (or infamous) General 'Tam' Dalyell, scourge of the Covenanters. A staunch Royalist, he played a leading and vehement part in the 'killing times' of political strife and religious fanaticism that racked Scotland in his lifetime. General Tam made quite a name for himself as a ruthless and implacable opponent of the Covenanters; legend – and Sir Walter Scott – made that name particularly lurid.

He was born around 1615, as far as can now be ascertained, and was educated at home at The Binns, probably by a tutor or chaplain, before doing the customary Continental tour from 1634 to 1637. He returned home in the year Scotland's political ferment began

to seethe, the year in which King Charles I tried to impose on Scotland's churches his new *Booke of Common Prayer* and Jenny Geddes threw a stool at the Dean of St Giles Cathedral for reading it aloud. In October 1637, in St Michael's Church, Linlithgow, both Tam and his father signed a petition to the Privy Council in protest against the forced introduction of the prayer book; but when this protest movement escalated into the drawing up of the National Covenant in 1638, and the Solemn League and Covenant of 1643 which supported the English Parliament against the king, Tam Dalyell took up a military career on the Royalist side. During the 1640s he saw service against the parliamentary forces in Ireland.

Tradition has it that when news of Charles I's execution in 1649 reached Ireland, Dalyell took an oath never to cut his hair or his beard until the monarchy was restored. He was now a proscribed outlaw from Scotland, but when Charles II was crowned in Scotland in 1651, Tam Dalyell hastened across to join the royal army under General Leslie as a Major-General of Foot. In the forlorn invasion of England that followed, General Tam was taken prisoner at the Battle of Worcester and committed to the Tower of London by Cromwell, five shillings a week being allowed for his maintenance. In May of the following year he contrived to escape – one of the few people who ever succeeded in doing so – and got away to the Continent. A committee of inquiry, set up to investigate the escape, failed to establish how he had done it.

Throughout the 1650s Scotland was under the firm rule of the English parliamentary forces. In 1654 there was an abortive rising in the Highlands; Tam Dalyell hurried back to join the Royalist forces, but the campaign fizzled out after a drubbing at Dalnaspidal at the head of Loch Garry. Dalyell, now with a price of £200 on his head, once again managed to make his way to the Continent to rejoin Charles II in exile in Cologne.

With the Royalist cause seemingly hopeless for the time being, Tam Dalyell embarked on a career as a professional mercenary soldier. Charles II gave him letters of recommendation to King Sobieski of Poland and to the tsar of Russia, Alexei Mikhaelovich (the father of Peter the Great). Dalyell opted for service with the tsar. He helped to reorganize the Russian imperial armies and gained high renown in various campaigns against the Poles, the Turks and the Tartars. He was promoted to full general and made a Noble of Russia, and apparently acquired a Russian wife called Anna Powski.

In 1665 the restored Charles II requested his return, and the tsar gave him a letter patent testifying that he was 'a man of virtue and honour, and of great experience in military affairs'. King Charles had need of that experience north of the border where the natives, particularly in the Covenanting strongholds in the south-west, were growing distinctly restless under the laws requiring universal church attendance to hear ministers appointed by bishops. In July 1666 General Tam Dalyell was appointed commander-in-chief of His Majesty's Forces in Scotland, charged with the suppression of all Covenanters.

He was a formidable and eccentric-looking figure by now, the sort of larger-than-life character around whom legends quickly accrete. Despite the Restoration, he still had not shaved off his beard, which was now white and bushy and reached almost to his girdle, according to contemporary accounts. His appearance at court in London occasioned considerable comment. He used a huge comb with teeth about six inches long to keep his hair and beard tidy (it's now on display in a showcase in the dining-room). He was laden with gifts from the tsar, including a massive fifteenth-century two-handed sword made in Passau on the Danube, which is now above the fireplace in the dining-room. There is a portrait of him by Paton above the fireplace in the blue room (so called because of the fine collection on the walls of blue and white Chinese export porcelain, English and Dutch Delft); the beard only reaches to his chest, but it looks pretty fierce nonetheless.

In Scotland, General Tam was soon in action. In November 1666 there was a Covenanter uprising in Dumfries. From there a ragged army of about 3000 marched through Ayrshire and Lanarkshire and headed for Edinburgh, determined to put an end to episcopacy. Just outside Edinburgh, at a place called Rullion Green near the Pentland Hills, General Tam and his royal troops fell upon them and routed them. It was the end of the so-called 'Pentland Rising', and King Charles II wrote Tam a letter of commendation in his own hand 'for the happy success you have had against the rebels in Scotland'.

But the success wasn't quite so happy in General Tam's eyes. At Rullion Green he had given quarter to some of the Covenanters' camp-followers, both women and children. However, when they were brought to Edinburgh they were shot out of hand. He was so enraged by this violation of his quarter that he resigned his commission and retired to The Binns, vowing that he would have no more to do with politicians. He was created a privy councillor, but over the next ten years he attended only ten meetings of the council. Instead, he spent his time developing his estate and cultivating 'curious flowers and plants'; he added a western wing to create a southern courtyard, and immensely high walls decorated with turrets at each corner.

His retirement from public affairs proved temporary, however. The Covenanter troubles had not disappeared, and in 1679 there was an armed rising in the west of Scotland. Charles II commissioned him as lieutenant-general of the forces in Scotland under the Duke of Monmouth (the king's natural son) as commander-in-chief. General Tam's self esteem was wounded by this apparent slight and he refused to go into action until he was mollified by a new commission from the king. This may be why he was not present at the fateful Battle of Bothwell Brig, near Hamilton, on 22 June 1679, when the Covenanters were crushingly defeated by Monmouth's forces.

From now on, the hunting down of Covenanters became a bloody and ferocious business. In November, General Tam succeeded Monmouth as commander-in-chief in Scotland, and it was now that his single-minded devotion to what he saw as his duty earned him his undying reputation for severity and cruelty. Nearly 150 years later, in *Old Mortality*, Sir Walter Scott presented him as a veritable monster, 'who, having practised the art of war in the then barbarous country of Russia, was as much feared for his cruelty and indifference to human life and human sufferings, as respected for his steady loyalty and undaunted valour'. The great Sir Walter had the grace to admit, in an anonymous review of his own novel in the *Quarterly Review* in 1817, that he 'had cruelly falsified history in representing Dalzell (*sic*) as present at the battle of Bothwell Bridge; whereas that "old and bloody man", as Wodrow calls him, was *not* at the said battle'. But the image presented by Scott stuck. General Tam Dalyell was 'Bluidy Tam' or the 'Bluidy Muscovite' to all Covenanters, a man who roasted people alive, a man in league with satanic powers who had frequent 'trookings (dealings) wi' the deil'.

His official portrait as commander-in-chief, attributed to one of the painting dynasty of Scougalls, hangs above the sideboard in the dining-room. It shows him in full armour, clean shaven, with a gaunt and stern face; a choleric man, not to be trifled with. It is a face of great character, an intensely forbidding face. No wonder the Covenanters feared and hated him. But he was clearly a much more complex man than the creature of legend. After his death in 1685 (appropriately from a fit of apoplexy the day after attending a meeting of the Privy Council), the Inventory of the Plenishing of The House of The Binns that was drawn up betrays a standard of living, both intellectual and material, unusually high for those times; in particular his library, which he kept in the bookcases still on view behind the panelling in the business room, indicates that his interests embraced Greek, Latin, philosophy and horticulture as well as military strategy.

And what of the legends, the folklore? The fascinating thing about folklore is that there is always *something* that triggers a tale.

It was said that General Tam frequently played cards with the devil, and the devil usually won; but on one occasion the General won, and the devil was so enraged that he hurled the card-table at Tam Dalyell's head. It missed him, and fell into the pond below the hill on the west. Some two hundred years later, during the very dry summer of 1878, when the pond was being cleaned, a very heavy object was recovered from the mud. It turned out to be a table of Carrara marble, possibly of seventeenth-century Florentine make.

It was said that he never wore boots, according to Sir Walter Scott; but in the dining-room at The Binns are the very riding boots he used, made of heavy Russian leather, square-toed, made to fit either foot (which was normal practice at the time) so that they could be pulled on quickly in a sudden crisis. Now they have generated their own legend; the boots are said to have walked on their own whenever they were not at The Binns, being restless to be there – and if water is poured into them, the water boils . . .

It was said that he roasted people alive. Why should anyone say that? In the 1930s the old barrel-vaulted bakehouse now known as the General's Kitchen was restored. It was discovered that the grate, hearth and ovens had been bricked up. Behind the brickwork was a large baking-oven, some seven feet in diameter. Could this have been the origin of the story? According to the present incumbent, Tam Dalyell MP, the roasting capacity of the oven is eighteen medium-sized Girl Guides!

Legend apart, General Tam Dalyell's major contribution to Britain's military history was the forming of a new cavalry regiment which would earn undying glory as the Royal Scots Greys. He received orders from the king to reorganize three independent companies and raise three new troops of dragoons to join them and so form the Royal Regiment of Scots Dragoons. He was appointed colonel of the new regiment, which held its first musters at The Binns. What was unique about the regiment at the time was their uniform; General Tam had seen how effectively the Polish army had used white uniforms as camouflage in the snow, and he thought that grey would be similarly effective to tone in with the Scottish landscape. So he got a licence to import from England 2536 ells of stone-grey Flanders serge for his dragoons' greatcoats. This, according to family tradition, is why the regiment came to be known as the Royal Scots Greys; but regimental historians claim that the grey uniforms were discarded a year after General Tam's death, to be replaced by the customary scarlet, and the name 'Greys' did not come into use until a few years later when the regiment was mounted exclusively on grey horses.

Above the Chippendale bureau in the Laigh Hall hangs a picture of the regiment receiving their grey mounts. Opposite it is a painting of one of the most famous moments in the regiment's history, when Sergeant (later promoted to ensign) Charles Ewart from Elvanfoot in Lanarkshire captured the Imperial Eagle Standard of the French 45th Regiment during the charge of the Union Brigade at Waterloo in 1815. The gallant ensign lived to the ripe old age of seventy-seven; he was buried in Manchester, but in 1938 his remains were moved to a fitting memorial on the north side of the esplanade of Edinburgh Castle.

General Tam also left for posterity a large brood of children. He had four wives but, eccentric as always, he never married them in church; they were all 'hand-fasted' – contracted to a trial marriage of a year and a day, after which, if a male heir had been born, or both parties agreed, the betrothed became a common law wife. His first wife in this manner was Elizabeth Ker of Cavers, by whom he had the requisite heir, Thomas.

Charles II had intended to bestow a baronetcy on General Tam but died before he could do so (February 1685). The General himself died later that year, so Charles II's successor, his hapless brother James VII of Scotland and II of England, conferred it instead on the General's eldest son Thomas in November 1685. The patent contained the highly unusual provision that the title should descend through 'heirs male and of tailyie' (entail), which meant that it could descend to or through the female line. This rare provision, which applies only to a handful of families in Scotland, ensured that the Dalyell name and title stayed attached to The Binns, because all too many male Dalyells of succeeding generations achieved the letters *ob.s.p.* after their names (*obiit sine prole* – died without

175

The dining-room at The Binns.

issue). This has caused the line of descent to swing disconcertingly at times from branch to branch of the family tree.

The second baronet, for instance, another Sir Thomas Dalyell, died without issue in 1719; whereupon his sister, Magdalene Dalyell, who had married James Monteith of Auldcathie, went to court to establish her right as the heir 'of tailyie'. She liked to be known as 'The Lady Binns', and it was her eldest son, James Monteith, who inherited the title and the name as Sir James Monteith Dalyell, third baronet. Their portraits are now in the dining-room.

His eldest son, Sir Robert Dalyell, became fourth baronet as a young man of twenty-one in 1747, and seems to have plunged straight into a programme of renovation and expansion at The Binns. What he did was to turn the house around, metaphorically speaking, changing its orientation from south to north.

Originally the house had faced south, with the driveway coming uphill to a cobbled courtyard that enclosed the main entrance. What is now the handsome ground-floor laigh hall was then two rooms, a laigh hall and a dining-room. Robert pulled down the partition wall, making it into one large chamber, and added an attractive arcade on three sides. He switched the main entrance to the north side of this new enlarged laigh hall, and on the south side, on part of the site of the old cobbled court, he added two elegant new rooms – the present morning-room and dining-room – with connecting doors. Then he terraced what was left of the courtyard. One striking feature of the old dining-room dominates the new laigh hall – the elaborate stone chimneypiece decorated with swags of fruit.

Sir Robert took his time about bringing a bride to the house he had thus improved, perhaps because he was simply content to leave the running of the household to his widowed mother, Dame Helen Campbell, who lived until 1774. At any rate he didn't get married until 1773, when he was in his late forties; but then he immediately started producing issue, as the phrase has it. And this was just as well for the Dalyell succession, for both his brothers had entered military service (as so many younger sons of landed gentry did in those days), and both had been killed in their thirties – Captain James Dalyell at Fort Detroit in 1763 during operations against the American Indians in the Seven Years' War, and Captain Thomas Dalyell RN in India two years later. Their portraits by Cosmo Alexander are in the dining-room, along with that by David Martin of the fourth baronet himself, resplendent as a Regency squire.

Sir Robert died in 1791, having belatedly fathered four sons and several daughters, who were destined to play a large part in the ravelled story of the Dalyell dynasty. The eldest, Sir James, who inherited as the fifth baronet, seems to have been a bit of a card – not to mention a bit of a rake as well. He was seventeen years old when his father died. In his lifetime he bridged the Georgian and Victorian eras, and left an unmistakeable contemporary stamp on The Binns. He would no doubt have thought of himself as Bulstrode's Continuer; but in fact he turned out to be rather a Ruiner instead.

In the 1820s he called in the rising young Edinburgh architect William Burn to give The Binns a facelift. He briefed Burn to give the house the appearance of a Regency country mansion in the Gothic style made fashionable by Robert Adam. To this end Burn altered the entire façade. The east and west ranges enclosing the south courtyard were extended; the main windows of the house were much enlarged and given rectangular hood moulds; all the walls were crested with battlements and crenellations; the dormer windows of the north façade, and the pepperpot roofs of the stair-turrets disappeared.

Sir James made one notable addition to the landscape – the tower on the hill behind the house, a real folly if ever there was one. He built it in 1826 as a result of an after-dinner wager with his cronies as to who could suggest the most fruitless and witty way of spending £100. Dalyell proposed building a folly to overlook the new wood that the neighbouring nouveau riche earls of Hopetoun had ostentatiously planted around their property – and he won hands down. He then showed a certain shrewdness by spending only £26 10s on it. Nearly a century later the ninth baronet added a windmill to the tower to generate electricity.

The fifth baronet's extravagance exhausted the family fortunes, and land had to be sold off. When he died in 1841 (without issue) there wasn't much except the title and house itself for his brother to inherit.

The sixth baronet, Sir John Graham Dalyell, had already been knighted in his own right for his services to literature and science. An Edinburgh advocate by profession, he was also a noted antiquary and naturalist, specializing in the marine biology of the Forth, particularly flat-worms and sea-anemones which he bred (one anemone he reared in captivity reached the ripe old age of sixty-six and merited an obituary notice in *The Scotsman* in 1887). He was a friend of Sir Walter Scott and mentor to the young Charles Darwin. It was the golden age of the gentleman amateur, and the golden age of publishing, and Sir John Graham Dalyell produced some superbly illustrated books that are now classics, like *Rare and Remarkable Animals of Scotland* (two volumes) and *The Powers of the Creator Displayed in the Creation* (three volumes). He also wrote widely on history, poetry, music and antiquities – and on 'the darker superstitions of Scotland'.

He never married, so when he died in 1851 the title passed to the fourth brother, Admiral Sir William Dalyell (the third brother, a general, had died three years earlier, also without issue). Sir William was a dashing fellow who had distinguished himself as a midshipman during the Napoleonic Wars in 'cutting out' expeditions on the French coast. On his last expedition, in January 1805, he was badly wounded and taken prisoner, half dead from nine fearful sabre cuts on the head. In his portrait in the morning-room one can still see two of the scars, above the left eyebrow and under the forelock. Above the fireplace in the laigh hall hangs the splendid presentation sword he was given by the Patriotic Fund on his return from captivity in 1814; only eighty such swords were made, varying in value according to the degree of valour displayed, and this was a fifty-guinea one.

By his beautiful Portuguese wife Maria Sampayo (her portrait is also in the morning-room) he had four children, two sons and two daughters. The eldest, Sir Robert Dalyell, inherited as eighth baronet in 1865; he died without issue in 1886. His brother and the elder sister had also died without issue by then, so the house went to the younger sister, Elizabeth Grace, who was married to Gustavus Cornwall, the head of the Post Office in Dublin (it was through this Irish connection that the magnificent mirror of greenish Waterford glass in the high hall came to The Binns). Cornwall adopted the name Dalyell, but the title remained dormant.

With her death in 1913, also without issue, the dynastic line took another swerve. It doubled back on itself, back through the eldest of Admiral Sir William's sisters Harriet, who had married a Wilkie of Foulden in 1804 and was now adjudged, posthumously of course, to have been the rightful heir 'of tailyie'. She had had a son, John Wilkie, and now in 1913 it was his elder son, James Bruce Wilkie, who adopted the Dalyell name and inherited The Binns and the title as the ninth baronet. Two-thirds of the plenishings of The Binns, however, went to his younger brother and sisters, and many of the Dalyell family possessions were dispersed at that time and never recovered.

Sir James, who had served in the Boer War and been mentioned in dispatches and would also serve in Egypt and Gallipoli with the King's Own Scottish Borderers in the Great War, had an only daughter, Eleanor Dalyell, who in turn inherited The Binns in 1935 as heir 'of tailyie'. In 1928 she had married Gordon Loch, who also obligingly changed his surname to Dalyell. Their rather formal portraits by Sir Stanley Cursiter – he in the heraldic tabard of the Unicorn Pursuivant of the Lyon Court of Scotland, she sentimentally pretty and not as vividly beautiful as she was in reality – are in the dining-room on either side of the connecting door to the morning-room.

They had an only child, Tam, who as a thirteen-year-old handed over his birthright to the National Trust for Scotland and is now a household name as Tam Dalyell, forthright MP for West Lothian since 1962 and Labour scourge of all political devolutionists. Had he ever regretted his parents' decision to hand over The Binns? Certainly not, he says; they had discussed the issues involved very thoroughly and openly with him at the time – and he would probably have done it himself by now anyway:

Theirs was a conscious and conscientious decision. They felt the house was a part of Scotland's history, and they saw themselves as its guardians rather than its owners, if I can make that distinction. They felt it ought to be open to the public, but they didn't want to make personal profit out of it. My father, and his father before him (he had been Governor of Nepal and latterly British Resident in Bahrein), were Anglo-Indian civil servants of the old school, and the concept of the 'common good' weighed very heavily with them.

When Eleanor Dalyell died in 1972 The Binns was metaphorically 'inherited' by Tam Dalyell MP and his vivacious wife Kathleen, who acts as resident Trust representative and organizes the small team of guides who deal with the 6000 visitors who come to see the house every year. But the baronetcy itself lies dormant again, thanks to Tam Dalyell's strictly socialist principles.

However, the Dalyells have a son, Gordon, and a daughter, Moira. So who knows? There could well be a tenth baronet of The Binns at some time in the future. General Tam, I am sure, would approve.

Kellie Castle from the south. The entrance is in the tower to the left.

KELLIE CASTLE
Fife

THERE ARE SOME FAMILIES on whom the angels seem to smile with extra benevolence, families at whose births the good fairy hands out gifts with almost excessive generosity. Such a family were the Lorimers of Edinburgh, who fell in love with Kellie Castle in 1877 and thus rescued it from ruin.

James Allan Lorimer, distinguished international jurist, was Professor of Public Law (and the Law of Nature and of Nations) at Edinburgh University. He had a beautiful and talented young wife, and six children so gifted that their home was like a miniature academy of arts, turning out musicians, artists, writers, a painter of international repute, and Scotland's foremost architect of his day.

Every summer the Lorimer family would leave their new baronial-style house in Edinburgh to holiday in rented country houses in the East Neuk of Fife, where the sea breezes were considered good for Professor Lorimer's asthmatic chest. One autumn day in 1877, when they were out on a family walk, they came across Kellie Castle, disused and forlorn, and promptly fell in love with it. Kellie had once been an outstanding example of Scottish castle-building in the sixteenth and early seventeenth century; but now it was all but derelict, practically a ruin. Every pane of glass in its eighty-two windows was smashed. Gaping holes let in rain and snow through the roof. The fireplaces were choked with fallen birds' nests, the ceilings sagged, the floors were covered with bird-droppings. Saplings grew out of some of the walls, and a local farmer was using the great hall as a granary. The garden was a wilderness. The old mansion was indeed a sorry sight, standing there among its trees, three miles inland from the picturesque little seaport of Pittenweem, looking out over the Firth of Forth and the Bass Rock, the distant Lothian hills beyond.

But the Lorimers saw its potential. They knew the owner, the Earl of Mar and Kellie, and persuaded him first to have Kellie Castle made wind- and water-tight and then to lease it to them as 'improving tenants' at a modest rent of £25 per annum. Their prospective neighbours thought them daft. Undaunted, Professor Lorimer took a thirty-eight-year lease on the castle, and they moved in on 1 September 1878. There was no gas or electricity and only pumped well-water; but they loved it, no matter how spartan the living-conditions. It was also the best thing that had happened to Kellie Castle for 250 years, if not in all its long and chequered history.

The castle was derelict not because it had a particularly violent history. There is no record of its having been stormed, battered or burned, like Brodick Castle on the island of Arran or some of the ancient tower houses of the north-east. The reason was that, unlike so many other great houses that were built and cherished by a single family down the centuries, Kellie Castle seemed to be forever changing hands, passed from this owner to that, from one branch of the family to another, its estates sold, its contents dispersed at massive auctions; and then it was abandoned altogether for forty-five years until a century ago, when the Lorimers came along.

Garden view of Kellie Castle from the north-east.

The first lairds of Kellie were called Siward. They were descended from Siward, Earl of Northumbria, leader of the great army with which Malcolm Canmore ('Big-head') invaded Scotland in 1057, to put an end to the reign of the usurper Macbeth. Three centuries later the Siwards parted company with Kellie when Sir Richard Siward's daughter, Helen, referred to as the *domina de Kellie*, resigned the lands of Kellie in favour of her cousin, Sir Walter Oliphant, who was married to a daughter of Robert the Bruce.

It was probably this Oliphant, inheriting the lands of Kellie in 1360, who was responsible for building the oldest part of Kellie Castle that can be seen today, the simple square tower, or keep, now known as the north tower. This seems to have been substantially remodelled in the fifteenth century, for the ground- and first-floor chambers are stone vaulted, as are the two small closets on each of the two floors above.

After two centuries of this Oliphant occupancy, in 1562 Kellie Castle and its estates were sold lock, stock and barrel to the head of the senior branch of the family, Lawrence, third Lord Oliphant. He was probably responsible for adding a top floor to the north tower, with delightful corbelled turrets at two of the corners to create circular lookout rooms.

It was his successor, the fourth Lord Oliphant, who started the building programme that was to give Kellie Castle its uniqueness of design. In 1573 he was to marry Lady Margaret Hay, a daughter of the Earl of Errol. Instead of rebuilding the old tower house for his bride, or adding an extension, as was the usual practice of bridegrooms to celebrate a good marriage, Lord Oliphant built a new four-storey tower house fifty feet away from the original one, with the initials of his bride, M H, and the date, 1573, carved in bold relief high on its southern front. This building is now known as the east tower. A top storey was added a few years later.

It was a curious decision, building a completely detached new tower like this. It split the Kellie home into two unconnected sections. There may have been some sort of wall enclosing the space between the two buildings, and an open passageway covered at best by a lean-to roof; but it was clearly neither a convenient nor an efficient domestic arrangement. So some time before 1605 the two towers, north and east, were linked together by a brilliantly improvized scheme that transformed Kellie into an architectural unity.

The problem of linking two separated towers was resolved by building a *third* tower, just to the south of the original north tower, with matching twin-corbelled turrets. There were now three towers that formed the points of a triangle, with the north and south towers at the base and the east tower at the apex. They were all then joined up into the shape of a long-stemmed T, with the east tower at the end of the stem of the T, and the old tower and its new companion forming the crossbar. The stem of the T was formed by the construction of a long and slightly lower building, comprising on the first floor a magnificent fifty-foot-long great hall with an equally splendid 'withdrawing-room' (or privy dining-room) opening directly off it, and on the floor above, up a handsome turnpike stair, two outstandingly beautiful bedchambers now known as the vine room and the earl's room. The new south tower provided an entrance hall with a staircase leading to the great hall, and to a further turnpike stair giving access to the earl's room and the rooms of that tower.

It is the south tower and this major 'link building' of the early seventeenth century that are open to the public today.

What was so innovatory about all this, as Schomberg Scott points out in *The National Trust for Scotland Guide* (1976), was that the old Scots tradition of building vertically had literally been turned on its side: between the three towers the master mason had built a horizontal mansion. As such, Kellie Castle represents a significant moment of transition between the old and the new, between the old tower houses of earlier times when defence considerations were paramount and the more amenable mansions of the seventeenth and eighteenth centuries.

The man responsible for this pioneering transformation of Kellie Castle seems to have been the fifth Lord Oliphant, who is described as 'a man of vast estates' but equally vast extravagance. His estates were apparently not vast enough to cope with the cost of his building project at Kellie; his cousin Patrick, the sixth Lord Oliphant who succeeded in 1613, promptly sold Kellie Castle and all its estates for the sum of 116,000 Scottish merks to pay off the debts.

The purchaser who thus brought a new name to Kellie was Thomas Erskine, Viscount Fentoun, a childhood companion of King James VI who had earned the king's gratitude for his part in the so-called Gowrie Conspiracy of 1600: in that rather mysterious episode, King James was menaced at knife-point in a house in Perth by the Master of Ruthven, brother of the Earl of Gowrie, and only saved from certain death when Erskine burst into the chamber and killed the would-be assassin.

It seems that when Thomas Erskine bought Kellie Castle the interior fittings had not been completed. It is not known what Erskine did to make it habitable; but at least he brought signal honour to the house when he was created the first Earl of Kellie in 1619. He died in 1639 in London, but was buried in Pittenweem, where his gravestone can be seen in the north wall of the parish churchyard.

This was the time when the civil wars of the Covenanter period were breaking out. The Erskines were Royalist to the core. The first earl was succeeded by his grandson, who died childless and was succeeded in turn by his brother, Alexander. This third earl followed Charles II on his foredoomed expedition into England in 1651 and was taken prisoner at the Battle of Worcester. Proscribed from Scotland, he married while he was abroad in the Dutch service; his bride was Anna, daughter of the governor of Bois le Duc. It was when he returned to Scotland with his wife after the Restoration of Charles II that he embarked on the redecoration scheme that gave Kellie Castle the splendid ceilings that miraculously survived the later years of neglect.

The combined coat of arms of Alexander and Anna is the centrepiece of the striking plaster ceiling of the 'withdrawing-room', which is now the dining-room. But the outstanding feature of the room is the painted wall panelling, which was in fashion in the time of Charles II. There are sixty-four rectangular panels, all painted with different romantic landscapes, of ruined castles and fortresses, bridges and waterfalls. All but four of the ones seen today are the originals installed by the third Earl of Kellie.

His wife Anna died very soon, and in 1665 the earl married again. His bride this time was Mary, younger daughter of Sir John Dalzell of Glenae in Dumfriesshire, and once again the earl celebrated his nuptials by putting his stamp on the ceilings of Kellie Castle. In the great hall (now the drawing-room), with its two square-pilastered fireplaces and great sash and case windows, he set three heraldic panels framed by fruit and laurel wreaths: his own coat of arms at one end of the room, his new bride's at the other, and in the centre a bravura combination of the two, with the date 1676. In the winter of 1980–1 this ceiling began to sag ominously – not surprisingly, in view of the conditions to which it had been subjected – but was saved by prompt and extensive rescue work by the National Trust for Scotland.

Upstairs in the earl's room immediately above the great hall he applied another central heraldic panel with their joint coat of arms, surrounded by winged cherubs' heads framed in laurel wreaths. No doubt the lovely vine room, separated from the earl's room by a dressing-room, was also decorated by the earl for his new bride. Here, the deeply coved ceiling is embellished with a profusion of pre-cast plaster vine branches laden with bunches of grapes, while the centrepiece is a circular painting of Mount Olympus, creating the effect of a skylight to heaven itself. The painting was done by the Dutch artist Jacob de Wet, who also painted a number of ceilings in the Palace of Holyroodhouse in Edinburgh as well as the series of Scottish monarchs in its long gallery. It was the beautiful vine room, with its simple pine panelling, that Professor Lorimer was to choose as his own room.

The earls of Kellie remained supporters of the Stuart dynasty to the bitter end. The fifth earl fought for Bonnie Prince Charles at Preston, Falkirk, and the crowning disaster of Culloden in 1746, and it did his estate no good at all. In 1769 the bachelor sixth earl, a noted violinist and composer, had to sell off all the estates around Kellie apart from the castle itself and a few acres of policies. When he died in Brussels in 1781 his bachelor brother Alexander inherited both the title and the castle, but very little else. He was succeeded by a kinsman, Sir Charles Erskine of Cambo, who also died unmarried, so the title and the castle were inherited by two childless bachelors in succession. In 1829, on the death of the tenth earl who had no obvious successor, a 'muckle roup' (a 'great auction') was held of the castle's contents. The earldom was claimed in 1830 by John Miller Francis Erskine, ninth Earl of Mar, as collateral male heir, and in 1834 he was eventually adjudged to be the rightful eleventh earl.

All he got was an additional title, to make him the first Earl of Mar and Kellie, and a shell of a castle. Kellie had been sadly neglected for years, what with a succession of bachelor and childless lairds, and the comprehensive 'muckle roup' in 1829. After that it was virtually abandoned, although one wing was used for a time as temporary lodgings for the manager of a coalmine that was opened at nearby Balcormo. And then in 1877 along came the Lorimers, who took the near-derelict old castle to their hearts, to bring Kellie to life again.

Professor James Lorimer had already achieved an international reputation by the time he acquired the lease of Kellie Castle. He was a remarkable man, a 'European' well ahead of his day. Born in 1818, he had graduated at Edinburgh University and then done the grand tour of Europe; he spent six months in Geneva perfecting his French (he was sketched there, none too skilfully, by the Countess de Pichon Longueville), followed by another six months studying German so that he could absorb lectures on law and philosophy at the universities of Berlin and Bonn. After three years on the Continent he returned home and was called to the Scottish Bar in 1845. He received few briefs to begin with, but in 1848 he was appointed Principal Lyon Clerk and Keeper of the Records of the Lyon Court, the office regulating the use of heraldic emblems in Scotland. He began to make his name as a writer on the philosophy of law and politics and on aspects of moral philosophy (his major works include *Handbook of the Law in Scotland* and *The Institutes of the Laws of Nations*). He was an advocate of university reform in Scotland – and, years before his time, a 'permanent congress of nations', to be backed by an international court of justice. In 1862 he was appointed to a Chair at Edinburgh University, and in 1873 he was one of ten founding members – all like himeself, international jurists of the highest standing – of the Institute of International Law. He had honorary degrees from half a dozen universities, and some of them are on display in the so-called professor's room at Kellie Castle.

In 1851, at the comparatively advanced age of thirty-three, he had startled his friends (and delighted his mother) by marrying a pretty and musical sixteen-year-old girl called Hannah Stodart, who was a granddaughter of the Robert Stodart who (along with John Broadwood) did so much to develop English pianoforte manufacture early in the nineteenth century. It turned out to be an idyllically happy marriage.

They had six children: James (1853), who became a businessman in South Africa; Hannah (1854), who was an able modeller, painter, and woodcarver; John Henry (1856), who became a painter of great distinction; Alice (1857), who played the piano, sketched and did embroidery; Louise (1861), who wrote verse and prose and was a keen gardener; and Robert (1864), always called Robin in his boyhood, who was destined to become Scotland's leading architect as Sir Robert Lorimer.

This was the lively, talented and engaging brood of children the Lorimers took with them when they moved into Kellie Castle in that September of 1878. Louise Lorimer was later to recall what it was like when they first saw it:

It was left to the rooks and the owls who built in its crumbling chimneys and dropped down piles of twigs which reached out into the rooms. Great holes let the rain and snow through the roofs, many of the floors had become unsafe, every pane of glass was broken, and swallows built in the coronets on the ceilings, while the ceilings themselves sagged and in some cases fell into the rooms … The garden, still encircled by a tumbledown wall, was a wilderness of neglected gooseberry bushes, gnarled apple trees, and old world roses, which struggled through the weeds, summer after summer, with a sweet persistence.

The Earl of Mar and Kellie kept his side of the bargain, and made the house wind- and weather-proof; Professor Lorimer kept his, and arranged for the basic cleaning of the castle and whatever modest improvements and restoration of the interior he could afford. One of his university colleagues, the principal, Professor Grant, commemorated the rescue of the castle with an elegant Latin inscription that was placed over the entrance door. In translation it reads:

This mansion snatched from rooks and owls is dedicated to honest ease amidst labours.

Here, for summer after summer, the elderly professor took his 'honest ease amidst labours', studying and writing learned books in his favourite vine room, and as a hobby he compiled the family history, which he dictated to his children in turn. As the castle warmed into life again, so the lives of this deeply artistic family seemed to blossom and flourish in the ambience of its lovely old chambers and turrets, its handsome turnpike staircases and splendid ceilings. There is no doubt that Kellie Castle had a profound influence on all of them; but they in turn left their lasting mark on it. This was the remarkable thing about the Lorimers and Kellie Castle: they all participated, contributing all their varied talents, with their adored mother as enthusiastic presiding genius.

The youngsters had their quarters in the north tower, the oldest part of the castle. One of its five rooms was used as a sitting-room by the three Lorimer daughters. Here they would spend hours embroidering bell-pulls and tablecloths. Hannah, the eldest, was a tremendously versatile artist, as happy with oils, watercolours, soft clay or hard wood as she was with music. She carved patterns on bookcases, chairs, plateracks and platestands. She copied Raeburn's portraits of the philosopher Thomas Reid and her great-grandfather Robert Stodart. After exhibiting at the Royal Scottish Academy she seemed destined for a career as a professional artist, but instead she married a celebrated mountaineer, Everard im Thurn, the first man to climb the spectacular Roraima peak on the borders of Venezuela and Guyana, who later became governor of Fiji.

The second daughter, Alice, later married Sir David Chalmers and was to commission some of her architect brother Robert's best early furniture and to embroider some of his designs. The youngest, Louise, spent hours at her Regency desk producing ballads, verses and descriptive essays. She was one of the first female students when Edinburgh University opened its doors to women in 1892. It was Louise, the one with the 'green fingers', who tackled the wild garden. She never married.

At the very top of the tower there is a rough-panelled room illuminated by one tall window and a northern skylight. This was used by the second Lorimer boy, John Henry, as his studio. He was a born painter. He produced his first watercolour as a small boy, and at the age of twelve produced his first oil-painting as a birthday present for his mother – a study of Holy Isle done on a sixpenny canvas with paints begged from the workmen who were redecorating their Edinburgh home. He sketched the family at their music-making, with Alice Lorimer as the muse of music. At the age of nineteen – just before the Lorimers discovered Kellie Castle – he had exhibited a portrait of his mother at the Royal Scottish Academy, and when the family moved into Kellie for their long summers he was training at the Royal Society of Arts school in Edinburgh. Just a year after the move, his brilliant portrait of his father was 'hung on the line' at the Royal Academy in London, and at the *right* The great hall, now the drawing-room. In the ceiling are heraldic panels of the third Earl of Kellie and his second wife, dated 1676. The right-hand door at the far end leads to the dining-room.

below The dining-room originally the withdrawing-room, showing some of the sixty-four painted panels that line the walls; all but four of them are the originals installed by the third Earl of Kellie during the reign of Charles II. On the back wall is a late sixteenth-century Flemish tapestry depicting 'Europa and the Bull'.

above left The earl's room with bed hangings designed and made by the late Mrs Mary Lorimer.

above A corner of the vine room ceiling at Kellie Castle with its beautifully wrought pre-cast plaster vines.

left The circular ceiling painting of Mount Olympus by Jacob de Wet, now in the vine room.

age of twenty-three 'JH' had definitely arrived as a painter.

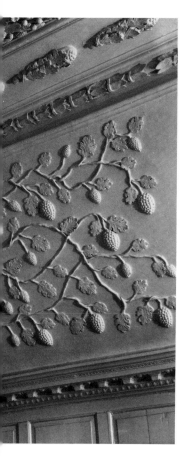

His output was enormous: over a hundred portraits have been identified as well as thirty large genre paintings and hundreds of landscapes, watercolour sketches and flower studies, and almost daily a collector reveals yet another Lorimer. Perhaps the most celebrated of his paintings is *Ordination of Elders in a Scottish Kirk*; one of his earlier works, it has been reproduced time and again and hung in ministers' studies all over the world. Today his paintings are to be seen in the National Gallery of Scotland, the Tate Gallery, the Louvre, the Kende Gallery in New York, the Victoria National Gallery in Melbourne, and many, many others.

Kellie Castle itself is featured in another celebrated painting now in the Louvre. It shows the Lorimer children at table in the 'withdrawing-room' with the painted panelling behind them, their heads bowed while Grandmother Lorimer says grace. It was bought by the French government and renamed *Le Bénédicité*.

Kellie was also to benefit greatly from the connection with J. H. Lorimer. It was he who found the Jacob de Wet circular painting of Mount Olympus and installed it in the vine room. It was he who painted and installed the four missing sections of the splendid seventeenth-century panelling in the 'withdrawing-room'. Several Lorimers grace the walls of the great hall today: a fine self-portrait above the door, a sepia drawing of his younger brother Robert at the age of twelve, a quarter-scale copy of Titian's *L'Homme au Gant*, a painting entitled *Homage to Cupid*, and over the tiled fireplace a large genre picture called *Bonnie Jean*, Lorimer's interpretation of the Scottish song of that name, with his sister Louise portrayed among the ladies.

But the Lorimer boy who was destined to become the most illustrious of the Lorimers was the youngest child, Robert. He chose the room above his sisters' sitting-room in the north tower as what he called his 'work room'. As befitted a multi-talented Lorimer he kept a variety of useful artistic equiment there – a rough deal drawing-desk which he had made with his own hands, a set of carving tools, a paint-box and a violin. By the age of fourteen he had announced that he was going to be an architect. It was the year the family had moved to Kellie Castle.

How much was his decision affected by his introduction to Kellie Castle, and how much was his style as an architect to be affected by it? He was too young to do much more than observe the work of repair and restoration that his father put in train at Kellie; but architectural historians are in no doubt that Kellie Castle had a profound influence on his later attempts to produce a modernized traditional style. Christopher Hussey, in his book *The work of Sir Robert Lorimer* (1931), wrote: 'The Scottish National War Memorial, the Thistle Chapel, and a score of lovingly restored castles would not have taken the shapes Sir Robert Lorimer gave them but for his father's romantic vision of Kellie.' More recently, Peter Savage in his definitive new book, *Lorimer and the Edinburgh Craft Designers* (1980), writes: 'The contrast between [the Lorimers'] Baronial town house and this genuine piece of Baronial history seems to have given him an insight which was to be the foundation of his success as an architect from which he went right to the top of his profession.'

There are specific examples that can be cited to show how much he was affected by the formative summers he spent at Kellie. For instance, one can see the ceiling decoration of the vine room echoed in the wood panelling of Hill of Tarvit, the mansion in Fife he designed for a wealthy Dundee jute financier and art collector in 1907 (it too is now in the care of the National Trust for Scotland). It was one of some fifty houses in Britain which he designed or extended. He also designed houses in France, Finland and Norway. He designed several churches, he revaulted the choir of Paisley Abbey, he designed shops, schools and university buildings and restored a score of famous Scottish castles such as Dunderave in Argyll and Dunrobin Castle in Sutherland. His most celebrated achievements were his work on the Thistle Chapel in St Giles Cathedral, Edinburgh (for which he was knighted in 1911), and the Scottish National War Memorial in Edinburgh

Castle in the 1920s, not long before his death in 1929 on his sixty-fifth birthday.

But he was more than simply an architect of buildings and monuments. He designed gardens (as he grew up he played his part in the development of the fine walled garden at Kellie Castle), and designed and made furniture. In the Lorimer room in the south tower of Kellie Castle there is a wooden cradle he designed, along with plans, drawings, photographs and other memorabilia associated with him. Peter Savage observes felicitously:

Lorimer chose to stay in Scotland because his heart was in Scottish architecture and he did not build much in the city ... but his designs for gardens, Rustic cottages, furniture and church woodwork are among the best of their kind and his 'Scotch' country houses have not been surpassed ... He loved the genius of the country and he came to believe that each building should grow naturally from its surroundings by making use of the materials of its locality, fashioned by its craftsmen to the forms traditional to it. As he found his inspiration in the people, the land of Scotland provided sites amid mountains for hill-top houses gazing on magnificent views across gardens striding the slopes in terraced banks; for mansions beside sea lochs like fiords and windswept moorlands and gardens in the far from flat lowlands like private arcadias sheltered behind high walls, as well as for long low unobtrusive cottages planted thick with rhododendrons and roses, the many dormers pushing against deep sheltering roofs.

Whatever Kellie Castle gave Sir Robert Lorimer, he returned the gift in rich measure. He designed the pilastered fireplace in the south wall of the great hall, with its stone hearth and lively seventeenth-century Dutch tiles. Also in the great hall he designed the showcase between the windows for the Lorimer collection of antique silver *objets d'art*. There is a lot of Lorimer furniture in the great hall (now set out as a drawing-room, as the Lorimers had it), including a pair of gilded wall mirrors and a secretaire, and a bow-fronted chest of drawers with a marble top. But the great hall/drawing-room is as much a family achievement as anything else in Kellie Castle. Its rehabilitation was a gradual process, and it is symbolized by the initials in the three cartouches over the west fireplace: those of Robert, of JH and, in the centre, of their mother Hannah.

Professor James Lorimer died in 1890, but his wife kept Kellie Castle on as the family's summer home. When she died in 1916 after a full and rich life, her painter son JH, a bachelor, extended the tenancy, dividing his time between Kellie Castle, his town house in Edinburgh, and a house he restored in Pittenweem called the Gyles, a seventeenth-century sea-captain's house overlooking the little harbour, which was later acquired by the Trust and rehabilitated for sale as a private residence.

J.H.Lorimer died in 1936 at the age of eighty, and the shadows closed in on Kellie Castle once again. There was another 'muckle roup' of the entire contents. Once again the old castle stood empty and forlorn, abandoned and neglected. It looked as if the long Lorimer association with Kellie, which had lasted precisely sixty years, was over, and that Kellie was doomed to sink into ruination once again. But then, five years later, a second Lorimer rescue operation began, this time by one of Professor Lorimer's grandsons, architect Robert's second son, the sculptor Hew Lorimer, and his artist wife, Mary McLeod Wylie.

Hew Lorimer, then in his mid-thirties, was later to achieve tremendous acclaim in the 1950s as one of Scotland's foremost sculptors; it was then that he designed and carved the seven allegorical figures on the frontage of the National Library of Scotland in Edinburgh; he designed the colossal twenty-seven-foot statue of sparkling Creetown granite of *Our Lady of the Isles* that now superintends the outlook from the island of South Uist in the Outer Hebrides (a two-foot-bronze model of it is in the 'withdrawing-room' at Kellie Castle), and he designed and carved the tympanum at St Francis Friary in Dundee.

Hew and Mary Lorimer were staying at the Gyles in Pittenweem at the time they took over Kellie Castle. They could see the old castle deteriorating, literally before their eyes, and could not resist the challenge. In 1941 they undertook to rent Kellie Castle on the same terms as before, and moved in with their two (later three) children. When the old Earl of Mar and Kellie died in 1955 he was succeeded by his grandson, who decided that he had to sell the castle and gave first refusal to the Lorimers. After reaching agreement with the Historic Buildings Council for Scotland, by which grants made for major repairs of the fabric of the castle would be matched by expenditure on modernization and internal redecoration, the Lorimers bought the castle outright in 1958. Furniture and furnishings from the Lorimer home in Edinburgh were moved in.

Long before this, however, a labour of love had begun such as the old castle had never known, not even in those years of rescue by the professor nearly a century earlier. Mary Lorimer was an exceptionally versatile artist with an instinctive understanding of domestic crafts. She used her sense of colour, of texture and of character to bring room after room alive again, and gradually, as Hew Lorimer writes in his affectionate guidebook, 'the old place began to smile again'. She painted, she embroidered, she made and lined nearly forty pairs of curtains, she recovered most of the upholstered furniture with her own hands. She designed and made the bed-hangings and the window curtains in the vine room to echo the 'fruits of the vine' theme on the ceiling. She and her husband together designed the wrought-iron circular ceiling-light in the dining-room. And throughout the year from spring to autumn she kept the castle alight with fresh flowers, more than twenty different arrangements, varying in size and character from a single choice bloom in a tear-glass to a magnificent centrepiece for the great hall.

Mary Lorimer died in 1970, and in that year Kellie Castle was acquired by the National Trust for Scotland, along with its essential contents, its gardens and eleven acres of land. Hew Lorimer stayed on as resident Trust representative, with his private quarters in part of the east tower and his sculptor's studio in the coach-house nearby. Mary Lorimer's influence still pervades the old place in the style and tact that informs the furnishings and works of art which complement its rooms so fittingly. A portrait by her of the Lorimers' only daughter, Monica, at the age of six, hangs in the earl's room. Right at the top of the north tower is her studio, which she inherited, so to speak, from JH.

The work of revival and rehabilitation still goes on steadily. 'Restoration' would be too strong a word, for very little replacement of old work has been necessary. Indeed, the old castle has been extraordinarily lucky, paradoxically: lucky to have fallen on hard times and been abandoned – because it happened during what Hew Lorimer calls 'the two middle and most dangerous quarters of the last century' for historic buildings, when wealthy Victorian owners spoiled or changed the character of so many Scottish castles and great houses by virtually rebuilding them to satisfy their delusions of grandeur; and lucky to have been rescued – twice – by a family like the Lorimers who had the good taste to appreciate it for what it was. Professor Lorimer had neither the means nor the inclination for massive 'improvement'; he liked Kellie Castle the way it was, with all its limitations for domestic convenience, and in that respect he was ahead of his time. His children all helped to embellish it; and *their* children carried on the labour of love, either living in it and loving it, like Hew and Mary Lorimer, or lovingly recording its story, like Esther Chalmers, the youngest daughter of Alice (Lady Chalmers).

So Kellie Castle lives on serenely, ghost and all. Yes, there's a ghost all right – perhaps even more than one of them. But it's no ordinary ghost. It's a pair of dainty red slippers that go pattering up and down the spiral stairs of the south tower. Legend has it that they belonged to a certain Anne Erskine, daughter of the house, who was betrothed against her will. To escape a fate worse than death she planned to elope with her true love one night. She leaped from an upstairs window to her waiting lover, but missed his outstretched arms and was killed by the fall.

In that same south tower, sleepers have also been woken by the tramp of heavy boots. Today they have been replaced by the tread of the 10,000 pairs of feet of the visitors who go each summer to enjoy the gardens and quintessential castle atmosphere of the old place that learned to smile again.

Leith Hall, north-west of Aberdeen.

LEITH HALL
Grampian

ARMA VIRUMQUE CANO – 'Of arms and the man I sing'; these opening words of Virgil's *Aeneid* are perhaps the most celebrated phrase in classical literature, introducing the epic story of the adventures of the Trojan warrior Aeneas after the siege and sack of Troy. Leith Hall, near the village of Kennethmont in north-eastern Grampian, sings a similar story – of arms and the *men* (and the women) who made Leith Hall a monument to a whole dynasty of 'bonnie fechters', and a microcosm of the history of British arms in many parts of the world.

Leith Hall was the first of the great houses in the Grampian Region to be handed over to the National Trust for Scotland. It was given to the nation in 1945 when the story of the Leiths of Leith Hall had come full circle; when the male line of martial Leith lairds had come to an abrupt and irrevocable end, when Leith Hall itself had fulfilled all its obligations to half a score of generations of Leith families who had lived in it and loved it and left on it marks of their affection which have endured to this day. It stands, modest and unpretentious, in the wide strath of Garioch, overlooked by the Tap O'North, some thirty-six miles west of Aberdeen and eight miles from Huntly. It is not by any means the grandest of the great houses of the north-east, nor the most impressive; but it has a special kind of grace, both of spirit and appearance, a beguiling intimacy of character reinforced by the intensely personal nature of the treasured mementoes that crowd its rooms. In Leith Hall, every single object has a story of its own to sing.

There have been Leiths at Leith Hall for three hundred years, ever since it was built in 1650. But there have been Leiths in this north-eastern shoulder of Scotland for six hundred years, even though the family originally came from Midlothian and took their name from the port of Edinburgh. They were once known as 'de Leyth' and were shippers and shipowners living in the lands of Restalrig, now a suburb on the eastern outskirts of Edinburgh. By the middle of the fourteenth century they had moved north and were firmly established as shippers in the growing port of Aberdeen, and various branches of the family were busily acquiring land outside the town and spreading west and north into the broad acres of Garioch.

The first Leith ancestor of whom there is any detailed record was William Leith, who rose to prominence and authority during the reign of the hapless King David II, (who succeeded his father Robert the Bruce in 1329). William was twice Provost of Aberdeen, in 1350-5 and again in 1373, and a member of the Parliament at Scone in 1367. Some of his extensive lands were given to him by Royal Charter for services to the Crown – including the part he played in achieving King David's release from imprisonment by the English after the disastrous rout at Neville's Cross in 1358. But his record of decorous public service was blemished during his second period of office as Provost; according to the *Memorials of Aldermen, Provosts and Lord Provosts of Aberdeen, 1272-1895*, he was involved in the murder of a certain Baillie Cattanach on the Moor of Backmill. It was a flash of the martial Leith spirit that would blaze in so many descendants.

His son Laurence showed no lack of fighting spirit, either. In 1411, at the grievously bloody Battle of Harlaw, Laurence was one of the leaders of the Aberdeen contingent that saved the town from a marauding army of Highlanders. The Provost of Aberdeen died in that battle, but Laurence survived and was made Provost in his stead. Laurence's younger brother John made even more of a name for himself – as 'Armiger and Scutifer' (Knight and Shield-Bearer). He went as ambassador to England in 1413 and 1416 when King James I was enduring his long captivity in England, and in 1423 and 1424 he was one of the commissioners appointed to discuss the terms of his ransom.

For the next two centuries a succession of Leith lairds peaceably and diligently tended their business affairs and their lands, extending their holdings and kinships by judicious marriages and purchases. It was the fourteenth of the line, James Leith of New Leslie and Peill, direct descendant of provost William Leith of Aberdeen, who began a new line – the Leiths of Leith Hall.

His father, James Leith of Barns, had bought the neighbouring estates of New Leslie and Peill at the upper end of the Garioch shortly before his death. It was not very good farming country, bleak and bare and almost treeless. Only about fifteen per cent of the land in the parish of Kennethmont was arable; the rest was rough hill-grazing or meagre moorland, with some peat-bogs to provide precious fuel. Presumably there must have been better farmland available elsewhere, but this seems to have been all that the family could afford at the time – enough to provide a living for laird and tenantry but not much more.

It was not the ideal estate on which to build a new laird's house; nor were the times exactly propitious for ambitious building projects. Scotland was still suffering badly from the privations of the Civil Wars of the Covenanter period, and many of the great houses still lay in ruins. But, nothing daunted, James Leith built his tower house in 1650, apparently on the site of an older tower that stood on the Peill estate.

Perhaps it was the troubled times that explain why the Leith Hall he built was the simplest kind of house imaginable, the kind of house a child draws – a tall rectangular block with a short sloping roof and a chimney at each end, but with four little corbelled turrets, one at each corner. It looked rather like an overgrown farmhouse with knobs on. Still, it was indubitably a tower house, nowhere more than one room thick and rising through four floors, complete with a carved stone panel over the entrance bearing the coat of arms of James Leith and his wife, Margaret Strachan of Glenkindie. The house faced south, overlooking a courtyard with bakehouse, brewhouse, stables, servants' quarters and other outhouses (the traditional 'laigh biggins') enclosed by a wall pierced by an arched entrance. Although later lairds amplified the plan by building handsome additions to replace the original walls and outhouses, James Leith's north tower has remained the nucleus of the crowded quadrangle that comprises Leith Hall today.

James, first Leith of Leith Hall, lived in his new house for some forty years. A relatively untroubled period followed the convulsions of the Civil Wars and there was never cause for him to draw his sword in anger. Instead, he displayed his Leith pugnacity in a series of wrangles and disputes with his neighbours and creditors; his chronic difficulties in making ends meet seem to have exacerbated an already litigious nature.

His son John, the second laird (known as John I to distinguish him from the line of Johns that followed), inherited Leith Hall in 1691 or 1692, and died in 1727. There is a portrait in the dining-room of a gentleman in a steel cuirass, looking suitably martial, which may possibly be of John I. He married Janet Ogilvie, a daughter of Lord Banff, by whom he had five sons and a daughter; and it was through them that the fighting spirit of the Leiths began to come to the surface.

The Leiths had always been Jacobite in their loyalties, and when Bonnie Prince Charlie raised his standard for the '45 Rebellion, four of the five Leith sons went to join him. After the *débâcle* they were all taken prisoner. Two of them were sentenced to deportation to

opposite The four major stages in the development and extension of Leith Hall. *Top left* the tower house built by James Leith (1650–1756). *Top right* expansion and development, with new pavilions at the corner, by John Leith and his wife Harriot (1756–97). *Bottom left* major rebuilding of the south range to match the old tower house opposite, by Sandie Leith-Hay (1797–1868). *Bottom right* major building-up of the west side with its arched entrance way, by Colonel Alexander Sebastian Leith-Hay (1868 to date).

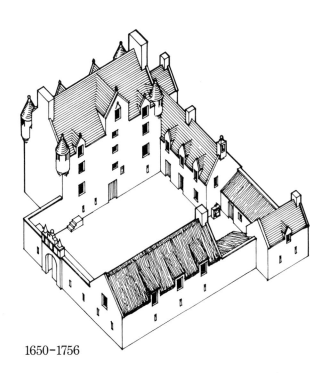

1650–1756

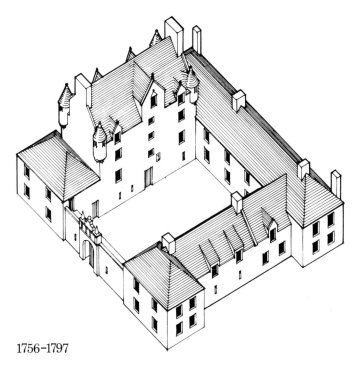

1756–1797

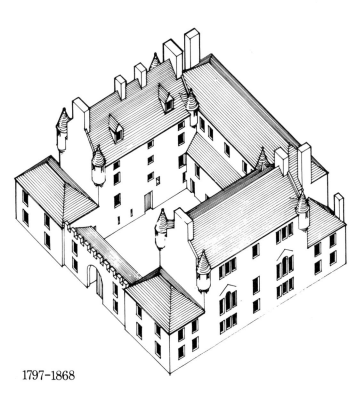

1797–1868

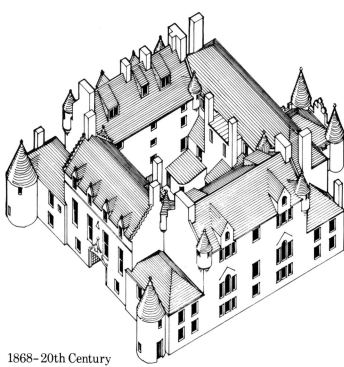

1868–20th Century

the American plantations. Only the eldest son, John II, who had become the third laird on his father's death in 1727 was spared the humiliation and despair of the failure of the '45; he had always been in poor health, and had died in 1736.

John II had been a Jacobite like his brothers. Indeed, in 1730 he had married into an even more ardent Jacobite family than his own. That marriage, despite his untimely death only six years later, was to prove the saving of Leith Hall in the most unpredictable way, and thereby hangs one of the most fascinating stories in the Leith saga. The young lady he married was called Mary Hay, of Rannes, near Elgin. Her portrait hanging over the door of the music room beside that of her young husband shows a gentle-faced girl seated soulfully at a harpsicord. She bore her husband a son, John III, and a daughter; but, just as important, she introduced on to the Leith Hall stage the man who would later change the family name – her brother, Andrew Hay of Rannes.

Andrew Hay is one of the most colourful and attractive characters in the whole Leith story. His portrait in the music room, painted when he was sixty-five, depicts a man of firm but good-humoured features, wearing a mauve coat with lace ruffles. But it does not show what a huge man he was. He was, quite literally, a giant, seven feet two inches tall (a pair of his hand-knitted silk stockings is on display in the music room). But he was a gentle giant, utterly devoted to his sister Mary and her fatherless children. John III was only five years old when he succeeded as the fourth laird of Leith Hall, and was sorely in need of help and guidance. His official guardian, or tutor, during his minority was the oldest of his Leith uncles, Patrick; but Uncle Patrick seems to have been a thoroughly bad character. Mrs Mary Leith brought a petition to have him removed from his office of guardian, claiming that he was 'ane habituall Drunkard . . . a weak man . . . a Man of no Religion and ane open Blasphemer . . . unfit for mannadgeing the affairs of any person . . .' Nevertheless, Uncle Patrick stayed on as John III's guardian.

Then came the Rebellion of 1745. John III was fourteen years old by then, old enough to get rid of Uncle Patrick and choose his own guardians, but too young to take up arms for the Jacobite cause. His uncles – the four fighting Leiths and, more apparently, Uncle Andrew Hay of Rannes – couldn't wait, however.

In 1747, when the worst of the proscriptions and victimizations were over, most of the Jacobite survivors were granted pardons through the Act of Indemnity and began to emerge from hiding and exile. But there was no pardon for Andrew Hay. His father had fought for the Old Pretender in the 1715 Rebellion; he himself had fought at Prestonpans, had led the victorious Scots into Manchester, had been with them at Derby, and he had marched back north with the Prince all the way to Culloden. On the eve of the battle the prince had given his faithful supporter an elegant little shagreen (leather) writing-case, which is one of the family treasures on display in the music room. It is about the size of a spectacle-case and contains a tiny silver pen and pencil, a pair of compasses, a folding ruler and a silver ink-pot. The prince wrote both their names in pencil on one of the set of ivory tablets that accompanied it.

A man as close to the Prince as Andrew Hay had clearly been was too dangerous a man to forgive or forget. After Culloden, Hay went into hiding in the hills. For five years he remained a fugitive – not an easy thing for a man as huge and easily recognizable as he was. When his father died in 1751 Andrew feared that his presence in Scotland might endanger his mother and the estate at Rannes, so in 1752 he decided to go abroad. For eleven weary years he wandered through Holland, Belgium and France with only a faithful servant to share his exile.

Throughout these years he kept up a regular correspondence with his mother; and through these letters he was able to keep in touch with what was happening at Leith Hall. The news was reassuring: his nephew John III was proving himself a capable laird and beginning to play a part in local affairs. He had started making improvements to the house, which had now stood for a century without change. He had removed the old stables to make more room for domestic offices around the courtyard and had rebuilt the stables in an elegant curving building apart from the house. But best of all he had married, and married well, in April 1756. His bride was Harriot Stuart, daughter and heiress of Alexander Stuart of Auchluncart – and what a marvellous woman she would turn out to be! Her portraits in the library and the music room show all the determination, character and courage that would be required of her in the future.

For a while all was domestic bliss at Leith Hall. The young couple immediately added a two-storey wing along the east side of the courtyard with a new entrance and new kitchen quarters across the south; then they added four little two-storey pavilions at the four corners of the courtyard, and inscribed their names on the window lintels of the north-west pavilion. Harriot bore her husband three sons – John IV, Alexander (Sandie) and James. Everything in the Leith garden seemed rosy.

Things were looking up for Uncle Andrew Hay as well. The giant Jacobite exile, tired and ill after his eleven nomadic years, resolved to come home, pardon or no. He was fifty years old, still unmarried, and desperately worried about his ageing mother's health at Rannes. In the spring of 1763 he came back. Although he was still officially proscribed, the law was not enforced and Andrew Hay was left in peace at Rannes, which his mother had had to rebuild during his absence after an accidental fire. He eventually received King George III's pardon in 1780, and this historic document now hangs framed in the music room, claimed to be the only pardon with its royal seal intact. The bill for it, which also survives, amounted to £76 13s 0d.

But hardly was Andrew home before tragedy struck the luckless Leith Hall family again. One night just before Christmas 1763, the laird of Leith Hall, John III, went to Aberdeen for a drinking party; an argument flared, and in the small hours of the morning John Leith was found dying in the street from a pistol shot in the head. Whether he had been killed in a bungled duel or simply murdered was never proved, for his assailant fled the country at once and was never brought to trial despite strenuous efforts by the widow of Leith Hall, Harriot Stuart of Auchluncart.

It was now that Harriot came into her own as one of the most remarkable women in the Leith dynastic story – and Andrew Hay came into *his* own as the quintessential uncle-figure. Andrew was a tower of strength to Harriot after her husband's killing, and to his three great-nephews. The fifth laird, John IV, was only six years old when he inherited the title, Sandie was five and James only months old. But Harriot never faltered; she might well have given up and moved out, but instead she bravely set about bringing up her children and running the estate with the help of the guardians her late husband had appointed. She planted a great number of fir trees, brought water to a new mill, and established flowers and flowering shrubs in the grounds of Leith Hall in keeping with the new fashion for making mansion gardens decorative instead of merely productive.

The new laird, alas, was consumptive from childhood, and Harriot was advised to keep him constantly on the move and away from the cold winds of Aberdeenshire. Summer after summer she travelled southwards with John and Sandie, organizing the hire of carriages and postilions, renting rooms, engaging tutors, buying asses and goats for John's milk, and always keeping an anxious eye on the expenses. For three years she stayed with the two older boys in Paris and the south of France, where they acquired flawless French accents and manners before going to Aberdeen University (there is a family tradition that John was for a time a page-boy at the court of King Louis XVI, a surmise that may have been suggested by the portrait of him in Leith Hall wearing a page's costume of blue and white with a ruff around his neck).

From an early age Sandie was determined to be a soldier – the fighting spirit of the Leiths was never far below the surface. When he was thirteen his mother sold her own inheritance of Auchluncart for £11,300 to help the Leith Hall finances, and with part of the proceeds she bought him a commission in the army for £400, although he was unable to take it up until four years later, when he was seventeen years old.

Meanwhile, John Leith IV was beginning to manage his own affairs and assume some of the duties of laird. But his health continued to deteriorate and, after yet another summer voyage with his mother from Aberdeen to London as a last-ditch remedy, he died at Cambridge Heath, Hackney, in October 1776. He was only nineteen years old.

His brother Sandie inherited, to become the sixth laird of Leith Hall. But he had by now embarked on his military career, and had little time to devote to the affairs of Leith Hall. A captaincy had been bought for him in the 21st Regiment for £2000, and he was seeing a good deal of service in Ireland. In 1780, four years after he inherited Leith Hall, his indomitable mother Harriot died. For seventeen appallingly difficult years she had held the Leith Hall dynasty together against all the odds. Now it was up to Andrew Hay to ensure that her valiant efforts had not been in vain.

Sandie Leith was destined to be laird of Leith Hall for longer than any of his predecessors or successors – sixty-two years, in fact; but for a time it was touch and go as to whether he would survive as laird at all. He was away on military service for much of the time, and he was ruinously extravagant; so, not surprisingly, he was soon in financial difficulties. He did not even seek to improve his position by courting an heiress: in 1784 he married Mary Forbes of Ballogie, who would make him a most devoted wife, even though 'the lady neither possesses fortune nor great beauty', as he confessed in an indiscreet letter to his great-uncle Andrew (her portrait in the music room by J. W. Chandler hardly bears out this ungallant remark, however). And in that same year he announced that he felt obliged to sell Leith Hall because the estate simply could not support his way of life. In effect, he was going bankrupt.

This was when Andrew Hay came to the rescue of Leith Hall in a last magnanimous gesture. He would no doubt have been flattered that the newly-weds' first-born, a son, was christened Andrew after his great-great-uncle; he presented the baby, the future seventh laird, with a gold and coral rattle-and-whistle combined which cost £9 8s 6d and is now on display in the music room. More to the point, the old Jacobite hero, who had sacrificed the best years of his life and the comforts of his home at Rannes for the cause he believed in so ardently, now made the supreme sacrifice: in 1789 he sold Rannes for £21,000 and bought Leith Hall in order to give it back, free of all debts, to the great-nephew from whom he had bought it. He himself died later that year, before he was due to quit his beloved Rannes. The only condition he attached to his gift was that the family should assume the name Hay as well as their own. Thus the childless old man, who had showered such parental affection on nephews and great-nephews alike, ensured that his own name would live on in conjunction with that of the family whose future he had now secured. Sandie Leith became Sandie Leith-Hay of Rannes and Leith Hall, which remained the full name and designation of the family from then on.

The fortunes of Leith Hall and of Sandie Leith-Hay now began to flourish. In his army career he rose in rank first to colonel and then to major-general, although he came near to resigning his commission in fury when the regiment he had raised in 1794, the 109th Aberdeenshire Regiment, was subsequently incorporated into the 53rd (Shropshire) Regiment; his only consolation for this blow to local and national pride was that he was allowed to retain the regimental colours, which are now on display in Leith Hall. At about the same time he received from a cousin a windfall legacy of a valuable sugar plantation in Tobago; this he sold for £29,000, some of which he used for making improvements on the estate.

He also made a major addition to the structure of Leith Hall in 1797 which more than doubled its size. On the south side of the courtyard he built a new block, almost a new house, matching it to the old tower house opposite, which was now relegated to service quarters. It was a plain rectangular block, white-harled, with flanking pavilions and turreted corners. It accommodated a new suite of reception rooms, including a charming

opposite Characters from the Leith Hall saga: *top left* Mary Hay of Rannes, wife of John Leith II. *Top right* Andrew Hay of Rannes, Mary's brother, the gentle Jacobite giant who saved Leith Hall. *bottom left* Harriot Stuart of Auchuncart, indomitable widow of John Leith III *bottom right* Sir Andrew Leith-Hay, the seventh laird.

above A ceremonial portrait of Colonel Alexander Sebastian Leith-Hay that dominates the music room.

above right The music room, originally built as a billiard room by Colonel Sebastian, now a museum of mementoes and keepsakes.

Right The library at Leith Hall.

oval drawing-room on the first floor; externally, the new elegance was emphasized by a pair of three-light Venetian windows with central arched heads surmounted by the suggestion of a classical pediment. A few years later he remodelled the two-storey 1756 east wing, adding a further storey, and created a new main entrance on the east façade.

This lavish expenditure on building projects, combined with his continued personal extravagance, ensured that he would never be entirely free from financial worries; but at least he could lead the life of a laird as he wanted and bring up a family of two sons and four daughters. The younger son, John, became a rear admiral; the elder, Andrew – the namesake of his great-great-uncle – continued the Leith tradition of taking up an army career.

Andrew Leith-Hay was fifty-three years old when his father died in 1838 at the age of eighty. He had joined the army nearly thirty years earlier as aide-de-camp to the most famous fighting Leith of them all, his uncle, General Sir James Leith, Harriot's third son, hero, under Wellington, of the Peninsular War, hero of Corunna, Vittoria and Salamanca, Commander of the 5th Division at the storming of Badajoz in 1812 and the celebrated siege of San Sebastian the following year. He died in 1816 as Commander of the Forces in the West Indies, laden with military honours, and was accorded the ultimate accolade of being buried in Westminster Abbey. Surprisingly, in a house so crammed with family and military portraits, there is no full-scale painting of him in Leith Hall; there is only a miniature of him among the display of family decorations in the music room, and a statuette which was the model for a life-size statue intended for Westminster Abbey but never completed.

His nephew Andrew Leith-Hay, the future seventh laird, became a dashing and courageous intelligence officer in the war against Napoleon in Spain; he was captured by the French but was released in time to rejoin his uncle for the siege of San Sebastian. A few years later he spotted a large painting of the battle and bought it at Christie's in London 'for almost nothing'. It is a huge canvas, ten feet by six feet; against a background of ferocious action it depicts General Sir James Leith in the bottom left-hand corner turning to speak to his young A.D.C., his nephew Andrew.

Andrew retired from the army soon after his uncle's death in the West Indies and settled in a rented cottage on Deeside. He was an immensely versatile and engaging man, and an artist of considerable talent whose drawings (sometimes coloured by other hands) profusely adorn the walls of Leith Hall. He was no mean writer, either; his detailed journals of his experiences with Wellington's army in the Portuguese and Spanish campaigns were published under the title *A Narrative of the Peninsular War*; he wrote a memoir of his famous uncle Sir James Leith, and later he used his own drawings to illustrate his book *The Castellated Architecture of Aberdeenshire*. He was a compelling speaker when he entered Parliament as Liberal MP for Elgin, and was knighted for his public services in 1836.

His portrait in Leith Hall shows us a man with a look of rumpled intelligence and intensity which slightly belies his open-hearted, devil-may-care character. He had inherited all his father's improvidence, and indeed exceeded it. In fact, he was a reckless and incurable spendthrift. When his father died in 1838, Sir Andrew Leith-Hay, now the seventh laird, was so impoverished that he could not even afford to live at Leith Hall. For two years he and his wife lived in Belgium, a favourite resort of the poor-rich in those days; and there Lady Leith-Hay busied herself with the many examples of exquisite needlework which are displayed in one of the corridors of Leith Hall today.

They returned to Leith Hall at a time when the economic tide for Aberdeenshire was well on the turn. Road and canal communications were opening up the county as never before, enabling landowners to make substantial improvements in agriculture. The first railway from Aberdeen to Huntly in 1854 passed right through the Leith Hall grounds, thus bringing the markets of Aberdeen to within ninety minutes of the estate, whereas before it had involved a journey of three days by horse and heavy cart. Sir Andrew was too shrewd a man not to foresee and exploit the advantages; the finances of the estate improved, he himself played a prominent part in Aberdeenshire affairs and lived to a contented and ripe old age – he was seventy-seven when he died in 1862, the father of five sons.

The eldest son, Alexander Sebastian, who would become the eighth laird, was another fighting Leith who chose the army as a career. There was little enough future for the others, so they all emigrated to Australia, like so many younger sons in the nineteenth century. Meanwhile, Alexander Sebastian (named, of course, in memory of his great-uncle's part in the great siege of 1813) joined the 93rd Sutherland Highlanders when he was seventeen years old; in 1854, twenty years later, he was a major who stood in the immortal Thin Red Line at Balaclava. Three years after that, in 1857, by then a colonel, he led his regiment to the relief of Lucknow in the Indian Mutiny before retiring from active service in 1860. Two years later he succeeded his father as eighth laird of Leith Hall.

Like many a retired colonel before and after him he developed his own peppery eccentricities, but his bark was always worse than his bite. In 1868 he made the final major addition to Leith Hall by building up the last unfilled side of the quadrangle, the west range; there he erected a new wing comparable in size with each of the other three, with an ornamented archway into the hollow centre of the quadrangle. This is the only block whose rooms are now open to the public, along with the south western pavilion of the 1756 additions. The original north wing of the house has a suite of rooms reserved for members of the Leith-Hay family, while the south wing (General Alexander's 1797 addition) and the east wing of 1756, remodelled and heightened by General Alexander, are now divided off from each other internally and let as self-contained dwellings.

The west block, built by the colonel in 1868, featured an imposing billiard room, which his successor converted into the present music room (although, as Schomberg Scott observes in his perceptive guidebook, it would more aptly be called the museum room nowadays). Here most of the Leith Hall treasures and keepsakes are on display — and of these the more quirky mementoes can be traced back to Colonel Alexander Sebastian Leith-Hay himself.

The room is dominated by a very large portrait of the good colonel in ceremonial dress: befitting his record of gallantry, it is the largest portrait in the house, and it is hard to dismiss the suspicion that he built the billiard room in part to house his portrait. The best trophies of war came from his Indian Mutiny days and included the throne of the King of Oudh (whose deposition by the British in 1856 was one of the direct causes of the Mutiny), as well as his banner, his signet ring, and a miniature of his queen. Another choice item is the Queen of Oudh's walking-stick, which has a phial of poison hidden in the ferrule. In the corner turret of the library there is another incongruous curio – the full costume of an American Indian chief. This was bestowed, along with an honorary title, on the young Alexander Sebastian in the province of Quebec during a tour of duty in Canada during his early days with his regiment.

'Colonel Sebastian', as people called him, had brought home a bride from Wigtownshire in 1860. She was Christina Hamilton, known as 'Teenie', and she immediately endeared herself to everyone. Theirs proved to be an extremely happy marriage, apart from one sadness – they never had any children. When 'Teenie' died in 1897, the old colonel would have been a lonely man but for the presence of his nephew and heir, Charles Edward Norman, son of his brother James who had emigrated to Australia fifty years earlier. When Colonel Sebastian died in 1900, Charlie Leith-Hay became the ninth laird.

He was something new in lairds, not a fighting Leith but a peace-loving, home-loving man. He combined the energy and versatility of his grandfather, Sir Andrew Leith-Hay, with tremendous charm and humour and a musical talent straight from his Irish grandmother, a Grogan, on his mother's side. He was also a product of the new world, with an Australian common touch that endeared him to his tenants: one of the most interesting mementoes in Leith Hall, tucked away in a passage, is a photographic collage of 194 tenants and feuars which they presented to him in 1902. He decided that not enough had been done to improve conditions for the workers on the estate and set about making enormous changes, personally supervising the rebuilding or modernization of dozens of farmhouses and steadings. He also added the last embellishment to Leith Hall itself, a grand new entrance hall adjoining the east side, flanked by two more turrets and panelled in old oak which for years Charlie had been collecting for that purpose.

It was a happy, busy household, full of music and laughter and active work for charity (it was turned into an auxiliary hospital in the First World War). Both he and his wife Henrietta, daughter of Lord O'Neill of Ireland, loved children, and children loved them. Alas, their first two children, who were daughters, died in infancy, and he and Henrietta must have lost all hope of producing a son and heir until a boy, Charles Arthur O'Neill Leith-Hay, was born in May 1918. His father was then sixty years old.

Young Charlie was a good-looking boy with a shock of fair hair and his father's flair for singing and acting. He also learned a trick from his father's Australian days – he could flick the end off a cigarette at thirty yards with a stockman's whip. After Eton and Gordonstoun he embarked on a military career, like so many of his forebears, and became an assistant adjutant in the Royal Artillery. His twenty-first birthday celebrations on 8 May 1939 were abandoned when his father died at the age of eighty-one.

Four months later, on 16 September 1939, 2nd Lieutenant Charles Leith-Hay was killed in a motor-cycle accident while on military business in Otterburn in Northumberland. He was the tenth and last laird of Leith Hall.

His widowed mother, Henrietta Leith-Hay, who died in 1965, devoted herself to researching the family's voluminous papers, and with the help of Marion Lochhead published in 1957 a delightful history of Leith Hall and its people, named after the family motto, *Trustie to the End*. She had already given the house and estate to the National Trust in 1945, and in her preface she explained why:

After the death of the two last lairds of Leith Hall in 1939 I felt certain the house would have to go the way of most other old country houses in Britain whose owners cannot afford to keep them up in these difficult times.

As it has never belonged to any but the Leith family since its building in 1650 I was most anxious that it should be preserved by some means or other. I therefore offered it to the National Trust for Scotland by whom it was accepted. I now have the satisfaction of knowing that it will continue for all time in some capacity as a lasting memorial to the old family of Leith, later Leith-Hay.

Her book is an enchanting evocation of the generations who built and embellished Leith Hall and lived in it through happiness and sorrow. Their family treasures, now cared for by the Trust representative Mr Sandy le Gassick and his wife (he is a former military man and has a special feeling for the place) embody a host of memories of Arms and the Men. As Henrietta Leith-Hay put it: 'There is no haunting; but their home is full of their presence as of their possessions; and some of them come out of the shadows into clear light, and live and speak.'

GLOSSARY

boss   rounded ornamental knob used as ceiling ornament, often at the intersection of the ribs of a vault.

caryatid   female figure used as supporting pillar.

corbel   projection of stone, brick or timber jutting from wall to support weight.

crenellation   notched or toothed defensive parapet; battlement.

feu   (Scot.) feudal tenure of land for which rent was paid in money or grain instead of by the performance of military service; the land so held.

feuar   the tenant of a feu.

harling   roughcasting; coating of lime and gravel applied to walls.

kist   (Scot.) large chest or coffer.

kenspeckle   (Scot.) easily seen or recognized; conspicuous.

laigh   (Scot.) low.

laigh biggins   (Scot.) low buildings.

policies   (Scot.) parkland, gardens etc. surrounding country house.

strapwork   ornamentation imitating interwoven straps.

telamon   heroic male figure, sometimes called *atlas* (pl: *atlantes*), used as supporting pillar.

ACKNOWLEDGMENTS

With the exception of those listed below, all the illustrations reproduced in this book have been kindly loaned by the National Trust for Scotland. The publishers would like to thank them, and especially their picture archivist Jean Gowans, for their cooperation, and would also like to thank the following agencies and other sources for permission to use material from their collections:

British Travel Association 22–3, 76–7, 79, 80, 82 top and bottom, 95 top, 137, 138

Peter Chéze-Brown 53

Country Life 94 top, 134, 188 bottom left

Department of the Environment, Edinburgh 159

National Galleries of Scotland 134, 199 (1, 2, 3 and 4), 200

Royal Commission on the Ancient and Historical Monuments of Scotland endpaper

INDEX